FUNDAMENTALS OF NONPARAMETRIC STATISTICS

FUNDAMENTALS OF NONPARAMETRIC STATISTICS

ALBERT PIERCE
The University of California at Berkeley

With problems by Jay Beaman

Dickenson Publishing Company, Inc., Belmont, California

L. C. Cat. Card No.: 71–90783

Printed in the United States of America

TO

ELLIE
TOM
DAVE
AND
LOUISE

CONTENTS

11 THE CHI-SQUARE STATISTIC 183

12 THE POISSON DISTRIBUTION 223

PREFACE

THIS CENTURY's revolutionary increase in the generality of mathematical concepts—and hence in the scope of things to which they apply—is of enormous benefit to the social and behavioral sciences. While a few years ago a social scientist might feel uneasy about the assertion that human characteristics cannot be measured, today such a pronouncement would betray either an archaic or a private language usage of the term "measurement."

To be sure, this broadened scope of mathematics does not mean that mechanically imitative concepts of measurement are suddenly legitimate. To construct models with algebraic symbols on the assumption that "someday these factors can be measured" is to fail to see that measurement cannot be separated from the premises of the model. Such *divertisements* Schumpeter aptly labeled "monkey mathematics." In point of fact, the new flexibility of modern mathematics demands considerable self-discipline from those who apply it.

Statistics has shared in the general growth of mathematics to the point where it can no longer be mastered except by specialists of extraordinary talent. However, the statistician's full-time preoccupation with his speciality makes it as difficult for him to acquire the special knowledge needed to apply statistics as it is for the scientist to master statistics while trying to keep abreast of the rapid growth of knowledge in his own field.

To bridge the "application gap," various how-to-do-it reference manuals present statistical topics within a context of intuitive explication. This book makes no attempt to supercede these fine works but seeks rather to contribute to sophistication in their use by offering a more in-depth presentation of strategic segments of their theoretical underpinnings.

Because its intent is essentially pragmatic, this book differs from those more concerned with the objectives of theoretical statistics, which subordinate problems of application in order to build a general logical structure from the fewest possible postulates. Too often, such abstractions obscure the relationship of the statistical models to the substantive conditions of empirical investigation—a fact acknowledged by one of the giants of modern mathematical statistics, Professor William Feller:*

> In principle, it is possible to restrict the theory of probability to sample spaces defined in terms of probability distributions of random variables. This procedure avoids reference to abstract sample spaces and also to terms like "trials" and "outcomes of experiments." The reduction of probability theory to random variables is a short cut to the use of analysis and simplifies the theory in many ways. However, it also has the drawback of obscuring the probability background. The notion of random variable easily remains vague as "something that takes on different values with different probabilities." But random variables are ordinary functions, and this notion is by no means peculiar to probability theory.

Feller translated this concern into a pari passus secondary discussion in the classic work from which this quotation is taken. However, he did not make corresponding concessions to the probable level of mathematical preparation of the reader to whom such a discussion might be of greatest interest—an omission that initially motivated the present effort.

This book undertakes a somewhat more detailed discussion of, and otherwise modified version of, the sample space approach to statistics for social and behavioral scientists. It seeks to develop a theoretical structure so as to be as homologous as possible with actual sampling procedures of substantive research. Since it is

* From *An Introduction to Probability Theory and Its Applications* (2nd ed.) (New York: John Wiley & Sons, Inc., 1950), Vol. I, p. 206.

assumed the reader has had only modest mathematical preparation, graduated mathematical requisites are introduced as an integral part of the exposition. The objective is not so much to teach statistical techniques as to impart statistical *literacy* and, hopefully, stimulate statistical creativity.

The mathematician's admonition to avoid becoming "a slave to notation" serves to develop the openness of mind needed to recognize essential similarities in transformed settings. This book deliberately omits certain terminology and forms of notation—for instance, such terms as "combinations" and "permutations" and their corresponding notations, ${}_nC_r$ and ${}_nP_r$, which can tend through past association to induce regressive thoughtways. Likewise, phrases such as "statistically significant" are played down in favor of less misleading terminology.

The notation of some important statistical tables is introduced, since a practical objective of this book is to familiarize the reader with tables which are invaluable for serious research—for example, Lieberman and Owen's *Tables of the Hypergeometric Probability Distribution.* Conveniently simplified symmetry instructions for the major tables are included in appropriate parts of the text, and it is recommended that the student be provided with access to major statistical tables in order to learn to use them as part of the general acquisition of serious skills.

The sample space concept is used throughout in order to contribute unity to the presentation and promote familiarity with this powerful conceptual tool. The concept "primitive sample space," which is somewhat innovative and provides a more generalized concept than "a perfect die" and the like, is presented in such a way as to show that its results are consistent with the more conventional axiomatic approach. Yet, unlike the axiomatic approach, it allows us to treat the material on a less abstract level and in such a way as not to obscure the relation of the theoretical premises to concrete sampling procedures.

Among other special features of this work are the following:

—A version of the Fisher exact test permitting its extension to three or more subcategories in one of its dimensions is included.

—Detailed instructions are given for using the χ^2 test for dealing with multiple variables by introducing the n-dimensional product space model.

—The often neglected Poisson distribution is given rather extended treatment.

—The "ball-and-cell model," whose power has been so ingeniously demonstrated by Feller, is given prominent treatment.

No attempt has been made to cover the same spectrum of nonparametric models available in such reference manuals as Siegel's *Nonparametric Statistics.* Certain distributions and corresponding models of salient importance have been developed to exemplify the rationale of nonparametric statistical analysis, and these should have considerable carryover value for understanding the use of nonparametric models not included here.

The instructor may exercise considerable discretion as to the prerequisites for a course in which this book serves as a text. The rock-bottom minimum is a good command of ordinary algebra, preferably on the college level. After that, the homogeneity rather than the level of previous preparation of the class becomes important. With minimal prerequisites, the pace must be slower, the coverage less, and supplementary material must be covered in more detail in the class lectures. On the other hand, a student with two or more years of college mathematics might still not find himself overprepared if the coverage proceeds at a pace sufficient to maintain his interest—provided, of course, it is not duplicating material he has already covered. The general structure of presentation is such that an instructor willing to devote some of his lectures to intuitive substitute coverage for some of the theoretical sections could cut down the assigned reading considerably. In classes with better prepared students, this would be both less necessary and less desirable. Another logical truncation would be to omit Chapters 12, 13, and all material after Section 14.1 in Chapter 14.

There has in the past been a marked tendency to regard statistics as "an approach." The author wishes to emphasize that statistics for him is not a philosophical position but a tool to be used only when applicable and, when used, used competently. It functions in the context of a much more general methodological interest—that is, the grounds on which evidence is assessed and the logic of proof in the validation of theory. Statistics are often important in such a context, but there are also areas of inquiry to which they are not applicable, and they are never sufficient when unsupplemented by qualitative and judgmental considerations. Conversely, the prevalent belief that one may ignore the problems to which statistics are addressed by using a "different approach" is sheer self-deception.

Tracing the myriad strands of one's intellectual indebtedness is a hopeless task, though it was Feller's *An Introduction to Probability Theory and Its Applications* that led to an appreciation of the power and elegance of the sample space approach around which the present work is organized. A place of special prominence must be given to Jay Beaman, who, in addition to contributing the problems and bibliographical materials, was my constant consultant in the many thorny conceptual problems entailed in the preparation of this manuscript.

I also owe much to the National Science Foundation for a fellowship that enabled me to enrich my fund of background knowledge and requisite skills. In this same connection, I am grateful to the departments of mathematics and statistics at the University of California at Berkeley for the hospitality extended during the tenure of my grant—and especially to Professor Lucien Le Cam, Chairman of the Statistics Department, and Mr. George Grosser of the Department of Mathematics. Suggestions made by Professor Warren Ten Houten of the Department of Sociology at the University of California at Los Angeles were most helpful in refining the first crude drafts of this work. For informal conversations some years ago which sharpened my appreciation of applied mathematics, I wish to thank Professors E. J. Polak and J. S. Gold of the Department of Mathematics of Bucknell University.

An author cannot avoid becoming aware of the countless ways in which "his" book is a cooperative effort of many people whose contributions do not relate directly to its particular content. To my good friend and colleague Lewis Yablonsky, I am deeply indebted for the generosity with which my efforts were encouraged and supported in his capacity as Chairman of my department. I am also grateful to Wendel Bell , whose considerate acts ultimately helped to make this book possible, and to Earl Bogdanoff, who helped to expedite production of the manuscript in a variety of ways and gave sympathetic encouragement.

I owe much to the students whose participation in my nonparametric statistics courses contributed indirectly to this book—particularly John Walton, Earl Mead, Patricia Blakeslee, Betty Harwick, Anthony Scalzo, Eugene Labovitz, and Maria Naujokaitis.

For preparation of the manuscript, I should like to express my gratitude to Anna Afetian, *primus inter pares* of the secretaries of my department, and to Pat Connally, Nancy Haupt, Bari Meiselman, Shelby Chapel, and Sheena-Ann Selkirk. If it were in my power to award a medal of valor, I would bestow one on Mrs. Bonnie Evenson for her extraordinary transformation of illegible handwriting into clean typewritten copy.

I am indebted to the Literary Executor of the late Sir Ronald A. Fisher, F.R.S., to Dr. Frank Yates, F.R.S., and to Oliver & Boyd, Ltd., Edinburgh, for permission to reprint Table IV, Distribution of χ^2 Probability, from their book *Statistical Tables for Biological, Agricultural and Medical Research.*

Finally, to all those colleagues and friends to whom I owe so much, my heartfelt thanks are extended.

ALBERT PIERCE

CHAPTER 1

INTRODUCTION

STATISTICS IS a branch of mathematics that scientists often use to help reach plausible conclusions from limited information—for instance, to help decide what to infer about the characteristics of a population from a sample of it and to determine the risk of error in making that decision.

Statistical analysis of data is accomplished by using mathematical functions called *probability distributions.* When these functions are used in such a way as to try to reflect the substantive conditions being described or tested for, they are called *statistical models*—models that allow one to use the mathematics of probability so that he can make rational decisions from and about substantive conditions.

One goal of this book is to show how the mathematics of probability are related to statistical models especially suited to research in the social and behavioral sciences. Although only a command of ordinary algebra is needed to understand it, the book also attempts to maintain a level of rigor that will sustain the interest of a reader with more mathematical preparation. A more general objective is to develop the understanding necessary to conduct serious social research.

Any type of reasoning (in fact, even the direct perception of objects) requires us to make assumptions, and statistical reasoning is no exception. However, some statistical models require rather restrictive assumptions about the observed data; such models fall into the category of "strong assumption" statistics. The contrasting category, sometimes labeled "weak assumption" statistics, is called *nonparametric statistics*—although this is a somewhat misleading term, since all mathematical functions embody fixed conditions, or *parameters*, which set the ranges of values the variables can assume. Nonparametric statistics are more suitable for analyzing data in the social sciences. For instance, in strong assumption statistics the only values that can be assigned to the variables are numbers, whereas in nonparametric statistics the values given variables are frequently *qualitative*—an advantage that allows additional scope while still maintaining mathematical rigor.

Yet, even if social and behavioral science data are such that the variables may be assigned real numbers, the strong assumption models impose special requirements on the composition of the populations from which the samples were drawn and on the samples themselves. Where the data actually satisfy these requirements, strong assumption statistics have a generally greater power to yield a given level of information from smaller samples. However, unless it has been determined that the data do comply sufficiently well with the restrictions, this greater power becomes irrelevant. The purpose of applied statistics is to delineate and justify the inferences that can be made within the limits of existing knowledge. That purpose is defeated if knowledge is assumed beyond that actually possessed. *Robust* models are those that work well even if an assumption limit is violated. However, the robustness deteriorates rapidly with each additional violation, and usually more than one assumption is made.

By contrast, the modest restrictions imposed by nonparametric models seldom present problems. Perhaps the most common hazard to the validity of these models is the failure to take samples in the required manner, but this hazard also occurs with strong assumption statistics.

Also, nonparametric models evolve directly out of the combinatorial foundations of statistical reasoning. An intelligent use of statistics requires a complete understanding of these foundations. To understand strong assumption statistics, one must have studied mathematics well beyond two years of calculus or else learned by analogy with nonparametric models. It is therefore hoped that this book will contribute to understanding beyond the confines of its formal coverage.

Another reason for studying nonparametric statistics as an introduction to statistical reasoning is that basic concepts are derived in terms of finite samples taken from finite populations. This conforms realistically to what we do in the social and behavioral sciences. Only Chapter 12, which deals with the Poisson distribution, requires the introduction of concepts of calculus beyond those given in ordinary algebra courses. More advanced concepts are necessary to study infinite populations.

Our pattern of organization is to present the mathematical foundations needed to derive certain important probability distributions, then derive the distributions, translate them into useful statistical models, and, finally, illustrate the application of such models.

Basic mathematical topics are covered extensively and no statistical models are presented until Chapter 7. The elementary set theory, sample space analysis, and probability theory presented in Chapters 2–6 are of intrinsic interest and should sustain the reader's motivation.

In presenting the foundational material, we will (1) develop a theoretical topic at the first point in the discussion at which it is needed so that the relevant material will be fresh in the reader's mind—this will free him from having to absorb more material than needed at any point, and (2) present only topics needed in this work, omitting some topics such as formal set algebra, which are available from other sources.

One word of caution: Statistical models are *mathematical* functions. Their valid use as research instruments involves many considerations that are *not* mathematical. These nonmathematical considerations, such as control of the experimental conditions and substantive interpretation of the statistical results, are known as *methodology*. Statistics and methodology should not be confused. To present the methodology that would make our statistical illustrations impeccable examples of scientific inference would quadruple the length of the book and detract from the *statistical* points. On the other hand, to deal with statistics without using terms that suggest application would mystify the reader as to what this has to do with social and behavioral science. The reader should thus be aware of methodological holes in the examples. Eliminating such holes is a necessary part of substantive investigation. The types of difficulties that arise in actual research cannot be anticipated, and we will make no pretense of doing so. The reader will benefit most if he assumes that any illustration is only a *segment* of an investigation that might involve merely having certain substantive conditions under control, but could possibly involve the use of a battery of additional statistical models of various types.

Having indicated our strategy and laid down some general ground rules, we will turn now to the business at hand.

PROBLEMS

These problems are designed around material given in the Introduction; for example, the first problem asks the reader to formulate definitions or to describe concepts discussed above. These concepts can be defined immediately, but a more precise definition emerges as the reader progresses through the book.

1. Define or describe the following terms: *statistical model*, *nonparametric statistics*, *qualitative values*, and *quantitative values*.

2. Describe the relationship between quantitative values and numbers. (For further information on this relationship, see books by Seigel and others in the Bibliography.) Discuss the relationship between real numbers and interval scales.

CHAPTER 2

FOUNDATIONAL TOPICS

THIS CHAPTER presents some topics from set theory which will serve as a foundation for the remainder of the book. The bibliography at the end of the book contains references for readers interested in pursuing these topics further.

2.1 A SOUPÇON OF SET THEORY*

A *set* is a jointly exclusive class or designation of distinct members—for example, any group of mutually distinguishable objects so designated or classified as to exclude all other objects, such as "American citizens." Members of a set must possess at least two attributes: one is the basis of their classification; the other distinguishes the particular member from all other members of that class. For instance, members of the class of U.S. citizens might be individually distinguished by their respective social security numbers. This second individual attribute need not be sufficient to distinguish

* *Soupçon*, the French culinary term meaning "just a trace of," has perhaps been best defined as a quantity midway between "hardly any" and "none at all."

the member from others that are not in the same set, but the combination of attributes must.

For generality, it is convenient to designate sets by such noncommittal symbols as letters of the alphabet. Thus we can speak of the set A, indicating that A is a specific category to which members belong because they possess certain common but collectively exclusive attributes.

The members of a set are called its *elements.* If some element, say x, belongs to the set A, we may designate this with the symbol $\in$, which means *belongs to.* Thus $x \in A$ means "the element x belongs to the set A," more concisely expressed as "x belongs to A." Usually a capital letter is used for the name of the set and a small letter for an arbitrary member.

Set theory requires that set be distinctly defined so that it is always possible to determine whether some element is or is not a member; for example, the set of natural numbers is clearly distinct. In practice, however, certain unclear instances can occur. If we speak of the set of all automobiles, we have no clear resolution of the point that a partly assembled or disassembled or somehow modified specimen still qualifies for membership. Are astronauts hovering in space members of the set "the world's population"? Set theory requires us to assume definite limits of sets.

Sets containing a finite number of elements are called *finite sets.* The number of elements in a finite set will be called its *size.* All sets that are not finite are infinite, such as the set of all real numbers.

Since elements may belong to more than one set, two or more sets may share some of the same elements. When this occurs, the sets are said to *intersect.* The elements belonging simultaneously to two or more sets are collectively designated as the *intersection* of those sets. For example, the set of all Methodists and the set of all Republicans share members that are both Methodists and Republicans. There are also of course, members of each that are not members of the other. The intersection of sets meets all of the conditions to qualify as a set itself and thus is a set. The operation of intersection is designated by the special symbol $\cap$. Thus the intersection of sets A and B is written $A \cap B$ and may be read "A and B" or "A intersect B." Since the elements belonging to A that also belong to B are identical with those belonging to B that also belong to A, the expression is commutative—that is, $A \cap B = B \cap A$.

It is important to be aware that sets, and hence their intersections, are ways of classifying elements. When sets are designated, elements either belong to them or they do not. If in a set of 100 persons each is either a Methodist or a Republican, then we might have 75 Republicans and 30 Methodists. These numbers do not mean that there are 105 people in the group. Some thought will show that there are at least five people who are both Methodist and Republican. If it were true that Methodists were never Republicans, then we could not have 75 Republicans and 30 Methodists in a group of size 100. Instead, the number of Republicans plus the number of Methodists would always total 100 people. Thus when sets do not intersect, the total number of elements in one set plus the number in the others is the total number of elements in all the sets. If they do intersect, the problem of calculating their combined size requires more information than the size of each. Obviously, then, classifying elements into sets implies neither the destruction nor the creation of elements.

When all of the elements of a set A are elements of another set B, we say that A is a *subset* of B. This may also be stated as "A implies B," and "B is implied by A." "Children" is a subset of "human beings"; hence being a child implies being a human being. There are special symbols to designate subset relationships, but we shall not use them.

The term "subset" is used when the fact of inclusion is to be stressed. Any subset is itself a set, by definition. A set containing other sets is called an *inclusive set* or *superset*; for example, motor vehicle is the inclusive set for automobiles, tractors, motorcycles, and so forth.

The broadest inclusive set for a particular analysis is frequently called the *universal set* or simply *universe*, and sometimes the *cannibal* set. All elements in a universe that are not contained in a specific subset are called the *complement* of that subset. If A is a set, its complement would be called "not A," often written as $\bar{A}$ or A'. We will have occasion to represent the complement as $\not{A}$. We shall call the universal set Ω in this work; hence $\not{A} = \Omega - A$.

A set may be represented either by a listing of its elements separated by commas or by a rule. An example of a listing would be $A = \{1, 3, 5\}$. The conventional form for defining a set by a rule is illustrated by

$$A = \{x \mid x \text{ an odd integer, } 1 \leq x \leq 5\}$$

The vertical line is interpreted to mean "such that." Hence the expression may be read "A is the set of all x such that x is an odd integer between 1 and 5 inclusive," or "A is the set of all odd integers in the closed interval 1 through 5." Some means of representing a set by a rule is necessary because it would not be practical to list all of the members of large sets, and it is impossible to list the members of infinite sets. "Curly" brackets are the standard notation for sets.

Sets are never distinguished by the order of their elements. For example, $\{a, b, c\}$ and $\{c, a, b\}$ are identical sets. Since every element in a set must be uniquely distinguishable and since order in a set is no basis of distinction, a set cannot contain repeated elements. For instance, $\{a, b, c, b, a, a\}$ is still only the set $\{a, b, c\}$. It will occasionally be convenient to use a general term that is noncommittal as to whether a collection of elements are ordered or unordered, or repeated or not repeated. For this, we will take the liberty of using the term *collocation.* Hence while all sets are collocations, not all collocations are sets. This term is used for convenience and is not an attempt to define a concept for general mathematical purposes.*

Since more than one symbol may be used to designate an element, the commas delineate what are to be regarded as elements. Thus $\{abe, cab, eba, abc\}$ is a four-element set.

The famous logician Venn used the device of intersecting circles to represent intersecting sets; such representations are known as *Venn diagrams.* It is instructive to consider the diagram below.

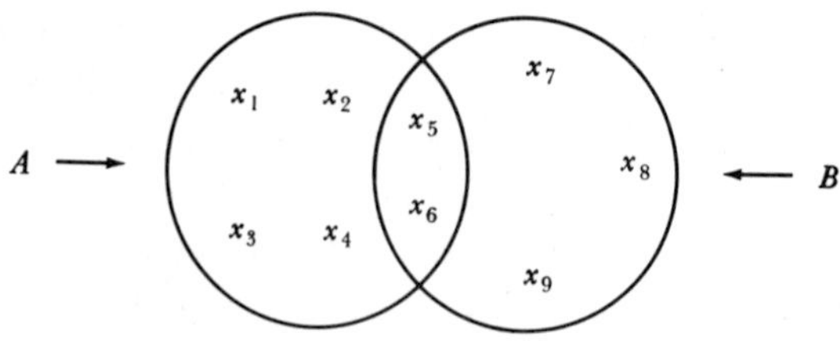

* Collocation will also be discussed under the general heading of arrangement. Here it will be pointed out that the problem of ordering or arranging disappears when we realize that the problem is due to the fact that "ordered sets" and "arrangements" are condensed notations for sets of ordered pairs where the ordering or arranging elements are not explicitly shown. The fact that the ordering or arranging set is not shown explicitly is usually indicated by changing the form of brackets setting off the set.

Some of the things we may note in this case are:

$$x_1 \in A$$

$$x_6 \in A$$

$$x_6 \in B$$

$$x_6 \in (A \cap B)$$

But

$$x_1 \notin B$$

$$x_1 \notin (A \cap B)$$

where the slant line indicates the negative "does not belong." $A \cap B$ then specifically means all of the elements that belong to both A and B. In this case, it means the elements x_5 and x_6.

We may write

$$A \cap B = \{x_5, x_6\}$$

$$A = \{x_1, x_2, x_3, x_4, x_5, x_6\}$$

$$B = \{x_5, x_6, x_7, x_8, x_9\}$$

Set theory sometimes uses a minus sign to indicate removal of elements from a set. For example,

$$A - (A \cap B) = \{x_1, x_2, x_3, x_4, x_5, x_6\} - \{x_5, x_6\}$$

$$= \{x_1, x_2, x_3, x_4\}$$

In words, we have elements in set A that are not in set B.

Just as $\cap$ indicates the intersection of sets, or the logical *and*, a similar symbol $\cup$ indicates the *union*, or logical *or*. $A \cup B$ reads "A or B," and it means all elements that belong to either A or B. Thus

$$A \cup B = \{x_1, x_2, x_3, x_4, x_5, x_6, x_7, x_8, x_9\}$$

Notice that x_5 and x_6 have not been repeated twice in the brackets—this would be redundant, since they meet the condition of being in either set. It should be remembered that $A \cup B$ is itself a set*

* $A \cup B$ may in fact be thought of as an inclusive set of which A, B, and $A \cap B$ are some of the possible subsets.

and hence may not contain elements that are indistinguishable from each other—which would be the case if the elements were repeated. Set elements, in other words, possess the algebraic property of *identity*; that is, any element is equal to itself.

Essentially the same reasoning that led us to conclude the commutativity of intersections would also establish that $A \cup B = B \cup A$.

Just as there is in arithmetic and ordinary algebra a neutral element for addition that is called "zero" and a neutral element for multiplication called "one," so there is an analogous concept in set theory. Its symbol is Φ (phi), and it is the set without any members or the "empty set." That is, Φ = *the empty set*. For reasons of logic, it is considered a subset of every set. Since it contains no members, it follows that $A \cup \Phi = A$ and that $A \cap \Phi = \Phi$.

It should be noted in particular that $\Phi = \{0\}$ is a false statement because $\{0\}$ contains the element zero *and hence has one member*. The expression $\Phi = \{\quad\}$ would be quite proper since it represents a set with no elements.

Two or more sets are said to be *disjoint* or *mutually exclusive* if they contain no elements in common. A Venn diagram would represent this as shown below.

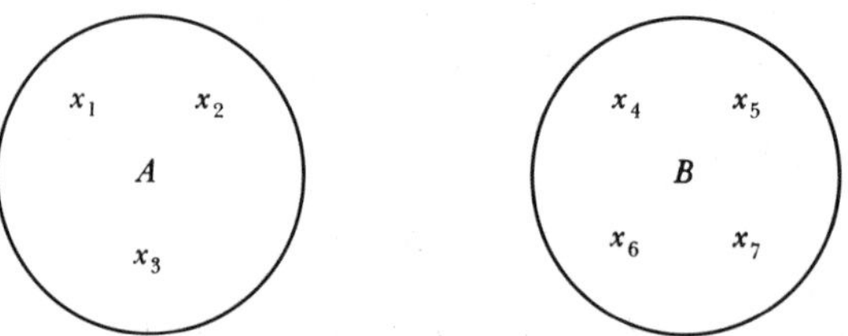

It is evident in this case that $(A \cap B) = \Phi$; that is, the elements that are common to A and B belong to the empty set. The sets "men" and "women" are mutually exclusive or disjoint.

When we speak of designated sets as being exclusive, it will be understood to mean relative to each other. In this case, the qualifier "mutually" becomes redundant, and we will simply use the phrase *exclusive sets*.

In the contrasting case in which, say, A is a wholly contained subset of B, then $A \cap B = A$. The Venn representation of this would be as shown opposite.

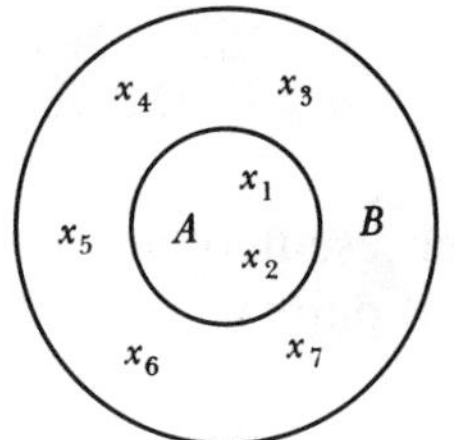

2.2 MULTIPLE SETS

When we are interested in operations involving more than two sets, it is often convenient to use subscript notation. For instance, the notation $A_1, A_2, A_3, \ldots$ can be used instead of speaking of sets A, B, C, D, and so on. This makes possible an economy of expression with set operators comparable to that of the summation sign. For instance, we can designate the intersection of events $A_1, A_2, \ldots, A_k$ as

$$\bigcap_{i=1}^{k} A_i = A_1 \cap A_2 \cap \ldots \cap A_k$$

We can designate the union of events B_i as

$$\bigcup_{i=1}^{k} B_i = B_1 \cup B_2 \cup \ldots \cup B_k$$

The reason for using such expressions will become apparent when we apply them to the analysis of probability.

Subscripts are general devices for making distinctions, and the distinctions to be made will vary in different contexts. Thus under some circumstances E_2 might be used to designate the fact that set E occupies position 2 in an arrangement of sets. In another context it might simply be a way of naming a set so that it can be distinguished from other sets named E_1, E_3, and so forth. Specific meanings derived from context are also common in nonmathematical communication. For instance, in one context the term "becoming" denotes a process of transition, whereas in another it means "flattering." Where the meaning of the subscripts is not explicitly stated, it should be obvious from context.

2.3 ORDERED PAIRS AND PRODUCT SETS

Ordered pairs are represented in the form (a, b). The fundamental property of ordered pairs is

$$(a, b) = (c, d) \quad \text{if and only if} \quad a = c \quad \text{and} \quad b = d$$

As a negative example, it is not true that

$$\{a, b\} = \{c, d\} \quad \text{if and only if} \quad a = c \quad \text{and} \quad b = d$$

The equality of these sets would also hold if $a = d$ and $b = c$.

Table 2.3.1 in this section displays the formation of all distinct ordered pairs of elements from two sets such that the first element in the pair is always from one set and the second element is always from the other set. These ordered pairs are the elements in a new set called the *product set*. Our definition may be stated more formally as follows.

With sets A and B, the product set $A \times B$ consists of all ordered pairs (a, b) where $a \in A$ and $b \in B$. This can also be written

$$A \times B = \{(a, b) \mid a \in A, b \in B\}$$

TABLE 2.3.1 / The Concatenation $\{1, 2, 3, 4\} X \{a, b, c, d, e\}$

	a	b	c	d	e
1	$(1, a)$	$(1, b)$	$(1, c)$	$(1, d)$	$(1, e)$
2	$(2, a)$	$(2, b)$	$(2, c)$	$(2, d)$	$(2, e)$
3	$(3, a)$	$(3, b)$	$(3, c)$	$(3, d)$	$(3, e)$
4	$(4, a)$	$(4, b)$	$(4, c)$	$(4, d)$	$(4, e)$

We see then that the ordered pairs in product sets preserve the identity of the sets from which the elements are drawn, even if the latter sets contain some identical elements. Furthermore, a set may form a product with itself as

$$A \times A = \{(a, b) \mid a \in A; b \in B; B = A\}$$

For example, if $A = \{1, 2, 3\}$, then

$$A \times A = \{(1, 1), (1, 2), (1, 3), (2, 1), (2, 2), (2, 3), (3, 1), (3, 2), (3, 3)\}$$

2.4 CONCATENATIONS AND ORDERED TUPLES

If we have two or more sets $A, B, C, \ldots$ such that $a_i \in A$, $b_i \in B$, $c_i \in C$, and so forth, then the distinct elements $(a_i, b_i, c_i, \ldots)$ that can be formed are the elements of a set which we shall call a *concatenation.*

Table 2.3.1 illustrates the concatenation of two disjoint sets. The concatenation of a collection of sets is the set whose elements are ordered n-tuples such that one element comes from each set and the order in the n-tuple indicates which set each element came from. Thus all of the elements in a given concatenation of disjoint sets must have the same number of components as there are sets to be concatenated. The only implication of the concept "concatenation" beyond what is already implied by "product set" is that of indifference to the order in which the factors are multiplied. That is, any one of the alternative orders in which the factors are multiplied will qualify as an acceptable concatenation of the elements of the factor sets. This further implies that no importance is attached to the particular order of elements that an n-tuple contains.

The case for concatenations or the product set generalizes into n-element collocations, as

$$A \times B \times C \times \ldots \times N$$
$$= \{(a, b, c, \ldots, n) \mid a \in A, b \in B, \ c \in C, \ldots, n \in N\}$$

If there is a constant factor in set multiplication, it can be abbreviated through the use of an exponent, or $A \times A \times A = A^3$. For convenience we may identify this type of expression as a *power product* of a set.

2.5 FUNCTIONS AND EQUIVALENT SETS

When there is a rule that determines for each and every element in set A, one and only one corresponding element in set B, we say that there is a *function* of A into B, written $F : A \rightarrow B$. In other words, such a rule provides for an unequivocal designation of a unique element in B for every element in A. Technically, the function is the complete set of correspondences designated by the rule. The set represented by A is called the *domain* and the set represented by B, the *codomain* or "target set," so that all functions are of the general form F: domain $\rightarrow$ codomain.

As an example, if we have a rule that all children are to be accompanied by their mothers, then we have a domain of children assigned to a codomain of mothers, that is, F: children $\rightarrow$ mothers. That a single mother may have more than one child illustrates the case in which more than one element in the domain may be assigned to a common element in the codomain. The converse is not permitted because the purpose of a functional expression is to provide for the unequivocal disposition of elements in the domain. One type of difficulty that might be anticipated is resolved by the fact that a set can be an element in another set. Suppose we had a set of four cars, one owned by a, one by b, a third owned jointly by a and b, and a fourth by c. Then a rule for assigning cars to their owners would imply a codomain as follows: $\{a, b, \{a, b\}, c\}$. We note that it is quite permissible for the set $\{a, b\}$ to be a unique element even in a set of which it is a subset.

An element in the codomain corresponding to a given element in the domain is called its *image*. If $a \in A$ and its image is $b \in B$, one may write $f(a) = b$. This reads "the image of a is b." Although every element in the domain has an image, not every element in the codomain need be an image. The subset of elements in the codomain that are images is called the *range* of the function. It is evident from previous considerations that an element in the domain can have only one image, but more than one element in the domain can have the same image.

Some implications of this may be stated. For instance, if the codomain is larger than the domain, then some of that codomain's elements must remain unassigned. If the codomain is equal to or smaller in size than the domain, then some of that codomain's elements may be unassigned. The minimum number of elements in the codomain that it is possible to assign is one, in which case, every element in the domain would have the same image.

It is quite common for a function to map a set into itself. Innumerable mathematical functions can map elements from the set of real numbers into itself. In this case, we would write $F: R \rightarrow R$. A simple typical example would be

$$f(x) = x^2$$

This represents the rule that the element in the set of real numbers corresponding to any number x in the domain of real numbers is a real number equal to x multiplied by itself. Examples are $f(2.0) = 4.0$, $f(-2.0) = 4.0$, and $f(1.0) = 1.0$.

If every element in the domain has an image that is exclusively its own in the codomain, the function is called a *one-one* function. If every element in the codomain is an image—that is, if the range and

FIGURE 2.5.1 / Types of Functions

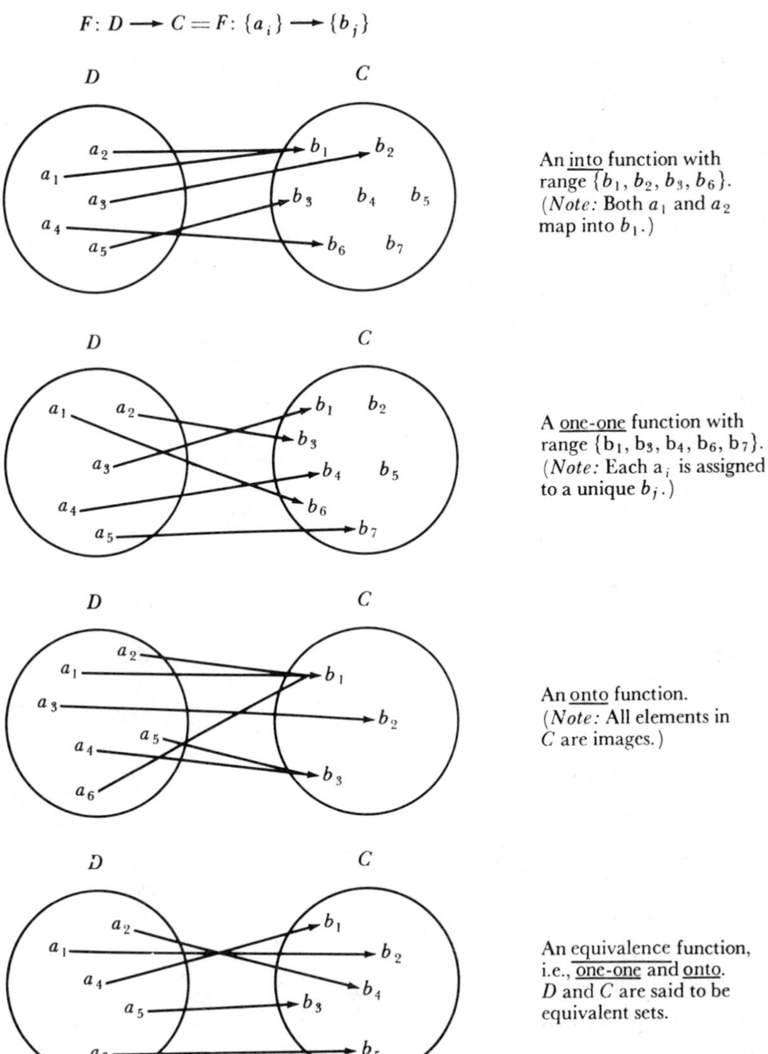

F: D → C = F: {a_i} → {b_j}
D
C
An into function with range {b1, b2, b3, b6}. (Note: Both a1 and a2 map into b1.)
A one-one function with range {b1, b3, b4, b6, b7}. (Note: Each a_i is assigned to a unique b_j.)
An onto function. (Note: All elements in C are images.)
An equivalence function, i.e., one-one and onto. D and C are said to be equivalent sets.

the codomain are identical—then the function is called an *onto* function. If a function is both one-one and onto, the sets are called *equivalent sets*. It is evident that the sets must be of exactly equal size in order for these two conditions to hold simultaneously.

Two equivalent sets D and C are said to be *isomorphic* if in $f(a_i) = b_j$ the a_i and the b_j differ at most in notation. In other words, if there is a function $F: D \to C$ so that operations defined on D are valid in the set C, then F is called an *isomorphism*.

Isomorphic sets are necessarily equivalent sets, but the converse is not true.

The concept of ordered pairs permits us to redefine function in an elegant way. If there exists a rule for forming ordered pairs from sets A and B under the condition that each and every element in A shall be used once and only once, then the resultant set of ordered pairs is called a *function* of A into B, written $F: A \to B$. Notice that this ensures an unequivocal assignment of every $a \in A$ and also determines that the number of elements in the function will exactly equal the number of elements in A. By way of illustration, if $A = \{1, 2, 3\}$ and $B = \{\text{odd}, \text{even}\}$, and the controlling rule is that numbers exactly divisible by 2 are to be assigned to even and all others to odd, then the complete function $F: A \to B$ is

$$\{(1, \text{odd}), (2, \text{even}), (3, \text{odd})\}$$

If $D = \{2, 3, 4\}$ and $C = \{\sqrt{4}, \sqrt{9}, \sqrt{16}\}$, then the function $\{(2, \sqrt{4}), (3, \sqrt{9}), (4, \sqrt{16})\}$ would be an isomorphism.

2.6 THE FUNDAMENTAL PRINCIPLE OF COMBINATORIAL ANALYSIS

The fundamental principle of combinatorial analysis states that a concatenation consisting of $m \cdot n$ elements may be formed from two disjoint sets of sizes m and n, respectively. We see from Table 2.3.1 that the four elements in the set $\{1, 2, 3, 4\}$ may be used to designate rows and the five elements in $\{a, b, c, d, e\}$ may be used to designate columns, to form a rectangular block of $4 \times 5 = 20$ cells, each of which contains a unique set of elements that consists of one from each of the two original sets. Also, for any finite values of m and n we could, in principle, arrange the m elements of one set in a marginal column and the n elements of another set in a marginal row, to generate a matrix of size mn whose elements are ordered pairs. The principle of combinatorial analysis is thus established.

Books of recreational mathematics (mathematics pursued for amusement) provide countless applications of this principle. For instance, if a man has three sport coats and four pairs of slacks, he can wear a distinct outfit for 12 consecutive days. We should not allow the recreational aspects of the principle to obscure the importance of its more serious applications—there are few places in which the adjective "fundamental" is so appropriately applied. It would hardly be an exaggeration to say that the whole field of combinatorial analysis consists of various ingenious applications of this principle. Since combinatorial analysis is the foundation for classical probability theory and classical probability theory undergirds applied statistics, its importance is evident.

It is important to understand that the order in ordered pairs and ordered tuples can be used as a notational device to identify the set from which any element was taken by the position of that element in the tuple; ordered need have no further implications. When so conceived, an ordered tuple is tantamount to a set whose elements have special identifiers, then (c, b, a, c) contains exactly the same information as $\{a_3, b_2, c_1, c_4\}$.*

The fundamental principle may be made into a general statement with the help of subscript notation and formulated as

> Given k sets of elements of respective sizes $n_1, n_2, n_3, \ldots, n_k$, we may form a concatenation consisting of $(n_1 \cdot n_2 \cdot n_3 \cdot \ldots \cdot n_k)$ distinct tuples each containing exactly one element from each of the original k sets.

To prove this we note that we can combine the elements from the first two sets in $n_1 \cdot n_2$ ways to form a new set of $(n_1 \cdot n_2)$ two-element tuples. We may in turn combine this newly formed set with the third set in $(n_1 \cdot n_2) \cdot n_3$ ways to generate a set of $(n_1 \cdot n_2 \cdot n_3)$

* Both cases imply the ordered pairs $\{(1, c), (2, b), (3, a), (4, c)\}$. This is some *ordering* function $F:\{1, 2, 3, 4\} \rightarrow \{a, b, c\}$. An *arranging* function could be illustrated by F:{red, yellow, blue} $\rightarrow \{a, b, c\}$, where the relevant rule might yield the function {(red, b), (yellow, c), (blue, a)}. An ordering function is an arranging function whose domain elements imply ranking.

three-element tuples, and continue this same process until we have

$$(n_1 \cdot n_2 \cdot n_3 \cdot \ldots \cdot n_k) = \prod_{i=1}^{k} n_i \quad k\text{-element tuples}$$

It follows that the fundamental principle may be used directly to determine the number of elements in a product set. That is, given that n_i is the size of set A_i, then the size of the product set

$$\prod_{i=1}^{k} A_i \quad \text{is} \quad \prod_{i=1}^{k} n_i$$

In the case of a powder product, since the sets constituting the factors are identical, they have to be equal in size. In this case, the n_i factor in the fundamental principle has a constant value, call it n, and the size of the power product set A^k is

$$\prod_{i=1}^{k} n = n^k$$

PROBLEMS

The problems below are designed to aid the reader in the transition between "usual terminology" and the terminology of mathematics encountered in journals and scientific publications with more specialized vocabularies. Technical terminology such as set theory terms permits precise expression in a way not usually possible with ordinary language.

1. Why must any member of a set be characterized by at least two attributes? *Answer:* Two attributes fulfill the definition of a member of a set as given in Section 2.1. Keeping the preceding question and answer in mind, discuss the problems of defining these three sets:

- **a.** The set of all living things.
- **b.** The set of Mexican-Americans.
- **c.** The set of "aged" persons in a given city.

2. What does it mean for a set to contain a finite number of elements? *Answer:* Intuitively, this means that the elements in this set may be counted. In other words, there is some number, for example, 1000, for which we can say that, if we have numbered points up to 1000, we have numbered all the points in the set. Which of the following sets are finite and which are infinite?* Explain.

a. The set of U.S. citizens.
b. The set of all people *anywhere.*
c. The set of all phone calls in a 1-hour period.
d. The set of all counting numbers: 1, 2, 3, and so forth.

The answers to Problems 3–5 use the sets defined below.

$A_1 = \{1, 2, 3, 4\}$
$A_2 = \{2, 3, 4, 5\}$
$A_3 = \{3, 4, 5, 6\}$
$A_4 = \{4, 5, 6, 7\}$
$A_5 = \{5, 6, 7\}$
$B = \{a, b, c, d, e\}$
$C = \{x \mid x$ is an Irish Roman Catholic$\}$
$D = \{y \mid y$ is a counting number$\}$
$E = \{(1, a), (1, b)$, etc., so that all pairs with first elements from A and second elements from B are included$\}$
$F = \{x \mid x$ is a Roman Catholic$\}$

3. Give three elements from each of the five sets A, B, C, D, E.

4. **a.** Draw a Venn diagram showing A_1, A_2, A_3, A_4, A_5. *Hint:* The diagram should resemble the pattern below. This diagram is correct but not complete, since it shows only sets A_1, A_2, A_5.

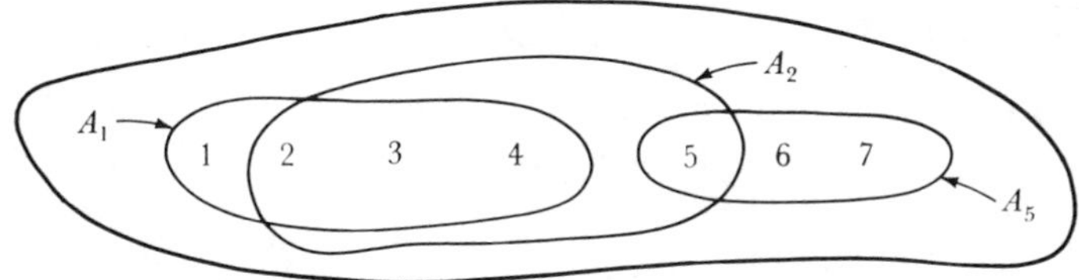

b. What is the universe for this collection of sets?
c. Which sets in this collection contain $\{4, 5\}$ as a subset?
d. Which sets are mutually exclusive with $\{4\}$s?

$A_1 \cap A_2, \qquad A_2$

f. Can you shade in $A_1 \cap A_5$? Why or why not?

* The moderately difficult book by Kamke in the Bibliography is an excellent discussion of transfinite counting.

5. Determine the following:

a. $A_1 \cup B$, $A_1 \cup A_2$, $B \cup A_3$, $C \cup D \bigcup_{i=1}^{5} A_i$, and $C \cup G$.

Hint: The answers may either give all the elements of the set or may express the composition of the set in words.

b. $A_1 \cap A_2$, $A_1 \cap B$, $A_1 \cap A_2 \cap A_3$, $C \cap G$ and $D \cap \{x \mid x$ is an even counting number$\}$.

c. $A_4 - A_5$, $D - \{x \mid x$ is an even counting number$\}$ and $G - C$.

6. Consider the following sets:

$$S_1 = \{x \mid x \text{ is a Catholic}\}$$
$$S_2 = \{y \mid y \text{ is Irish}\}$$
$$S_3 = \{z \mid z \text{ is a U.S. citizen}\}$$
$$S_4 = \{w \mid w \text{ is a male}\}$$
$$\Omega = \{x \mid x \text{ is a human}\}$$

Give the meaning of the sets defined in parts a to c below.

a. $S_1 \cap S_2$, $S_1 \cap S_2 \cap S_3$ and $S_1 \cap S_2 \cap S_3 \cap S_4$.

b. $\Omega - S_4$ and $\Omega - S$.

c. $(\Omega - S_1 \cap S_2)$, $S_2 \cup S_3$.

d. Explain why $S_1 \cap S_2$ is or is not a subset of S_1, S_2, S_3, S_4, and Ω.

7. Given the array X (ethnic group, religion, occupation) and given the following codes:

ETHNIC GROUP	RELIGION	OCCUPATION
1. British	1. Roman Catholic	1. White collar
2. French	2. Protestant	2. Blue collar
3. Other	3. Other	3. Other
	4. No religion	
	5. No religion given	

Interpret the following points or sets:

a. $X(1, 1, 1)$.

b. $X(2, 1, 2)$.

c. $X(3, 4, 2)$.

d. $\{X(1, 1, i) \mid i = 1 \text{ or } i = 2\}$.

e. $\{X(2, k, j) \mid k = 3, 4, \text{ or } 5 \text{ and } j = 1 \text{ or } 2\}$.

8. Use an elementary text (see Bibliography) or, preferably, make up examples of the following:

a. A function with domain $\{1, 2, 3, 4\}$.

b. An into function with codomain $\{a, b, c, d, e\}$.

c. An onto function.

d. A one-one and onto function.

e. Give a different one-one and onto function having the same domain and codomain as the function given in part d.

9. Give examples of the application of the fundamental principal of combinatorial analysis in calculating the following:

a. The number of religion-ethnic group categories defined by the codes in Problem 7.

b. The number of religion-occupation and ethnic-occupation categories defined by the codes in Problem 7.

c. The number of combinations of religion-ethnic group, and occupation possible with the codes of Problem 7.

10. Given $M = \{a, b, \{c, d\}, e\}$, is it true that $c \in M$? Is $\{c, d\}$ a one-element or a two-element subset of M?

CHAPTER 3

SOME BASIC DEFINITIONS

PROBABILITY THEORY can be rewarding for one who is willing to prepare himself for it. Such are its subtleties, however, that even a dull-normal wool-gatherer can redefine a very simple problem as a highly complex one by proposing an innocuous-appearing change in a single condition. The novice will save himself a lot of unproductive wheel-spinning if he restrains the impulse to raise anticipatory questions of the sort that start out, "What if . . . ?" One must exercise a certain amount of self-disciplined effort to acquire the necessary conceptual tools to manage the complexities. It is not easy for an untrained person to frame an unambiguous question about the probability of an event. For instance, if there are nine passengers on an elevator, then the question "What is the probability that two of them will be discharged on the same floor?" may seem perfectly straightforward. However, there are at least eight or nine equally correct answers to it, depending upon which of a number of additional and unstated conditions one assumes to be the case—for example, two *specified* persons, or any two persons; a specified floor, or any floor; exactly two persons, or at least two persons; exactly one floor on which exactly two persons get off, or at least one floor.

The set theory discussed in the previous chapter will prove

useful in formulating unambiguous expressions. Another helpful step is to frame precise definitions—a task to which we now turn.

3.1 ESSENTIAL CONCEPTS

Since we will later define the concept of a "sample space," it is necessary to know what a space is. Not long ago the term "space" evoked a physical image as something that is occupied by objects which have extension (volume). It was that general medium occupied by the physical universe. On a more abstract level, space also referred to the geometric representation in the traditional three dimensions. With the emergence of set theory as the dominant style of mathematical thinking, the concept of space has been enormously generalized. A *space* consists of a nonempty set together with the rules, axioms, conditions, or restrictions that apply to its elements. Once the set of rules has been specified, the set elements may be called *points* in the space. If the number of points in a space is finite, we shall call it a *finite space* and shall refer to the number of points in it as its *size*. Otherwise, we shall call it an *infinite space*. If the elements in an infinite space can be placed in a one-one correspondence with the set of natural numbers, it will be called *countable* or *denumerable*. In this book we shall be concerned, with occasional exceptions, with finite spaces.

The older mathematical conceptions of space have not actually been eliminated by the new definition—they are special cases of it. For instance, since every point in a three-dimensional Euclidean space can be located by distances along three orthogonal (perpendicular) axes through a common point called the *origin*, and since the set of points on a Euclidean line corresponds to the set of real numbers, then conventional Euclidean space has been redefined as a space whose points are the set of all ordered triplets of real numbers, for example, (7.9, 3.2, −2.77). Such points are called *vectors*, and certain rules specify their properties. Lines (whose points are subsets of the elements in the space) are defined by such rules as "If P and Q are distinct points in the space, there is only one line in the space through both P and Q." One might define a "chess space" as elements called "pieces" and "squares" together with the set of rules governing "moves." A "social space" could be defined as a subset of elements from the set "human population," whose relationships can be delineated by certain rules. These are all perfectly acceptable spaces by modern mathematical standards.

Since we shall be using sets to study spaces, we can agree that when we refer to a set as a space and to its elements as points, it is assumed that some set of rules necessary to qualify the elements as points in a space exists.

By a *statistical investigation* we shall mean an investigation in which a statistical model plays an instrumental role rather than the investigation of the logical rationale of such models, although it is the latter that is the subject matter of this book. The scope of statistical investigation is limited to *events*.

For any phenomenon to qualify as an event it must be possible to decide whether it occurred. That is, it must have characteristics that make it possible for a neutral observer to determine unequivocally whether the assertion that the event has occurred is true or false. The statement "Joshua fought the Battle of Jericho" describes an event, because observation at the time it is alleged to have occurred could have determined that it was true or false. On the other hand, "God moved Joshua to fight the Battle of Jericho" states a nonevent, because disagreement as to its veracity could not have been resolved by observation at the time of its alleged occurrence.*

By an *experiment* we mean the complete act of observation required to determine whether or not a specified event has occurred. The word "complete" indicates that the observation may have to be conducted in segments and the information from all the segments collated to determine whether the event has occurred. The irreducible or "quantized" segments of observation are called *trials*, and we shall call the phenomenon observed during a single trial an *elementary event*. For example, if we conduct the experiment of tossing a coin three times to see if three heads will occur, three trials are required to observe the three elementary events from which the conclusion may be drawn that the outcome was as specified. We shall call any event whose outcome requires or might require more than one trial a *composite event*. The event "at least one head in three tosses of a coin" might conceivably be determined on the first trial; nevertheless, we shall think of it as a composite event requiring three trials.

With "experiment" now defined, we may state our definition of

---

* We are not evaluating here the relative merits of events and nonevents but merely delineating the categories of phenomena to which probabilities may properly be assigned.

"event" more mathematically, by again using ideas introduced from set theory. An *event* is any designated set of outcomes that could result from the performance of an experiment. The particular set of outcomes whose occurrence or nonoccurrence is designated may also be called the *event set*. The event will be said to have occurred if any point in the event set occurs. For example, the space of ordered outcomes of the experiment of observing two tosses of a coin is $\{(H, H), (H, T), (T, H), (T, T)\}$. The event set for the event "the same face will show on both trials" is $\{(H, H), (T, T)\}$, and the event will be said to have occurred if either (H, H) or (T, T) occurs. Conversely, if any event not in the event set occurs (that is, any point in the complement of the event set), the event will be said not to have occurred. We shall make frequent use of the symbol E to represent an event or event set and $\not{E}$ to represent its complement.

When the event set contains more than one element (alternative outcome) of the space it is defined on, we shall call it a *compound event*. Compound events may be represented by such notation as

$$\bigcup_{i=1}^{k} E_i$$

where if any of the outcomes $E_1, E_2, \ldots,$ or E_k occur, the event will be said to have occurred. Thus a compound event can be thought of as a union of qualifying outcomes. Note that, unlike "composite," the concept of "compound" has no reference to the number of trials required for the experiment. For instance, "an odd face shows in one toss of a die" involves only a single trial, but any outcome of one, three, or five dots meets the condition that defines the event. We note that a qualifying outcome of a compound event could be either elementary or composite; that is, the notions of "compound" and "elementary" are not contradictory.

To *decompose* an event means to display the elements of that event—that is, indicate all of the alternative outcomes that qualify as occurrences of it. Thus "both faces the same" decomposes into HH and TT.

$$\bigcup_{i=1}^{k} E_i$$

decomposes into E_1, E_2, and so on. An event that can be decomposed only into itself and Φ is called a *simple event*. As a matter of convenience, we shall sometimes refer to an event as "nondecomposable," with the implicit understanding that this means it can be decomposed only into itself and Φ. For instance, the event "in three tosses of a die, each face will correspond to the number of its trial" is a simple event because only the exact sequence of outcomes 1:2:3 fulfills the condition; it cannot be realized in any other way.

The concepts of "compound event" and "composite event" should never be confused nor should "simple event" be confused with "elementary event." In the example above, one should never make the error of saying that such an event decomposes into the elements 1, 2, and 3. In a three-trial experiment, every alternative outcome has to contain three elements; for example, 1:3 simply cannot be an outcome. We will comment on these distinctions in the next section, after we have defined the concept of "sample space." The matter can be understood more fully in terms of "events involved in determining the attributes of the points in a sample space" and "events defined on the sample space."

Any ordered tuple will be called an *order*. It is a special case of an *arrangement*. In the present book, order and arrangement may, to all intents and purposes, be used interchangeably. For example, an ordered outcome of five tosses of a die might be 6:2:5:2:6. An exactly equivalent arrangement could be obtained from the simultaneous throw of five distinguishable dice (say, different colored), specifying that the red and the green dice each show face 6, the orange and blue each show face 2, and the yellow one shows face 5. Similarly, throwing a coin three times, specifying the outcome for each throw, is equivalent to throwing a nickel, a dime, and a quarter simultaneously and specifying, say, that the quarter land tails, the dime tails, and the nickel heads.

For our purposes, the following definition should suffice. Given a set A of at least two elements, to be called "arranging elements," and a set of elements B, then any function arranging or identifying B according to A designates a unique arrangement of B elements. For example, given

$$A = \{\text{orange, red, yellow, blue, green}\}$$

$$B = \{1, 2, 3, 4, 5, 6\}$$

then one $F: A \to B$ could be

$$\{(\text{orange}, 2), (\text{red}, 6), (\text{yellow}, 5), (\text{blue}, 2), (\text{green}, 6)\}$$

This is seen to represent the order of outcomes of the dice as specified above. Ordered refers to an ordinal arranging set. In this presentation, "arrangements" will generally be exemplified by orders.

It should now be evident that for the outcome of an experiment to be ordered there must be some basis on which the trials can be distinguished, such as "first trial" or "second trial." In other words, the trials must qualify as elements in an "ordering set." Conversely, if the trials of an experiment are *indistinguishable*, the outcome must be *unordered.* If a set of students drawn from a class were {Tom, Dick, Mary}, one could not tell which student corresponded to which trial, so it is an unordered outcome. For experiments, then, one may think of ordered outcomes as being associated with distinguishable trials, and unordered with indistinguishable.

There are still two important things that are relevant to this discussion of order. First, although there might happen to be a *de facto* order to the outcome of an experiment, we shall regard such an outcome as ordered only if the order is of consequence to our investigation. In other words, order is dependent upon the attitude of investigator toward the outcome rather than the actual outcome itself. He might know the order in which Tom, Dick, and Mary were drawn, but it might not matter; hence the outcome is unordered.

Finally, it is important to recognize that, paradoxically, *unordered* means the union of all orders that qualify as an occurrence. That is, the condition "unordered" is met by any order that occurs. Thus an unordered outcome of an experiment will always be a compound event on some space, if the decomposition has any meaningful interpretation.

Collocation will be used as a general designation for any representation of elements that are to be thought of as belonging together. Thus sets, ordered tuples, or unordered collections containing repeated elements would all be examples of collocations.

3.2 POPULATIONS AND SUBPOPULATIONS

A *population* is a nonempty set; it is *not* a space. As a set, a population is a collection of separately identifiable objects that share at least one characteristic that serves as a basis for their collective distinction.

A *subpopulation* is a subset of a population, and just as subsets are themselves sets, subpopulations are populations. The prefix serves to call attention to the existence of an inclusive set. "People" is a population and "women" is a subpopulation of it. "Even integers" is a subpopulation of the population "integers."

As social scientists we shall be interested primarily in human populations and populations of their attributes. Certain important concepts can be grasped easier if we use decks of cards and the faces of coins and dice for our illustrations.

3.3 SAMPLE SPACES AND SAMPLE POINTS

A *sample space* is a space whose points are the set of all possible outcomes of the experiment of drawing a sample of elements from one or more populations according to stipulated rules or restrictions. Examples of rules that are often used are "the same element may not be drawn more than once in the course of a single experiment" or, conversely, "any element may be drawn as many times as there are trials in the experiment." "Drawing a sample" is used in a broad sense to include recording a set of observations that could be defined as isomorphic to a set of outcomes of sampling from a population. For instance, the set of outcomes of the experiment of tossing a coin five times can be defined as isomorphic to that implied by drawing a sample of size five with replacement between trials from the population $\{H, T\}$.

Certain attributes characterize a sample space. First, since the points constitute a set, each point is a distinct element in that set. If we had an original population $P = \{a, b, c, d, e\}$, examples of points in different sample spaces formed according to different rules might be (c, b, b), $\{b, c, e\}$, $[c, b, b]$, and so forth. In these cases, each total parenthetical expression is a point in its own particular space. In a sample space, no operation may be performed to alter the internal composition of a point without implicitly defining a new space.

Second, because set elements are by definition separate identities, they are nonintersecting or mutually exclusive. Ambiguity can be avoided if we represent certain notations for points in brackets, as $[a, b]$ rather than $\{a, b\}$, since the former clearly occurs only if both a and b occur, whereas the latter might be taken to imply that either a

or b is sufficient to constitute an occurrence. Furthermore, the notation for two points like $\{a, b\}$ and $\{a, c\}$ implies an intersection which is contrary to the notion of mutually exclusive, whereas $[a, b]$ and $[a, c]$ imply merely that two points exist, one which occurs when both a and b occur and the other which occurs when both a and c occur. Finally, $\{a, b, b\} = \{a, b\}$, whereas $[a, b, b] \neq [a, b]$.

Confusion may be avoided if one recognizes the distinction between the "events that define the sample space" and "events defined *on* the sample space." Each point in a sample space represents one possible outcome of an experiment. Each such point is either an elementary or a composite event; that is, its identity is established by either the outcome of one trial or more than one trial. "Elementary" and "composite" have reference only to this internal composition of points in the sample space. Such a point is never to be regarded as anything but a single element *in its own space*. Therefore the experiment and the number of trials involved in the experiment *define the sample space*.

Once such a sample space is explicitly or implicitly defined, one may arbitrarily classify the outcomes (points) on the basis of selected attributes that may characterize more than one of the outcomes. If one defines the event of interest only in terms of those attributes, then more than one point may qualify as an outcome. The specification of outcomes or points that will qualify is called "defining an event *on* the sample space." If only one point in the space satisfies this definition, we call it a *simple event*. That is, it is a one-element subset of the sample space. If more than one point satisfies this definition, then one has defined an event set larger than size 1 and such an event set is called a *compound* event. Thus just as "elementary" and "composite" have reference to the internal composition of the points in the space, so do "simple" and "compound" have reference to classes of outcomes defined on the space. This distinction, one it is understood, will be obvious from the context of the problem. After "probability" is defined in Section 3.5, it will be obvious that "the probability of an event" will always mean an event defined *on* a sample space. "Probability" will have no meaning until a space has been defined.

As previously noted, since a sample space is a set and its points are its elements, they are mutually exclusive. Events defined separately on a sample space, however, need not be mutually exclusive; they may be intersecting sets. For instance, if we have a space defined as the set of all five-card poker hands, we might define event

E_1 as the subset of hands containing exactly three kings and E_2 as the subset of hands containing at least one club. Then E_1 and E_2 are intersecting sets, since at least one hand in the space, a fair number in fact, will contain both three kings and at least one club.

3.4 THE "PRIMITIVE" SAMPLE SPACE

The concept of a "primitive sample space" is of basic theoretical importance to this work, although there does not appear to be any precedent for this terminology. This space is only a theoretical construct since there is not, even in principle, a noncircular way of determining whether such a space exists other than conceptually.

First, *a primitive sample space* has all of the characteristics of a sample space with four additional restrictions.

1. By postulation no point in it has any greater *de facto* tendency to be observed than any other.* This implies that if the experiment were conducted repeatedly, no regular recurrence pattern would emerge.

2. It is finite.

3. Its points are each intrinsically nondecomposable; that is, none of them could be represented as a multiple element subset. For instance, a point like $[a, b]$ could be expressed as $\{(a, b), (b, a)\}$, whereas (a, b) could only be resolved into itself.† Another way to state much the same thing is that the set of points constituting a primitive space could not be defined as isomorphic to a set of exclusive exhaustive subsets of a larger space. Of course, no point is decomposable within its own space, since every point in a space is an integral element of that space. We shall loosely use the terms "decomposable" and "nondecomposable" spaces, meaning only that they either can or cannot be defined as isomorphic to an exhaustive set of nonintersecting subsets of a larger space.

All primitive spaces then are nondecomposable although the converse is not true.

* To postulate an empirical property is not tantamount to supposing it to be true. Thus one might postulate that the earth is flat and then reject the proposition that the earth is flat by virtue of discrepancies between its observed characteristics and those implied by the postulate. This is in fact a common type of inference in statistics, as we shall see.

† A convention being used to aid intuitive understanding.

4. Every point in the space must represent an outcome requiring the same number of trials as every other. Thus every point in a primitive space is either an elementary event or, alternatively, a collocation, ordered tuplet, or array, of the same size and type as every other point.

It might be thought that to postulate a uniform tendency to be observed is to postulate equiprobability surreptitiously. This is not the case since probability denotes an attribute of a state of knowledge of an observable phenomenon and not an attribute of the phenomenon itself. A uniform tendency to be observed is an attribute of an event identified with a sample point, not a state of knowledge about it.

Many nonprimitive sample spaces may be decomposed into primitive sample spaces. For example, the space of ordered points for the investigation of three tosses of a coin could be the primitive space obtained by the decomposition of the unordered space

$$[3H]$$

$$[2H, 1T]$$

$$[2T, 1H]$$

$$[3T]$$

This is a four-point nonprimitive (and as we shall see, nonuniform) space that decomposes into an eight-point primitive space as follows (with the equivalent subsets indicated):

$$\{\{HHH\}, \{HHT, HTH, THH\}, \{TTH, THT, HTT\}, \{TTT\}\}$$

3.5 PROBABILITY

Now we can define probability in a manner that will be valid for many of the spaces we shall be considering in this book. For others it will suffice by intuitive extrapolation. An important advantage in this definition, as opposed to definitions more important for other purposes, is the ease that actual values of probabilities can be obtained by its use. This is related to the fact that this is a "natural" definition to use in conjunction with the concept of "sample space." These are highly desirable features when the application is the end in view rather than the economy of postulates in the development of a theoretical system.

DEFINITION 3.5.1. When one assumes a primitive sample space \$ of size S that contains a subset E of size $\mathscr{E}$, with E defined as all points in \$ qualifying as occurrences of a specified event, then the probability of that event is defined as

$$P[E] = \frac{\mathscr{E}}{S}$$

Probability is thereby defined as the ratio of the size of a specified subset called an *event set*, to the size of an inclusive set known as the primitive sample space. Thus we have given probability a sort of operational definition. It is extremely important to remember that this definition is in terms of the *primitive* space and its subsets. Errors of great magnitude may occur if this fact is ignored.

The reader should divest himself of previous conceptions of probability during this discussion. He should think of probability as nothing more than the mathematical ratio of the sizes of two sets. The result of the most complex problem in probability is, at least implicitly, a ratio of this sort. Conversely, it is a useful assumption that determining the value of a probability involves two separate tasks—determining the size S of the relevant primitive sample space, and determining the size $\mathscr{E}$ of the subset of its points that constitute occurrences of the event of interest.

For the time being, we shall settle for one simple illustration of our definition. In the previous section we saw that the primitive sample space for three tosses of a coin contained eight points. Suppose we wish to know the probability of the event "all faces show the same." We already know that $S = 8$. The subset of sample points meeting the required condition is $E = \{HHH, TTT\}$ and contains two elements; hence $\mathscr{E} = 2$. From our definition,

$$P[\{3H\} \cup \{3T\}] = \frac{\mathscr{E}}{S} = \frac{2}{8} = .25$$

3.6 STOCHASTIC EVENTS AND RANDOM VARIABLES

A stochastic event is an event defined on a sample space and hence an event for which a probability may be determined. If one forms a function for which the domain consists of stochastic events, and the codomain is a set of probabilities to which they have been appropriately assigned, then the function may be called a *random variable.* If X is a general symbol for the function, it is usual to speak of X as a random variable. If an element in the codomain corresponding to X_i is p_i, then $f(X_i) = p_i$.

If we think of the experiment of a single toss of a die, X_i may assume any of the values 1, 2, 3, 4, 5, or 6, to each of which a probability attaches. X_i is thus a random variable. The alternative values of a random variable constitute a set, but these values and their corresponding probabilities are not necessarily equivalent sets. In the example of the die, for instance, the set of corresponding probabilities is only a one-element set,* and that element is $\frac{1}{6}$. On the other hand, if we tossed two dice, the various sums of their faces would have to be assigned to different probabilities in the codomain. For example, "sum 2" would be assigned to $p = \frac{1}{36}$ and "sum 7" to $p = \frac{1}{6}$.

PROBLEMS

1. Give the definition of a space and explain why the space that was studied in Euclidean geometry qualified as a space. In other words, what are the rules involved in defining this as a space?

2. Discuss the differences between a space and a sample space.

3. Discuss briefly why the point *abc* written without brackets is referred to as an event, yet $\{abc\}$ is the same event. Your discussion will be aided by explaining the statement "$\{abc, bac, cba\}$ is the union of the points *abc*, *bac*, *cba*, or equivalently, it is $\{abc\} \cup \{bac\} \cup \{cba\}$."

4. Give examples of experiments that are elementary events and experiments that are composite events. For each composite event tell how many trials it requires. Using Table 4.1.1 (page 39 in Chapter 4), formulate a compound event and give an example of a simple event in this compound event. Explain how many trials it takes to achieve the simple event just specified. What is the elementary event at each stage of this given simple event?

* Or, if one prefers, a one-element range in the set of rational numbers.

5. Decomposition is used in a uniquely restrictive way in this text. Probabilities are always associated with sets or events. The same sets may be defined as events on different probability spaces. Many new spaces could be created, and decomposition only has meaning in context where there is a unique decomposition. A set of rules has been given which defines a unique way of breaking up a given set or element. List these rules.

6. Given $\{(p, h), (n, t), (d, t), (q, h)\}$, answer the following:

a. What is the arranging set?

b. This event could be given as $HTTH$ or by using $N = \{1, 2, 3, 4\}$ as the ordering set. Write this event using N as the ordering set. Why is "arranging" used in one case and "ordering" in the other?

c. Express $HHTH$ using both N and $\{p, n, d, g\}$ as arranging sets.

d. Define a function mapping the two arranging sets into each other.

e. If p refers to a penny, n to a nickel, d to a dime, and q to a quarter, explain how p, n, d, q could be used as an ordering set as well as an arranging set.

f. Give three examples of arranging sets which are not ordering (ordered) sets.

7. How may the arrangements given in the previous problem be related to composite events and trials? See Feller's discussion (page 33 in his book—see Bibliography) concerning Bose–Einstein statistics, which makes it clear that decompositions and unions of ordered sets do not necessarily lead to the concept of unordered events.

CHAPTER 4

EVENTS AND THEIR PROBABILITIES

IN THIS CHAPTER, we will (1) illustrate the application of sample space analysis to the determination of probabilities; (2) show that the premises we have adopted lead to results that are consistent with those derived from the postulates of axiomatic theory; (3) derive, while implementing the two objectives above, some very important principles and identities.

There are many alternatives to the proofs and derivations presented in this chapter, but they would not be consonant with our desire to demonstrate a general method of great power that is minimally dependent upon *ad hoc* devices.

Perhaps the main type of event with which this book is concerned is the event known as a sample, and a sample space is, in fact, a type of "event space." The nature of these events and the probabilities associated with events is very much affected by the rules under which the samples are drawn. First we shall consider a classical sample space and the rules that determine its properties.

4.1 ORDERED SAMPLES TAKEN WITH REPLACEMENT

The sample space for ordered samples taken with replacement does not find much direct application in the social sciences, but it is a primitive sample space of great theoretical importance. Our decision to study arrangements primarily when they are ordered will be recalled from Section 3.1. Since strings of letters are more convenient to write, we shall use them whenever there is no special need for the ordered tuple notation. Many types of simple experiments yield ordered sample points; for example, tossing a coin some specified number of times. Such physical examples as tossing coins and dice or drawing cards from a deck may seem remote from humans and social problems, but important formal characteristics of statistical models can be conceived through these physical phenomena when they are used to depict randomness. Incongruously enough, the very people who object to comparing human beings with such physical objects are the ones who insist on the uniqueness of the human individual. An indispensable quality of uniqueness or individuality is randomness. Even more ironically, the statistical test of social conformity is its dissimilarity to the behavior of coins and dice.

We shall use the problem of determining the size of our primitive space as a convenient point of departure for consideration of both its qualitative and quantitative aspects. Suppose we wish to find the number, S, of distinct ordered points for a sample of size $r = 3$ that may be drawn with replacement from the $n = 5$ element population, $P = \{a, b, c, d, e\}$.

From the specification of the problem, we know that the length of a string or the number of elements in the n-tuple of each point in the sample space will be 3. Since the sampling is done with replacement, this means that any element may be drawn repeatedly up to the maximum number of trials in the experiment.* Thus to give examples of two contrasting cases, one point in the space will be *ccc* and another will be *cab*. Since the conventional way to represent any outcome involving sequential trials is with a linear string in which the element shown for a specified trial occupies the position corresponding to its trial number, we have a space whose points are *arrangements*, and any two points consisting of the same array of elements are still distinguishable by the orders of those elements. Thus *cab* and *abc* are different points. In order for every possible arrangement to be realized, every element in the population will

* Equivalent conditions are that there be n dice or n decks or n urns and that independent "draws" be made from each of these.

occupy every position in a sample point the same number of times as every other. Thus the set of points in the sample space is the power product of the population—in this case, $\mathbb{S} = P \times P \times P = P^3$, but in general P^r. We have seen in Section 2.5 that the size of a set formed as a power product is the size of the constant factor set raised to the power of the exponent of the power product. In the present case, then, $S = 5^3$ and, in general, $S = n^r$. Table 4.1.1 reproduces all of the points in the space of our special case.

TABLE 4.1.1 / Sample Space of Ordered Sample Points of Size 3 that Could Be Drawn with Replacement from a Population of Five Elements, $P = \{a, b, c, d, e\}$

aaa	*baa*	*caa*	*daa*	*eaa*
aab	*bab*	*cab*	*dab*	*eab*
aac	*bac*	*cac*	*dac*	*eac*
aad	*bad*	*cad*	*dad*	*ead*
aae	*bae*	*cae*	*dae*	*eae*
aba	*bba*	*cba*	*dba*	*eba*
abb	*bbb*	*cbb*	*dbb*	*ebb*
abc	*bbc*	*cbc*	*dbc*	*ebc*
abd	*bbd*	*cbd*	*dbd*	*ebd*
abe	*bbe*	*cbe*	*dbe*	*ebe*
aca	*bca*	*cca*	*dca*	*eca*
acb	*bcb*	*ccb*	*dcb*	*ecb*
acc	*bcc*	*ccc*	*dcc*	*ecc*
acd	*bcd*	*ccd*	*dcd*	*ecd*
ace	*bce*	*cce*	*dce*	*ece*
ada	*bda*	*cda*	*dda*	*eda*
adb	*bdb*	*cdb*	*ddb*	*edb*
adc	*bdc*	*cdc*	*ddc*	*edc*
add	*bdd*	*cdd*	*ddd*	*edd*
ade	*bde*	*cde*	*dde*	*ede*
aea	*bea*	*cea*	*dea*	*eea*
aeb	*beb*	*ceb*	*deb*	*eeb*
aec	*bec*	*cec*	*dec*	*eec*
aed	*bed*	*ced*	*ded*	*eed*
aee	*bee*	*cee*	*dee*	*eee*

We have proven the theorem that is presented below along with a slightly different proof that may be valuable in visualizing applications.

THEOREM 4.1.1. The size, S, of the space for ordered samples of size r drawn with replacement from a population of size n is n^r.

PROOF. There are r order categories (trials, places, color codes) to be occupied. The first can be occupied by any of the n population elements. Since the element chosen in any trial is replaced, all of the n elements are also available to fill the second order category, and so forth, until the process has been repeated r times. By applying the fundamental principle of combinatorial analysis, we obtain $n \cdot n \cdot n \ldots$ through r factors to obtain

$$S = \prod_{i=1}^{r} n = n^r \qquad \text{Q.E.D.}$$

Throwing a die r times and observing which face appears is conceptually equivalent to drawing with replacement an ordered sample of size r from the population of elements $P = \{1, 2, 3, 4, 5, 6\}$. Tossing a coin is conceptually equivalent to drawing a sample with replacement from the two element population, $C = \{H, T\}$. If we toss a coin three times, we might observe the point THT, for example. Here we note that the sample is larger than the population itself. This is possible because replacement occurs between trials. The sample may be many times larger than the population as, for example, if we rolled a die or tossed a coin a million times. The method for finding the size of the sample space is still $S = n^r$.

Examples

1. If a coin is tossed 50 times, the size of the primitive sample space is $S = n^r = 2^{50}$.

2. The number of possible ordered outcomes for the toss of a pair of dice is $6^2 = 36$. For the toss of 48 dice, it is 6^{48}.

3. The number of ways in which 12 distinguishable elevator passengers may be distributed among seven floors is 7^{12}, if we base our distinctions on the particular set of passengers on each floor rather than just the number. Since our passengers are distinguishable, we may think of them as ordered trials. Thus the first passenger (trial 1) could be discharged on any of seven different floors. For each

of these, passenger 2 could be discharged on any of seven different floors and so on through 12 factors of $7(= 7^{12})$. It is frequently asked why the answer is not 12^7; that is: why don't we think of the floors as the trials and assign them to the passengers? The answer is that we are not interested in the number of different floors that can be simultaneously assigned to a passenger. Obviously, the only number possible would be 1. It makes no sense at all, for instance, to think of a sample point in which the third, fifth, and seventh floors are simultaneously occupied by, say, John Smith. On the other hand, it does make sense to say that the first, seventh, and ninth passengers simultaneously occupy the fifth floor.

4. In how many distinguishable ways may r distinguishable balls be distributed among n cells? Since the balls are distinguishable, we may arbitrarily number them $1, 2, 3, \ldots, r$ to correspond to the first, second, ..., rth trials. The first ball may be assigned to a cell in any of n different ways. For each of these, the second may be assigned in n different ways, and so on through r factors of n whose continued product equals n^r. We may note for future reference that this is exactly the same magnitude as the sample space for ordered samples drawn with replacement.

Although not all of the above illustrations make explicit use of the term "sample space," it should be fairly evident that the answer in each case is the size of a sample space for experiments conducted under the stipulated conditions.

Since the sample space concept is used in determining probabilities, it may be instructive to consider a few simple problems at this time.

Consider tossing a pair of dice under the less common condition that the dice are separately identifiable as die 1 and die 2. The appropriate sample space, which is a primitive one, is completely represented as follows:

1:1	2:1	3:1	4:1	5:1	6:1
1:2	2:2	3:2	4:2	5:2	6:2
1:3	2:3	3:3	4:3	5:3	6:3
1:4	2:4	3:4	4:4	5:4	6:4
1:5	2:5	3:5	4:5	5:5	6:5
1:6	2:6	3:6	4:6	5:6	6:6

It will be recalled that probability is the ratio of the number of points $\mathscr{E}$ in the subset of events E that qualify as elements in it, to the number of points S in the sample space \$. That is,

$$P[E] = \frac{\mathscr{E}}{S}$$

where E is a subset of \$. For the time being we shall determine the size of E by simply counting its elements in \$ above.

Suppose we wish to know the probability that both faces will show the same value. The number of points in \$ is $S = 6^2$. The elements in subset E as our problem defines it are 1:1, 2:2, 3:3, 4:4, 5:5, and 6:6. By count, these are six in number; that is, $\mathscr{E} = 6$. Hence

$$P[E] = \frac{\mathscr{E}}{S} = \frac{6}{36}$$

We could, if we wished, reduce our answer to $\frac{1}{6}$ or even state it decimally as .1666.... To stress the actual size of the sample space, we shall not, for the present, reduce the fractions.

If we ask for the probability that for two dice the sum 7 will be thrown, we see that the relevant subset is

$$E = \{1:6, 2:5, 3:4, 4:3, 5:2, 6:1\}$$

which also happens to contain six points and to yield $P[E \mid E = \text{sum } 7] = \frac{6}{36}$. For the probability of sum 3, however, only the points 1:2 and 2:1 belong to E, and $P[E \mid E = \text{sum } 3] = \frac{2}{36}$. Interpretively, we may state that sum 7 is three times as likely as sum 3.

4.2 THE LEAST UPPER BOUND AND GREATEST LOWER BOUND OF PROBABILITY VALUES

The inequality we will derive from our definition of probability is characteristically regarded in mathematical statistics as a postulate and hence does not require proof. We will prove it here because it is an implication of our postulates.*

* In other words, in mathematical statistics it is postulated directly while here it is derivable. The proof of this fact reinforces our intuition that our model or postulates are good since we would be embarrassed if $0 \leq P[E] \leq 1$ did not hold.

THEOREM 4.2.1. The probability of any event is never greater than 1 nor less than 0.

PROOF. By definition,

$$P[E] = \frac{\mathscr{E}}{S}$$

where $\mathscr{E}$ and S are the sizes, respectively, of sets E and $\$$, and where E is a subset of $\$$, a primitive sample space. A subset may contain at most the same number of elements as its inclusive set. Hence the maximum size of $\mathscr{E}$ occurs where $\mathscr{E} = S$. In this case,

$$P[E_{\max}] = \frac{S}{S} = 1$$

Since a sample space is defined as all possible outcomes of an experiment, then at least one of those outcomes has to occur; and since $P[E] = 1$ implies $\mathscr{E} = S$, a probability of 1 is inconsistent with the notion of no occurrences, and we interpret such a probability to mean certainty.

We may recall that Φ, the empty set, is a subset of every set. Since it contains no members, it is the smallest subset of any set and for it $\mathscr{E} = 0$. Hence

$$P[\Phi] = \frac{0}{S} = 0$$

and we may write

$$0 \leq P[E] \leq 1$$

Since $P[E] = 0$ is the probability of an element in a set containing no elements, we interpret it as the probability of an impossible event.*

4.3 THE PROBABILITY OF THE UNION OF EXCLUSIVE EVENTS

THEOREM 4.3.1. The probability of one or another of a set of exclusive events is equal to the sum of their respective probabilities.

* This statement must be understood in terms of the specific postulates given. In presentations based on different postulates—for instance, in studying distributions with an infinite number of points—the fact that $P[E] = 0$ does not mean $E = \Phi$.

PROOF. To ask the probability of one or the other of exclusive events is in effect to ask the probability of a compound event containing all of the elements of the exclusive sets that comprise it. If events are exclusive, their combined size is the sum of their sizes. In short, it is an inclusive and exhaustive set of the exclusive subsets that comprise it, and as such, the total number of elements (simple events) in it is the sum of those in the subsets it contains. If we let E_i stand for the ith event, we thus see that

$$P\left[\bigcup_{i=1}^{k} E_i\right] = \frac{\sum_{i=1}^{k} \mathscr{E}_i}{S} = \frac{(\mathscr{E}_1 + \mathscr{E}_2 + \cdots + \mathscr{E}_k)}{S}$$

$$= \frac{\mathscr{E}_1}{S} + \frac{\mathscr{E}_2}{S} + \cdots + \frac{\mathscr{E}_k}{S}$$

$$= P[E_1] + P[E_2] + \cdots + P[E_k]$$

$$= \sum_{i=1}^{k} P[E_i]$$

and the theorem is proved.

The identity should, for subsequent use, be committed to memory in the following form.

IDENTITY 4.3.1.

$$P\left[\bigcup_{i=1}^{k} E_i\right] = \sum_{i=1}^{k} P[E_i]$$

This relationship does not hold for nonexclusive events.

THEOREM 4.3.2. The sum of the probabilities of an exhaustive set of exclusive events is 1.*

PROOF. If k exhaustive events E_i in \$ is given, then

$$P\left[\bigcup_{i=1}^{k} E_i\right] = \frac{\sum_{i=1}^{k} \mathscr{E}_i}{S} = \frac{S}{S} = 1$$

* Exhaustive means, of course, the universal set

$$\Omega = \bigcup_{i=1}^{n} E_i$$

But in our proof of Theorem 4.3.1 we saw that

$$\frac{\sum_{i=1}^{k} \mathscr{E}_i}{S} = \sum_{i=1}^{k} P[E_i]$$

whence

$$\sum_{i=1}^{k} P[E_i] = 1$$

as claimed.

This is another instance in which a theorem in this exposition would characteristically be a postulate in axiomatic mathematical statistics and hence would not require proof.

4.4 THE PROBABILITY OF ONE OR THE OTHER OF NONEXCLUSIVE EVENTS

Consider the investigation of the drawing of a single card at random from a poker deck. Our population elements will be the 52 alternative cards. Drawing a heart and drawing a spade in a single draw are exclusive events, since drawing of the one precludes the drawing of the other. There are 13 cards to a suit, so the probability of drawing either a heart $[E_1]$ or a spade $[E_2]$ is

$$P[E_1 \cup E_2] = \sum_{i=1}^{2} \frac{\mathscr{E}_i}{S} = \frac{(13 + 13)}{52} = \frac{26}{52}$$

Now consider the probability of drawing either a red card $[E_1]$ or a card higher in value than 7 $[E_2]$. The probability of drawing a red card is $\frac{26}{52}$ and of drawing a card higher than 7 is $\frac{28}{52}$. Thus

$$P[E_1 \cup E_2] = P[E_1] + P[E_2] = \frac{26}{52} + \frac{28}{52} = \frac{(26 + 28)}{52} = \frac{54}{52}$$

is a false statement since we know that $\frac{54}{22} > 1$, and without exception $0 \leq P[E] \leq 1$, by Theorem 4.2.1.

The anomaly is caused by an implicit overcount of the elements. The events are not exclusive because 14 of the cards (elements) simultaneously meet the conditions of being both red and greater than 7. In other words, E_1 and E_2 are intersecting sets. Thus identical elements were counted once with the 26 red cards and again with the 28 cards $x \mid x > 7$. In other words, the subset $(E_1 \cap E_2)$ was counted twice when it should have been counted only once. We can rectify the overcount by subtracting $E_1 \cap E_2$ once from $E_1 \cup E_2$. Thus we get

$$P[E_1 \cup E_2] = \frac{\mathscr{E}_1 + \mathscr{E}_2 - \mathscr{E}_{(1\cap 2)}}{S}$$

$$= \frac{\mathscr{E}_1}{S} + \frac{\mathscr{E}_2}{S} - \frac{\mathscr{E}_{(1\cap 2)}}{S}$$

$$= P[E_1] + P[E_2] - P[E_1 \cap E_2]$$

This identity should also be learned, but strictly for the two-event case; higher order cases cannot be obtained by simple formal extrapolation of the two-event case. Notice that

$$P[E_1 \cup E_2] = P[E_1] + P[E_2] - P[E_1 \cap E_2]$$

applies equally to exclusive and nonexclusive events. Recall that for exclusive events, $E_1 \cap E_2 = \phi$; hence

$$P[E_1 \cup E_2] = P[E_1] + P[E_2] - 0 = P[E_1] + P[E_2]$$

In the example of a card that is either red or greater than 7, we have

$$P[E_1 \cup E_2] = \frac{(26 + 28 - 14)}{52} = \frac{40}{52}$$

which is both meaningful and valid. Probability is defined in terms of numbers of *elements*. The fact that an element happens to be classified in two or more ways does not increase the probability that it will be drawn.

The general formula for

$$P\left[\bigcup_{i=1}^{k} E_i\right]$$

where the E_i are not exclusive, is discussed in Section 13.2. For the present, however, we may state the following relationship, which is known as Boole's inequality.

$$P\left[\bigcup_{i=1}^{k} E_i\right] \leq \sum_{i=1}^{k} P[E_i]$$

If all of the events are exclusive, the equality holds, as we have already seen. If two or more of the E_i are not exclusive then

$$\sum_{i=1}^{k} \mathscr{E}_i$$

is greater than the total number of simple elements in the compound event

$$\bigcup_{i=1}^{k} E_i$$

If we let $\mathscr{E}'$ represent the number of elements in the union set, then

$$\mathscr{E}' < \sum_{i=1}^{k} \mathscr{E}_i$$

and

$$\frac{\mathscr{E}'}{S} < \frac{\sum_{i=1}^{k} \mathscr{E}_i}{S}$$

whence

$$P\left[\bigcup_{i=1}^{k} E_i\right] < \sum_{i=1}^{k} P[E_i]$$

which completes the proof.

4.5 THE PROBABILITY THAT AN EVENT WILL NOT OCCUR

THEOREM. The probability that an event will not occur is equal to 1 minus the probability that it will occur. If we represent the event by E and its nonoccurrence by $\not{E}$, then

$$P[\not{E}] = 1 - P[E]$$

PROOF. If we remove from the sample space $\$$ all of the points that constitute an occurrence E, we will have left all the points belonging to its complement $\not{E}$. Therefore $\not{E}$ is the subset of all nonoccurrences of E, and its probability is

$$P[\not{E}] = \frac{S - \mathcal{E}}{S} = 1 - \frac{\mathcal{E}}{S} = 1 - P[E]$$

Thus the theorem is proved.

4.6 CONDITIONAL PROBABILITIES AND STATISTICAL INDEPENDENCE

If we ask the probability that a randomly selected American male will die in a given future year, our answer will be some probability p. If, however, we impose a condition on the way we draw the "selected American male"—for example, that he be over 80 years of age at the beginning of the year—the value of p would be quite different. Similarly, if we ask the probability that a card drawn will be the ace of hearts, the probability will be $\frac{1}{52}$, but if we stipulate the condition that the card drawn is red, then the probability is $\frac{1}{26}$. Here we can see the dependence of the outcome on the condition. We can say, for instance, that the probability of drawing the ace of hearts depends on whether a red card is drawn. In this case, "heart" is a totally contained subset of "red," but dependence can also exist as a consequence of only partial intersection.* For example, the probability that an American will have colonial ancestry will be increased if we add "under the condition that he be a Negro." In this case, "colonial ancestry" only partially intersects "Negro" instead of being a wholly contained subset. However, a higher proportion of the American Negro population than of the Caucasian (but not a greater number, necessarily) are of colonial ancestry; hence, the condition affects the probability.

The conventional representation of a conditional probability is $P[A \mid B]$, which is read, "the probability that an event belongs to set A under the condition that it belongs to set B." It might more inconveniently but more precisely be represented as $P[x \in A \mid x \in B]$.

* In the context of statistical independence and dependence, sets will be said to intersect only if they contain at least one element whose removal from any of those sets implies its removal from the others.*

It should be noted that the definition of probability in Section 3.5 includes probabilities on subsets of a set, whether or not the probabilities are conditional; thus it may be used to define a probability space on any set. To impose the condition is, in effect, to define a new sample space as a subset of the old one and merely restricts the universe of possible outcomes.

This is pictured as below, with Ω being the universal set on which both E_1 and E_2 must be defined. We will suppose that $E_1 \cap E_2$

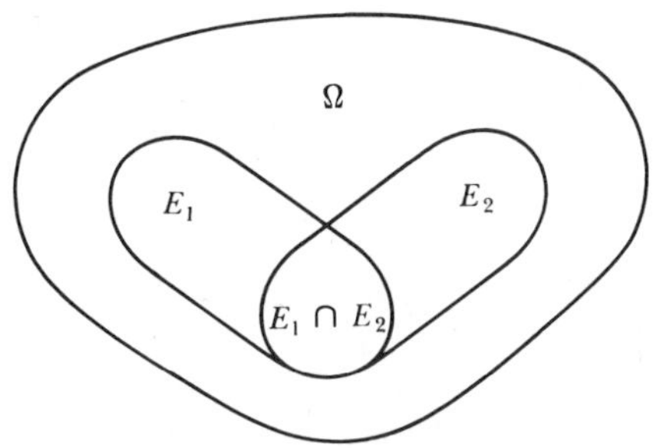

is not Φ (thus neither E_1 nor E_2 equals Φ). Then if we know E_1 occurred, the primitive space postulate may be used to determine probabilities with respect to E_2.

$$P[E_2 \mid E_1] = \frac{\text{no. of points in } E_1 \cap E_2}{\text{no. of points in } E_1}$$

Multiplying the right-hand side of the expression by 1 in the form of (no. of points in Ω)/(no. of points in Ω) gives

$$P[E_2 \mid E_1] = \frac{\text{no. of points in } E_1 \cap E_2}{\text{no. of points in } \Omega} \times \frac{\text{no. of points in } \Omega}{\text{no. of points in } E_1}$$

$$= \frac{P[E_1 \cap E_2]}{P[E_1]}$$

By multiplying by $P[E_1]$, this can be written as

$$(P[E_1])(P[E_2 \mid E_1]) = P[E_1 \cap E_2]$$

This is a basic identity, because it is instrumental in defining independence. The main thing to note is that as long as $P[E_1] \neq 0$, conditional probability is meaningful. For finite event spaces, if $P[E_1] = 0$, it means E_1 is impossible, so that it is meaningless to try to determine conditional probabilities.

We are now in a position to define independence and dependence of events in the framework of conditional probability.

Event E_2 is *independent* of E_1 if $P[E_2 \mid E_1] = P[E_2]$. This says that event E_2 is independent of event E_1 if its probability remains unaffected by the occurrence of E_1.

Example

If a die is tossed twice, is the event E_2, "face 3 on the second toss," independent of the event E_1, "an odd face on the first toss"?

$$P[E_2 \mid E_1] = P[E_2 \mid \not{E}_1] = \tfrac{1}{6}$$

This implies that $P[E_2] = \frac{1}{6}$ unconditionally, or

$$P[E_2 \mid E_1] = P[E_2]$$

We therefore conclude that E_2 is independent of E_1.

This is a somewhat stylized way of saying that the probability of the outcome of the second toss is unaffected by what happens on the first toss. It is apparent that the trials of a sequence drawn from a single population are independent if replacement occurs implicitly or explicitly after each trial. We thus see that the multiple-trial coin and dice experiments that have concerned us thus far exemplify spaces composed of concatenated independent events.

Our definition of dependence emerges naturally from our definition of independence. Event E_2 is said to be *dependent* on E_1 if $P[E_2 \mid E_1] \neq P[E_2]$.

Example

A card is drawn and then replaced if it is not a spade. If it is a spade, it is discarded, and a joker is put into the deck in its place. Is event E_2, "a spade on the second draw," independent of event E_1, "a spade on the first draw"?

$$P[E_2 \mid E_1] = \tfrac{12}{52}$$

$$P[E_2 \mid \not{E}_1] = \tfrac{13}{52}$$

Therefore $P[E_2 \mid E_1] \neq P[E_2]$, and the events are dependent.

We shall now develop these ideas more rigorously.

If $P[E_2 \mid E_1] = P[E_2]$, then we substitute into the expression $(P[E_1])(P[E_2 \mid E_1]) = P[E_1 \cap E_2]$ and determine $P[E_1 \cap E_2] =$

$P[E_1] \times P[E_2]$. As long as $P[E_1]$ and $P[E_2]$ are not equal to zero, we can see that if events are independent, probabilities multiply and $P[E_2]$ does not depend on E_1, and that the converse is true. When events are dependent, the probability of E_2 depends on whether E_1 occurred.*

Considerations of symmetry with $P[E_1 \mid E_2]$ also justify the conclusion that E_1 is dependent on E_2, and the events may be said to be statistically dependent events without reference to any direction of the dependence.

DEFINITION 4.6.1. If $P[E_2 \mid E_1] = P[E_2]$, then E_1 and E_2 are said to be *statistically independent.*

This says that the events are statistically independent if the conditional probability of E_2 is equal to its unconditional probability. In words, this means that the set Ω has been broken up so that the points of E_2 in E_1 are in the same ratio as the number of points in E_2 to Ω. This means that E_2 must also have a number of points in $\not{E}_1$ so that $P[E_2 \mid \not{E}_1]$ is equal to $P[E_2]$. All this makes it clear that independence is quite a "strong" condition.

DEFINITION 4.6.2. If $P[E_2 \mid E_1] \neq P[E_2]$, then E_1 and E_2 are said to be *statistically dependent.*

Let E_1 and E_2 be independent; their probabilities are determined from a primitive product space. Then the concatenation $E_1 \times E_2$ is of size $\mathscr{E}_1 \cdot \mathscr{E}_2$ by the fundamental principle of combinatorial analysis of Section 2.6. Similarly, the number of points in the concatenation of their universe sets $\$_1 \times \$_2$ is $S_1 \cdot S_2$. Recognizing that $E_1 \times E_2$ is the subset of all points in $\$_1 \times \$_2$ representing the joint occurrence of E_1 and E_2, we have

$$P[E_1 \cap E_2] = \frac{\mathscr{E}_1 \cdot \mathscr{E}_2}{S_1 \cdot S_2} = P[E_1] \cdot P[E_2]$$

In point of fact, $P[E_1 \cap E_2] = P[E_1] \cdot P[E_2]$ is often used as the mathematical definition of statistical independence. It is a useful computational formula if one knows by other criteria that the events are independent. We shall state it in its general form.

* Some confusing examples of dependence exist, but they will not be discussed here.

THEOREM 4.6.1. Given that $E_1, E_2, \ldots, E_k$ are defined on a product space and it is primitive, then

$$P\left[\bigcap_{i=1}^{k} E_i\right] = \prod_{i=1}^{k} P[E_i]$$

PROOF. The case for $k = 2$ has already been established by previous discussion. Since the E_i are from a product space, then $E_3 \cap (E_2 \cap E_1)$ and, in general,

$$E_k \cap \left[\bigcap_{i=1}^{k-1} E_i\right]$$

are concatenations of sets, as are

$$\$_k \cap \left[\bigcap_{i=1}^{k-1} \$_i\right]$$

Since we may define

$$\bigcap_{i=1}^{k} E_i \quad \text{as an event set in} \quad \bigcap_{i=1}^{k} \$_i$$

then

$$P\left[\bigcap_{i=1}^{k} E_i\right] = \frac{\prod_{i=1}^{k} \mathscr{E}_i}{\prod_{i=1}^{k} S_i} = \frac{\mathscr{E}_1}{S_1} \cdot \frac{\mathscr{E}_2}{S_2} \cdots \frac{\mathscr{E}_k}{S_k}$$

$$= P[E_1] \cdot P[E_2] \ldots P[E_k]$$

$$= \prod_{i=1}^{k} P[E_i]$$

Q.E.D.

COROLLARY. Since an ordered tuple implies the conjoint occurrence of all the elements it contains, then

$$(E_1, E_2, \ldots, E_k) = \bigcap_{i=1}^{k} E_i$$

whence

COROLLARY 4.6.1

$$P[(E_1, E_2, \ldots, E_k)] = \prod_{i=1}^{k} P[E_i]$$

If the sets from whose elements ordered k-tuples or arrangements are formed are independent, Corollary 4.6.1 holds, for example, for any elements in sample spaces whose points are product sets or subsets of product sets, even in the extreme case where

$$\$_1 = \$_2 = \cdots = \$_k \quad \text{in} \quad \prod_{i=1}^{k} \$_i = \$^k$$

For instance,

$$P[HTH] = P[H] \cdot P[T] \cdot P[H] = \left(\frac{1}{2}\right)^3 = \frac{1}{8}$$

This agrees with the probability obtained by regarding HTH as a single point in the eight-point primitive space C^3, where $C = \{H, T\}$. We note then that Theorem 4.6.1 and its corollary provide an alternative means for finding the probability of a point in a space whose points are composite events. It should perhaps be stressed that it is applicable to the probability of the concatenation of any events that are defined respectively on independent sample spaces. A simple example occurs in finding the probability that one throw of a pair of dice and one draw of a card from a standard poker deck will result in a sum of 3 and an ace, respectively. Call "sum 3" E_1 and "an ace" E_2. Substantive considerations indicate that $\$_1 \cap \$_2 = \Phi$, which establishes the independence of the events. Hence Theorem 4.6.1 applies. $E_1 = \{(1, 2), (2, 1)\}$ with $\mathscr{E}_1 = 2$, where E_1 is an event set defined on $\$_1$ with $S_1 = 36$. Also, we have $E_2 = \{A_H, A_S, A_D, A_C\}$, a subset of size $\mathscr{E}_2 = 4$ defined on $\$_2$ of size $S = 52$. We apply the theorem to obtain

$$P[E_1 \cap E_2] = \left(\frac{2}{36}\right)\left(\frac{4}{52}\right) = .00427$$

A result similar to Theorem 4.6.1 holds regardless of whether the events involved are independent or dependent, but dependence does affect the values of the probabilities constituting the terms. We shall not attempt to develop the rationale involved but will give a brief indication of its form and meaning.

First note that we may represent the independence of an event E_k from a concatenation of $k - 1$ prior events as follows

$$P\left[E_k \,\middle|\, \bigcap_{i=1}^{k-1} E_i\right] = P[E_k]$$

The same expression with an inequality sign would, of course, indicate dependence. Incorporating this notation into the Theorem 4.6.1, we get

$$P\left[\bigcap_{i=1}^{k} E_i\right] = P[E_1] \cdot P[E_2 \mid E_1] \cdot P[E_3 \mid E_1 \cap E_2] \cdots P\left[E_k \,\middle|\, \bigcap_{i=1}^{k-1} E_i\right]$$

This modified form of Theorem 4.6.1 applies equally to independent or dependent probabilities since if any term (call it the rth) is independent of the prior terms, then

$$P\left[E_r \,\middle|\, \bigcap_{i=1}^{r-1} E_i\right] = P[E_r]$$

That is, the conditional probability is equal to its unconditional probability.

We can see that statistical dependence and conditional probabilities are highly interrelated and important topics, particularly for statistical investigations involving what is known as "stratified sampling." No attempt will be made in this book to cover the models for stratified sampling, but we will include a few remarks and examples which will hopefully be provocative enough to encourage inquiry into other sources.

In general, statistical dependence will be discerned more conveniently from substantive considerations since it is not always obvious which sample spaces are involved and what their interrelations are. For instance, suppose we have three boxes of marbles such that the first box contains a green, a red, and a white marble; the second box contains two reds and a green; and the third, three greens, a red, and a white. It is intuitively obvious that the probability of drawing a red marble from a box during one random trial depends upon which box is selected, but it is less obvious that the three boxes of marbles may be considered as an exhaustive set of exclusive subsets in the population of available marbles that intersect with elements in the exhaustive subsets of marbles classified by three colors. Finding, say, the probability that a red marble will be picked if in the first trial a box is randomly chosen and then a marble is randomly chosen from that box involves the consideration of two dependent trials, which makes it a composite event, but it additionally happens to be a compound event. It is the probability of drawing box 1 multiplied by the probability of drawing a red marble under the condition that box 1 is drawn, plus the probability of drawing box 2 multiplied by the probability of drawing a red marble under the condition that box 2 is drawn, and so forth. The probability for each of the boxes will by postulation be $\frac{1}{3}$, and the probability that any marble will be taken from a selected box of n marbles will be $1/n$. Thus each term will be a product of the form

$$P[\text{box } X] \cdot P[\text{red marble} \mid \text{box } X]$$

and we have

$$P[\text{red marble}] = (\tfrac{1}{3})(\tfrac{1}{3}) + (\tfrac{1}{3})(\tfrac{2}{3}) + (\tfrac{1}{3})(\tfrac{1}{5}) = .40000$$

Removing a marble from one box has no effect on the elements in any other box; hence the boxes contain nonintersecting sets.

We may cite another example. If we ask the probability that one draw from a poker deck will yield the king of hearts, the obvious answer is obtained from the ratio of the size of the event set (= 1) to the size of the sample space to yield $P[A_H] = \frac{1}{52}$. However, this same result could be obtained as a dependent conditional probability as follows:

$$P[A \cap H] = P[H] \cdot P[A \mid H] = (\tfrac{1}{4})(\tfrac{1}{13}) = \tfrac{1}{52}$$

4.7 PSEUDO-DEPENDENCE

It was noted in the preceding section that the relevant sample spaces are not always obvious, and it was suggested that substantive considerations might be a more convenient test of dependence. However, there are situations in which intuition might lead one to conclude dependence when technically it does not exist. Consider the following example.

Toss a coin. If a head shows, toss a die. What is the probability that the coin will show a head and the die will show face 1 or face 2? Tossing a coin and throwing a die imply a given sample space, but since whether or not the die will be thrown "depends" upon the outcome heads, intuition might suggest that the events are dependent. The correct probability is obtained by

$$P[H] \cdot P[\text{face 1 or } 2 \mid H] = (\tfrac{1}{2})(\tfrac{2}{6}) = \tfrac{2}{12}$$

but also by

$$P[H] \cdot P[\text{face 1 or 2}] = (\tfrac{1}{2})(\tfrac{2}{6}) = \tfrac{2}{12}$$

which indicates independence.

The relevant sample space is

$$\{T, [H,1], [H,2], [H,3], [H,4], [H,5], [H,6]\}$$

which is nonprimitive and also nonuniform,* since $P[T] = \frac{1}{2}$, and the probability of any other point is $(\frac{1}{2})(\frac{1}{6}) = \frac{1}{12}$. T appears to be nondecomposable, but this is an illusion created by the notation. The actual sample space is

$$\{[T,1], [T,2], [T,3], [T,4], [T,5], [T,6], \\ [H,1], [H,2], [H,3], [H,4], [H,5], [H,6]\}$$

which is quite evidently uniform and for less obvious reasons may be regarded as primitive. This space contains 12 points, of which two comprise the event set. Hence we get $P[E] = \frac{2}{12}$, which agrees with our previous results. The key lies in the fact that a condition terminating an experiment only defines an *event set* on the primitive sample space. The sample space itself in our problem is implicitly defined by experimental outcomes requiring a uniform number of trials for each and every outcome even though the information required for some events may be known before the experiment has run its course. Many sample spaces that make time trial discriminations can be decomposed into primitive spaces that do not. Understanding this may be easier if one conceives ordered outcomes in the more general sense of arrangement as defined in Section 3.1, rather than as an order reflecting the time sequence of the trials. It was stated in the same section that "The event 'at least one head in three tosses of a coin' might conceivably be determined on the first trial; nevertheless we shall think of it as a composite event requiring three trials."

A condition that calls for the termination of an experiment before it has run its course is called a *stopping condition*. In our coin and die experiment, the stopping condition is "face T on the coin," but the problem is stochastically unchanged if the die is thrown first and the event set is defined as $(\{1\} \cap \{H\}) \cup (\{2\} \cap \{H\})$. In this case, the coin toss would not stop the experiment. We might refer to

* Uniform spaces will be discussed in Section 5.1. For the present, it suffices to note that the points in a uniform space must be equiprobable.

the failure to recognize the implicit extension of the trials beyond the stopping condition as *premature truncation of the primitive sample space.*

It should be stressed that the space points are integral composite elements. These points are nondecomposable even though their form may tempt one to think otherwise. These particular elements are arranged in the more general sense in any case, since the points preserve the identity of the initial sets of the conjoined elements. With these possible sources of misunderstanding under control, we may note that the concatenation $C \times D$, where

$$C = \{H, T\} \quad \text{and} \quad D = \{1, 2, 3, 4, 5, 6\}$$

generates the required space. Since C and D are nonintersecting, we may correctly conclude the independence of the events.

It will be recalled from Section 3.4 that the primitive sample space calls for postulation of an empirical tendency of each point in the space to be observed as often as any other on the average. It must not be thought, however, that postulation implies the freedom to be capriciously arbitrary. When a postulation is made for scientific purposes, there must be a rational justification, and the postulation must be internally consistent; that is, it must be neither self-contradictory nor patently absurd, although it may in fact be untrue.

4.8 A WAITING TIME PROBLEM

Let us consider now a certain problem that happens to fall into the category of "waiting time" problems. This problem will be instructive at this point for a number of reasons. (1) It introduces a sample space whose points clearly do not all have the same tendency to occur and hence is an excellent contrasting example to the uniform sample space. (2) It offers an example of a sample space with an infinite number of points that can qualify as countable. (3) It puts to use a number of the basic rules we have previously considered.

If we throw a coin until for the first time, we get a sequence of two identical outcomes, what is the probability that our investigation will not go beyond the kth toss? As an intermediate step, let us consider the probability that the investigation will end at exactly the kth toss. The first toss will obviously not produce a stopping point so we proceed directly to the case of $k = 2$.

Either HH or TT will cause us to stop at the second toss. If either HT or TH occurs, we will go on for a third. The probability of any of these four outcomes could be obtained from the application of the product rule presented in the previous section. Thus in each of the four cases the first event will be either a head or a tail with a probability of $\frac{1}{2}$ and the second event will be either a head or a tail with probability $\frac{1}{2}$, and

$$P[\text{any particular sequence of 2}] = \tfrac{1}{2} \cdot \tfrac{1}{2} = \tfrac{1}{4}$$

Since any sequence of two identical outcomes will stop the game, then either HH or TT will suffice, and the probability that the investigation will stop with the second throw is

$$P[HH] + P[TT] = \tfrac{1}{4} + \tfrac{1}{4} = \tfrac{1}{2}$$

With the third throw the trials will stop with HTT or THH and continue with HTH or THT. Thus the probability of any one of these sequences would be

$$P = (\tfrac{1}{2})(\tfrac{1}{2})(\tfrac{1}{2}) = 2^{-3} = \tfrac{1}{8}$$

and

$$P[HTT \cup THH] = \tfrac{1}{8} + \tfrac{1}{8} = \tfrac{1}{4}$$

and so on, so that the probability that the trial will stop at exactly k trials is

$$P[x = k] = 2 \cdot 2^{-k} = 2^{-k+1} = 2^{-(k-1)} = \frac{1}{2^{k-1}}$$

If we represent all points that constitute occurrences of the terminating condition up to, say, $k = 6$, we would get with their corresponding probabilities in parentheses, and the number of the trial in brackets

[2]	[3]	[4]	[5]	[6]
$HH(\frac{1}{4})$	$HTT(\frac{1}{8})$	$HTHH(\frac{1}{16})$	$HTHTT(\frac{1}{32})$	$HTHTHH(\frac{1}{64})$
$TT(\frac{1}{4})$	$THH(\frac{1}{8})$	$THTT(\frac{1}{16})$	$THTHH(\frac{1}{32})$	$THTHTT(\frac{1}{64})$

The probability that the experiment would end no later than the sixth toss is then

$$P[(HH) \cup (TT) \cup (HTT) \cup (THH) \cup \ldots \cup (THTHTT)]$$
$$= (\tfrac{1}{4} + \tfrac{1}{4}) + (\tfrac{1}{8} + \tfrac{1}{8}) + (\tfrac{1}{16} + \tfrac{1}{16})$$
$$+ (\tfrac{1}{32} + \tfrac{1}{32}) + (\tfrac{1}{64} + \tfrac{1}{64})$$
$$= \tfrac{1}{2} + \tfrac{1}{4} + \tfrac{1}{8} + \tfrac{1}{16} + \tfrac{1}{32}$$
$$= \tfrac{31}{32} = .9687$$

And, in general, for the kth toss,

$$P[x \leq k] = \sum_{i=2}^{k} \frac{1}{2^{i-1}} = \sum_{i=1}^{k-1} \frac{1}{2^i}$$

It is a standard topic in elementary calculus to show that the sum of terms of the geometric progression is of the form

$$\sum_{i=1}^{\infty} ar^i = \frac{a}{1-r}, \quad \text{if} \quad 0 \leq r < 1$$

where a is the first factor of the geometric progression ar^i and r is the common factor. Thus

$$\sum_{i=1}^{\infty} \frac{1}{2^i} = \frac{\frac{1}{2}}{1 - \frac{1}{2}} = 1$$

This indicates that the sum of the probabilities of the infinitely large number of points in our sample space is equal to 1, which is as it should be.

We could also ask the probability that the tosses will continue beyond the kth toss. This equals, of course,

$$P[x > k] = 1 - P[2 \leq x \leq k]$$

In the case of $k = 6$, $P[x > k] = 1 - .9687 = .0313$, which is perhaps a more statistically interesting problem.

PROBLEMS

1. In a group of 100 people, a sample of size 4 is drawn with replacement.

a. How many points are there in this sample space?

b. How many times may the same person be drawn?

c. Give a typical point for the space in some adequate notation.

d. Assume the sample space is primitive. What is the probability of the point given in part c?

e. Using the notation adopted above for a point, give examples of a simple event and examples of three compound events with three, four, and five outcomes, respectively.

Note: In later chapters it will be possible to compare the results obtained with samples with replacement and samples without replacement and to note that the two approach each other under certain conditions. The problems are chosen to guide the reader in understanding the differences between sampling with and without replacement and also to achieve an understanding of why these differences occur and how they affect sampling.

2. Use the space given in Table 4.1.1 (page 39) to answer these questions:

a. What is the probability that no letter occurs more than twice in any given composite event—in other words, in any sequence of trials?

b. What is the probability that no element occurs more than once? Note again that this is related to the problem of replacement and nonreplacement. Assume that the space made up of the 120 points in Table 4.1.1, where no letter occurs three or more times in a point, is a primitive space. Use this space to answer parts c, d, and e.

c. What is the probability of the event that no letter occurs more than twice in a composite event (point) of this space?

d. What is the probability that no symbol occurs more than once in a composite event? Compare this answer with the answer obtained in part b and explain why the probabilities are different.

e. Calculate the probabilities of a occurring at any trial, of a occurring on the first trial, and of a not occurring. Note that the probability of a not occurring can be determined as indicated in Section 4.5.

3. The outstanding athletes in football, baseball, track, golf, and tennis are chosen in each of four schools. Then an overall popularity contest is held in each of the schools to determine which of that school's four athletes is the most popular. A physical education teacher wishes to examine the hypothesis that it is not the person but the sport that is popular. Formulate a primitive probability space based on this example in which the points are strings of letters. For example, an observation might be *fbfb*, referring to a football player, a baseball player, a football player, and another baseball player as the most popular athletes. Write the points in this space and answer these questions:

a. What is the probability that a football player will be the most popular in at least two schools? Note that "at least two" means in two or more schools.

b. Use the results that are given in the section on the probability of an event not occurring to check your work. The negation of this is: "What is the probability that a football player will be chosen in one or fewer schools?"

c. What is the probability that no single sport will be most popular in all schools? How do you formulate this hypothesis? A hint is given by considering what is meant by "the most popular in all schools." In this case, a collection of points will be considered which corresponds to athletes in the same sport being in a majority in each point in the collection. Select those points which meet the above condition. Then calculate the ratio of the number of these points to the number of points in the space.

d. What is the probability that football will be the most popular sport in a majority of the schools? Show four example points in this event and explain why football is the most popular for these points. The term "football is the most popular" applies to the points which are shown. It is possible to employ the term "football is the most popular" in two different ways. One may wish to include *ffbb* as a case where football is most popular or one may allow points of only the type *ffbf*. It may help to compare results with other readers and to compare definitions of the term "most popular."

4. This problem is meant to illustrate theoretical points raised in this chapter, although the applied problems presented are limited by the space and time required to explore the ideas. For all of this problem, consider the space generated by using Table 4.1.1 (page 39); however, omit the first collection of points. In other words, omit the upper block of numbers. Assume that this space with 100 points is a primitive sample space. Table 4.1.1 completely defines the sets below. Several examples are given which should help the reader to understand the general notation N_K. The notation $\overline{N}_K$ will refer to all elements in the universe but not in N_K.

$$A_2 = \{x \mid a \text{ is the second element in the triple } x\}$$

(*Note:* x refers to an element in the space. This is the same as saying that x is any triple from the table, say *abc* or *dec*. x cannot be *bac* since it is not in the table.)

$$\begin{aligned} \bar{A}_3 &= \{x \mid a \text{ is not the third element}\} \\ B_2 &= \{x \mid \text{the triple } x \text{ has } b \text{ as its second element}\} \\ C_2 &= \{x \mid c \text{ is the second element}\} \\ D_3 &= \{x \mid d \text{ is the element in every triple } x\} \end{aligned}$$

Although the words defining the sets given above vary slightly, all the sets are covered by the general notation, which is now defined.

$$N_K = \{x \mid n \text{ is the } k\text{th element of all triple } xs\}$$

For example, E_1 has $N = E$ and $k = 1$ so that $n = e$, and we can write

$$E_1 = \{x \mid e \text{ is the 1st (first) element of all tuples } x\}$$

In the problems below, calculate probabilities by making the best use you can of the result

$$\begin{aligned} P(A \cup B) &= P(A) + P(B) \quad \text{if} \quad A \cap B = \phi \\ P(A \cup B) &= P(A) + P(B) - P(A \cap B) \quad \text{if} \quad A \cap B \neq \phi \end{aligned}$$

a. Obtain probabilities for the sets or unions of disjoint sets given the following:

(1) A_2, B_2, C_2, D_2, E_2.

(2) $\bar{A}_2$ and $\bar{B}_2$.

(3) $A_2 \cup B_2, B_2 \cup D_2, C_2 \cup E_2$.

(4) $A_2 \cup B_2 \cup C_2$ and $A_2 \cup B_2 \cup C_2 \cup D_2 \cup E_2$.

b. Obtain probabilities for the following sets, which may or may not be disjoint.

(1) $A_2 \cup D_3, A_1 \cup D_3, B_2 \cup D_3$.

(2) $E_3 \cup D_3$ and $E_3 \cup D_3 \cup B_2$.

(3) $A_1 \cup B_2 \cup C_3$ and $A_1 \cup B_2 \cup A_1$.

c. Calculate probabilities of the following sets by making the best use you can of previous results and the result

$$P(\bar{A}) = 1 - P(A)$$

(1) $\overline{B_2 \cup D_2}$, $\overline{A_1 \cup D_3}$ and $\overline{C_2 \cup E_2}$

(2) $\overline{A_1 \cup B_2 \cup C_2}$ and $\overline{A_1 \cup B_1 \cup C_1}$

d. The following problems are based on the section on conditional probabilities and independence. The sets referenced are those defined at the beginning of this exercise.

(1) Calculate the following:

$$P(x \in A_1 \mid x \in B_2),$$
$$P(x \in C_3 \mid x \in B_2),$$
$$P(x \in C_2 \mid x \in B_2),$$
$$P(x \in A_2 \mid x \in B_2).$$

(2) In each case in part 1, is the conditional probability the product of the nonconditional probabilities?

e. Are the following events independent?

(1) A_3 and E_1.

(2) A_2 and E_1.

(3) A_1 and A_3.

(4) $\{x \mid \text{one element is an } a\}$ and $\{x \mid \text{two elements are the same}\}$.

(5) Using the space defined for this exercise, give two examples of independent events and two examples of dependent events.

f. In these problems, *c* or *d* being drawn refers to a triple in the space having *c* or *d* or both.

(1) Is the event "*b* or *c* are drawn" independent of the event *d* and *e* are drawn?

(2) Is the event "*b* or *c* is drawn" independent of the event "*c* or *d* is drawn"?

(3) Is the event "*b* is drawn" independent of the event "*c* is drawn"?

CHAPTER 5

DEPENDENT TRIAL EXPERIMENTS—SPACE FOR SAMPLES TAKEN WITHOUT REPLACEMENT

WE HAVE SEEN that if an experiment is to consist of r independent trials such that, for every performance of the experiment, n_i is the size of the population from which the ith element is to be taken, then the size of the sample space may be obtained as

$$S = \prod_{i=1}^{r} n_i$$

If $r > 1$, the points are composite. The condition of independence of the trials is fulfilled if the populations for each and every trial may be considered as a replica of a master set.

This means that if the population for each and every trial contains no elements whose removal would alter the size or composition of the population for any other trial the trials will be independent.

Sampling from a single population with replacement of the element drawn in each trial before proceeding to the next is a special case of sampling with independent trials, since replacing the element drawn between each of the r trials is tantamount to making one drawing from each of r identical sets.* Thus we have the apparent

* Many experiments have been devoted to showing that actual replacement rarely produces independence in the case of cards or other game devices involving shuffling.

anomaly of identical sets that are nonintersecting, because the removal of elements from any of them has no effect on the size or composition of any of the others. This seeming contradiction exists because the elements for each trial receive an additional dimension of identification in being implicitly associated with separate trials, even if the trials cannot be identified. If the same element appears twice in the same composite point, we know that the instances are from two different trials, even if we do not know which trials they were. We saw that in this special case of independent sampling the size of the sample space may be obtained as $S = n^r$, where n is the constant population size from trial to trial. Moreover, the sample space itself may be generated as the set power product P^r.

On the other hand, if the fact that an element drawn in one trial is on that account unavailable for another, then the trials are dependent. One should be cautious and not jump to the conclusion that replacing the element drawn for each trial always guarantees independent trials, however. For example, one might ask for the probability of drawing two hearts under the following conditions: If a heart is drawn on the first trial, replace it and discard all the spades for the second trial. This is actually an ambiguous instruction, because it is silent as to what should be done if a heart is not drawn the first time. If nothing is to be done other than to make the second draw, the trials are dependent, since the removal of the nonheart after the first draw would make it unavailable for the second. If, on the other hand, one supposes that the spades are also to be discarded and the card that is drawn replaced if it is a nonheart, then the drawing of a nonheart is only a stopping condition, and the trials are independent. While stipulating what is to be done if a heart is not drawn may not appear to make much practical sense, it is theoretically necessary in order to complete the definition of the primitive sample space, which requires a uniform number of implicit trials. It must be remembered that *events are defined on a space* whether or not one needs the full information about a point to implement the stopping condition.

So far, the specific spaces that have commanded more than our passing attention were for ordered samples drawn with independent trials, with the independence achieved by conceptually replacing the elements between trials.* Later chapters will discuss *unordered*

* Since we have related these to the power set we have also used the concept of n replicas of a set A to get A^n. Thus implicitly we have used two formulations of ordered sample spaces.

samples taken with replacement. In this chapter, we shall consider two particular, important types of sample spaces for experiments in which the trials are dependent. One is the space for ordered samples drawn from a single population without replacement. The other is the space for unordered samples drawn from a single population, also without replacement. Among the things that will be exemplified by the first is that a sample space may be primitive even if its samples are formed with dependent trials. The second will constitute an example of a special type of space that may be used as though it were primitive even though it is not. In anticipation of this second case, we shall first consider the concept of a "uniform" space.

5.1 UNIFORM SAMPLE SPACES

A sample space is *uniform* if its decomposition is by definition an exhaustive set of equal-sized nonintersecting subsets of a primitive space. We could say the spaces are by definition "isomorphic" if each point in the uniform space contains exactly the same information as the subset of the primitive space that is its image, and that the converse is true.

For example, suppose we have a primitive space $\$_p$ that consists of all ordered samples of size 2 that can be taken without replacement from $P = \{a, b, c\}$. Then

$$\$_p = \{ab, ba, ac, ca, bc, cb\}$$

Now consider the space $\$_u$ of all unordered samples of size 2 that can be drawn without replacement from P. This is

$$\$_u = \{[a, b], [a, c], [b, c]\}$$

If we now form an exhaustive set of nonintersecting subsets of $\$_p$ as

$$\$'_p = \{\{ab, ba\}, \{ac, ca\}, \{bc, cb\}\}$$

it is now possible to define the function

$$F: S_u \rightarrow \$'_p = \{([a, b], \{ab, ba\}), ([a, c], \{ac, ca\}), ([b, c], \{bc, cb\})\}$$

Since the points in each ordered pair in the function represent identical information that differs only in notation, $\$'_p$ and $\$_u$ are isomorphic. If I is the size of the subset represented by any element in $\$'_p$, then the probability of an event E defined on the primitive space $\$_p$ as that same subset would be

$$P[E] = \frac{\mathscr{E}_p}{S_p} = \frac{\mathscr{E}_p/I}{S_p/I} = \frac{\mathscr{E}'_p}{S'_p} = \frac{\mathscr{E}_u}{S_u} = P[E_u]$$

where E_u is a one-element event set in $\$_u$. Recall that the relationship $P[E_u] = P[E]$ holds also where E_u is a compound event; this includes the case where E_u defined on the uniform space might be composed of intersecting sets. All this implies that in calculating probabilities, uniform sample spaces may be treated exactly as though they were primitive spaces. That is,

DEFINITION 5.1.1

$$P[E_u] = \frac{\mathscr{E}_u}{S_u}$$

We shall not, in general, write the subscript u in future calculations, but we must caution against the inconsistency of using the size of the event set defined in one sample space and the size of the other sample space in calculating probabilities. Specifically,

$$P[E] \neq \frac{\mathscr{E}_u}{S_p} \quad \text{and} \quad P[E] \neq \frac{\mathscr{E}_p}{S_u}$$

This may seem obvious in abstract statement, but sample space inconsistency is a common error.

We will clarify the concept of uniform space by showing its relation to a primitive space. The diagram below shows a primitive

Primitive Space Showing Equal-Size Subsets Uniform Space Having A, B, C as Points

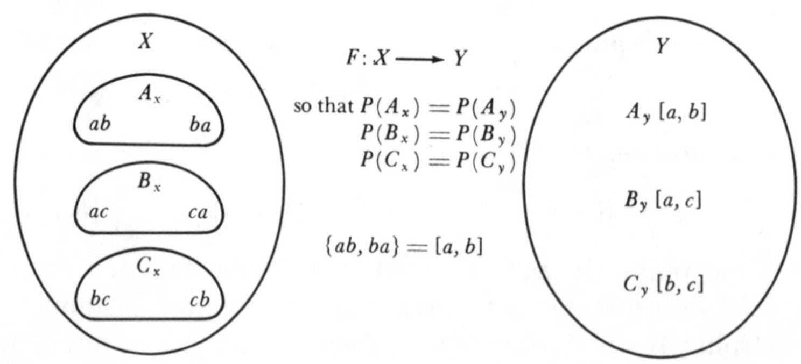

space that is a logical decomposition of the uniform space. The primitive space is determined by the postulates (1) an unordered point is the union of all ordered points, (2) Y is uniform. These postulates are necessary for the probabilities in the one space to hold in the other space. By changing rule 1 through the use of "selection rules" or by changing rule 2, we can arrive at other spaces. Feller gives an interesting discussion of this.*

5.2 ORDERED SAMPLES TAKEN WITHOUT REPLACEMENT

We have noted in Section 3.1 that order with respect to sample elements is defined sufficiently as separate identifiability of the trials. To avoid unnecessarily cumbersome exposition, we shall continue to represent points composed of ordered elements as strings of letters.

The fact that we are concerned here with samples taken without replacement implies necessarily that no point will display any repeated elements. *caebd* would exemplify an appropriate point but *ccabb* would not. Since the sample is drawn from a population which is by definition a set, then the fact that an element is not replaced after it is drawn makes it unavailable to fill subsequent positions in the sample point.

We see that the trials here are clearly dependent, since the removal of an element from the set of elements available for any trial implies its unavailability for any other, so that the trial sample spaces are intersecting.

For subsequent use we shall at this point introduce a most convenient notation used by Feller. It is of the form $(n)_r$, where n and r are positive integers and $r \leq n$. It means "n through r descending factors." Thus $(7)_3 = 7 \cdot 6 \cdot 5 = 210$, and, in general

$$(n)_r = n(n-1)(n-2)\dots(n-r+1)$$

It should be noted that $(n - r + 1)$ refers to the magnitude of the rth factor, not its position in the sequence. $(n - r + 1)$ may be thought of as a rule for determining the value of the factor from its position. For example, in $(7)_3$ the third factor is 5. That is, $(n - r + 1) =$

* William Feller, *An Introduction to Probability Theory and Its Applications*, Vol. I (2nd ed.). New York: John Wiley & Sons, Inc., 1950, pp. 38–40.

$7 - 3 + 1 = 5$. In the case where $r = n$, we get a more familiar form:

$$(n)_r = (n)_n = n(n - 1)(n - 2)\ldots(n - n + 1) = n!$$

For example, $(5)_5 = 5 \cdot 4 \cdot 3 \cdot 2 \cdot 1 = 5!$ We are now in a position to state the following theorem.

THEOREM 5.2.1. If an ordered sample of size r is to be drawn without replacement from a population of n elements, the size of the corresponding sample space is $(n)_r$.

PROOF. There are r positions to be filled in the sample point. An element may be selected from the population to fill the first place in any of n different ways. For each of these, a different element may be selected from those remaining in the population in $(n - 1)$ ways, and so forth, through a final selection from among $n - r + 1$ elements. Applying the general form of the fundamental principle of combinatorial analysis, we get

$$n(n - 1)(n - 2)\ldots(n - r + 1) = (n)_r$$

and the theorem is proved.

COROLLARY 5.2.1. The number of distinct arrangements of size r that can be formed from a set containing r elements with no elements repeated is $(r)_r = r!$

An example of the space for ordered samples of size 3 drawn without replacement from the five-element population $P = \{a, b, c, d, e\}$ is shown in Table 5.2.1. According to our theorem, this space should contain $(5)_3 = 5 \cdot 4 \cdot 3 = 60$ points; a direct count will confirm this.

We may note that the points in Table 5.2.1 are a subset of the points in Table 4.1.1, which is a primitive space consisting of points for samples drawn with replacement from $P = \{a, b, c, d, e\}$. Spaces whose points consist of samples of a specified uniform size drawn without replacement of the elements between trials will always be a subset of the set of points of the same size drawn with replacement from the same population. *A sample space whose points consist of a subset of elements from a primitive space will also be a primitive space,* since it meets all the conditions to qualify as such. Hence sample

TABLE 5.2.1 / Space of Ordered Sample Points of Size 3 that Could Be Drawn without Replacement from the Five-Element Population $P = \{a, b, c, d, e\}$

abc	*bac*	*cab*	*dab*	*eab*
abd	*bad*	*cad*	*dac*	*eac*
abe	*bae*	*cae*	*dae*	*ead*
acb	*bca*	*cba*	*dba*	*eba*
acd	*bcd*	*cbd*	*dbc*	*ebc*
ace	*bce*	*cbe*	*dbe*	*ebd*
adb	*bda*	*cda*	*dca*	*eca*
adc	*bdc*	*cdb*	*dcb*	*ecb*
ade	*bde*	*cde*	*dce*	*ecd*
aeb	*bea*	*cea*	*dea*	*eda*
aec	*bec*	*ceb*	*deb*	*edb*
aed	*bed*	*ced*	*dec*	*edc*

spaces formed as indicated in Theorem 5.2.1 are primitive sample spaces. Thus as previously indicated, we see that drawing samples with dependent trials does not automatically disqualify the sample space as primitive.

Examples

We may now illustrate the use of Theorem 5.2.1 with some simple problems.

1. What is the probability that a sample of size 3 drawn without replacement from the seven-element population, $P = \{a, b, c, d, e, f, g\}$ will contain the elements a, b, and c *in any order*?

By Theorem 5.2.1, $S = (7)_3$. The three elements from the subpopulation $\{a, b, d\}$ may, by corollary 5.2.1, be arranged in $(3)_3 = 3!$ distinguishable ways to give us $\mathscr{E}$. Therefore

$$P[a, b, c] = \frac{\mathscr{E}}{S} = \frac{3!}{(7)_3}$$

2. What is the probability that a number selected from all three-digit numbers containing the integers $1, 2, \ldots, 9$ will contain no repeated digits?

The size of the sample space of three-digit numbers containing no zeroes is $S = n^r = 9^3$, since the repetition of digits in the sample points implies that sampling occurs with replacement. Three-digit numbers can be formed from the same integers with no elements repeated (that is, without replacement) in $\mathscr{E} = (9)_3$ ways. Therefore

$$P[E] = \frac{(9)_3}{9^3} = \frac{9 \cdot 8 \cdot 7}{9 \cdot 9 \cdot 9} = \frac{504}{729} = .6913$$

Subpopulations are distinguished only by the elements in them, but arrangements are distinguished by both their elements and their particular order. Thus *abc* and *abd* are distinct arrangements whose elements are from distinct populations (or subpopulations), even though they contain elements in common. Suppose we have the following sets which could, for instance, be sample points belonging to some space not fully represented here.

SETS	NUMBER OF DISTINCT ARRANGEMENTS
$\{a, b, c\}$	$3!$
$\{a, b, d\}$	$3!$
$\{a, c, d\}$	$3!$
$\{e, f, g\}$	$3!$

There are four points, each of which can be decomposed into $3!$ distinct arrangements; hence the total number of arrangements that can be generated from them is

$$3!(4) = 3 \cdot 2 \cdot 1(4) = 6(4) = 24$$

The fact that the form of the number 6 in this case is $3!$ should not obscure another fact—that it is simply a number that can be thought of as a single factor whose value is 6. That is, $3!(4) = 24$. More abstractly, if we have x unordered sample points of size r drawn without replacement from a population P, we may decompose them into $r!x$ distinct ordered points. This will be useful in the next section.

5.3 UNORDERED SAMPLES TAKEN FROM A SINGLE POPULATION WITHOUT REPLACEMENT

As previously noted, a sample taken without replacement from a population can contain no repeated elements. If, additionally, order is of no consequence, then from the standpoint of its internal composition every point will be a set, although that set will of course be regarded as a single element in the sample space of which it is a point. The set of all points in a space for unordered samples of size r taken without replacement from a finite population P can be made isomorphic with the set of all distinct subpopulations of size r that can be formed from the elements in P. This follows from the fact that each is an exhaustive set of the alternatives for unordered arrays of identical numbers of unrepeated elements drawn from the same population. Since even the notation is identical for each element in any ordered pair in the equivalence function of points and subpopulations, the sets are considered identical. Subpopulations are technically not *ipso facto* points, but it would be absurd to insist that we explicitly notice the distinction between subpopulations on the one hand and points and spaces on the other.

For the distributions derived in this book, a sample point constituted of unordered elements means exactly the same thing as the union of all possible orders. This applies to models where the substantive meaning of "unordered" is that any observed order meeting the stipulated conditions will constitute an occurrence. This attribute applies to the cases when order or arrangement is defined as an *attitude* toward the actual outcome. This could be illustrated for a representative point as*

$$[a, b, c] = \{abc, acb, bac, bca, cab, cba\}$$

We see then that such a point decomposes into a set of non-decomposable elements. It should be apparent that an exhaustive set of such points would decompose into a set of equal-sized non-intersecting sets whose union would constitute a primitive sample space. A space whose points decompose in such a manner automatically qualifies as a uniform space.

In order for two populations or subpopulations to be distinguishable, they must differ by at least one element. Hence $\{b, c, e\}$ and $\{a, c, e\}$ are different populations. At the other extreme, the maximum difference that can exist between two populations of the

* Here again we use a notation that is in line with our convention (or abbreviation). The above expression would be written more precisely as

$$[a, b, c] = \{\{abc\}, \{acb\}, \ldots, \{cba\}\}$$

We have not defined *abc* as an event (thus a one-element set or point), but we have adopted definitions which imply that *abc* is a one-element set so that we need not be overly involved in notation.

same size occurs when they have no elements in common. In other words, two subpopulations drawn from the same population may range from almost completely intersecting to exclusive sets. Subpopulations have a special importance because this is the kind of sample that is most commonly drawn in practice by social science researchers.

We shall at this point introduce a new symbol which for the time being should have no mathematical meaning other than that it represents some number. It should be thought of as a shorthand symbol for the verbal statement with which it is equated.

$\binom{n}{r}$ = the number of distinct *unordered* samples of size r that may be drawn *without replacement* from a population of size n
= the number of distinct subpopulations of size r that can be formed from the elements of a population of size n.

Other than being a number, then, we shall regard $\binom{n}{r}$ as only verbally defined and proceed to see if we can also define it mathematically.

Recall from the previous section that if we have x sets or subpopulations of size r, we may decompose them into $r!x$ distinct arrangements of size r. Thus if we know that the number of unordered sample points of size r that can be drawn without replacement from a population P of size n is $\binom{n}{r}$, then the product $r!\binom{n}{r}$ is the number of arrangements of size r that can be formed without repeated elements from the elements in P. It takes account of every possible order of the elements in every possible r-sized subset of P.

The number of such arrangements could also be obtained directly by Theorem 5.2.1 as $(n)_r$. That is, the number of ordered sample points (arrangements) of size r that can be drawn without replacement (and hence no elements repeated in any single point) from a population of n elements is $(n)_r$. It follows that

$$r!\binom{n}{r} = (n)_r$$

whence

$$\binom{n}{r} = \frac{(n)_r}{r!}$$

and $\binom{n}{r}$ is *mathematically* defined. We have thus proved the following theorem.

THEOREM 5.3.1. The size of the space for unordered samples of size r that may be drawn without replacement from a population of size n is

$$\binom{n}{r} = \frac{(n)_r}{r!}$$

This is also the number of distinct subpopulations of size r that can be formed from a population of n elements.

The size of the space for unordered samples of size 3 to be drawn without replacement from the five-element population, $P = \{a, b, c, d, e\}$ is

$$\binom{n}{r} = \binom{5}{3} = \frac{(5)_3}{3!} = \frac{5 \cdot 4 \cdot 3}{3 \cdot 2 \cdot 1} = 10$$

This may also be seen in Table 5.3.1. The 10 unordered sample points appear in brackets in the table. Beneath each unordered point are the $3! = 6$ arrangements into which it decomposes. Since the union of these arrangements constitutes a primitive space, the original space is uniform.

TABLE 5.3.1 / Decomposition of the 10-Point Uniform Space for Unordered Samples Drawn without Replacement from $P = \{a, b, c, d, e\}$ into the 60-Point Primitive Space of Table 5.2.1

$[a, b, c]$	$[a, b, d]$	$[a, b, e]$	$[a, c, d]$	$[a, c, e]$
abc	abd	abe	acd	ace
acb	adb	aeb	adc	aec
bac	bad	bae	cad	cae
bca	bda	bea	cda	cea
cab	dab	eab	dac	eac
cba	dba	eba	dca	eca

$[a, d, e]$	$[b, c, d]$	$[b, c, e]$	$[b, d, e]$	$[c, d, e]$
ade	bcd	bce	bde	cde
aed	bdc	bec	bed	ced
dae	cbd	cbe	dbe	dce
dea	cdb	ceb	deb	dec
ead	dbc	ebc	ebd	ecd
eda	dcb	ecb	edb	edc

IDENTITY 5.3.1

$$\binom{n}{r} = \frac{n!}{r!(n-r)!}$$

This identity is of considerable theoretical importance, although it is generally less useful for actual computation than the previous form. Its proof is

$$\binom{n}{r} = \frac{(n)_r}{r!} = \frac{n(n-1)\ldots(n-r+1)}{r!} \cdot \frac{(n-r)!}{(n-r)!} = \frac{n!}{r!(n-r)!}$$

Q.E.D.

We multiplied the right-hand side of the original expression by the number 1 in the form $(n-r)!/(n-r)!$. Since $(n-r)$ is one unit less in value than $(n-r+1)$, then $(n-r)!$ supplies all of the remaining factors required to produce $n!$. A numerical example is

$$\binom{7}{3} = \frac{(7)_3}{3!} = \frac{7\cdot6\cdot5}{3!} \cdot \frac{(7-3)!}{(7-3)!}$$

$$= \frac{7\cdot6\cdot5\cdot4!}{3!4!} = \frac{7\cdot6\cdot5\cdot4\cdot3\cdot2\cdot1}{3!4!} = \frac{7!}{3!4!}$$

An extremely useful identity for computational purposes is

IDENTITY 5.3.2

$$\binom{n}{r} = \binom{n}{n-r}$$

For example,

$$\binom{5}{3} = \binom{5}{5-3} = \binom{5}{2}$$

PROOF 1. By formal substitution of $(n-r)$ for r in $\binom{n}{r}$, we get $\binom{n}{n-r}$, which by Identity 5.3.1 gives

$$\binom{n}{n-r} = \frac{n!}{(n-r)![n-(n-r)]!} = \frac{n!}{(n-r)!r!} = \binom{n}{r}$$

A different form of proof may be more illuminating.

PROOF 2. Each time we extract a subpopulation of size r from an n-element population, the remaining elements constitute a residual subpopulation of size $(n - r)$. There are evidently exactly the same number of subpopulations in the residual set as in the extracted set, a fact which is expressed in the relationship

$$\binom{n}{r} = \binom{n}{n-r}$$

and the theorem is proved.

The computational convenience of this identity may be seen in the following example. If we need to find $\binom{52}{48}$, then $(52)_{48}/48!$ would give us a string of 48 factors each in the numerator and denominator, but

$$\binom{52}{48} = \binom{52}{52-48} = \binom{52}{4} = \frac{(52)_4}{4!} = \frac{52 \cdot 51 \cdot 50 \cdot 49}{4 \cdot 3 \cdot 2 \cdot 1}$$

We proceed to develop some useful definitions.

IDENTITY 5.3.3

$$\binom{n}{n} = \frac{(n)_n}{n!} = \frac{n!}{n!} = 1$$

Also,

$$\binom{n}{n} = \binom{n}{n-n} = \binom{n}{0}$$

We therefore define the following identity.

IDENTITY 5.3.4

$$\binom{n}{0} = 1$$

We may now write

$$\binom{n}{0} = \frac{n!}{0!(n-0)!} = \left(\frac{n!}{n!}\right)\frac{1}{0!} = 1 \quad \text{or} \quad 0! = 1 \cdot \frac{1}{1} = 1$$

Therefore we have the following identity.

IDENTITY 5.3.5

$$0! = 1$$

Finally

$$\binom{n}{0} = \frac{(n)_0}{0!} = \frac{(n)_0}{1} = 1$$

Hence the following:

IDENTITY 5.3.6

$$(n)_0 = 1$$

For the sake of completeness, we may also recall from elementary algebra that $n^0 = 1$.

5.4 ILLUSTRATIVE PROBLEMS

With the three very fundamental sample spaces now at our disposal, we can illustrate their application to some elementary problems of probability. The trivial subjects of the illustrations should not obscure the importance of the principles they illustrate. These problems are intended to encourage the reader to think in terms of sample spaces.

1. Suppose a die is tossed six times.

a. What is the probability that the face on each trial will correspond to its order; that is, 1 on the first throw, 2 on the second, and so forth?

Solution. For six throws of a die, the sample space is $S = 6^6$. Only one point in the space has the arrangement 1:2:3:4:5:6. Hence $\mathscr{E} = 1$ and $P[E] = 1/6^6$.

b. What is the probability that each face will be different?

Solution. S will remain as before. E will be the subset consisting of all possible arrangements of the elements 1, 2, 3, 4, 5, 6. We know that $r!$ arrangements of r distinct elements are possible. Therefore $\mathscr{E} = 6!$, and $P[E] = 6!/6^6$.

c. What is the probability that *at least* two faces will show identical values?

Solution. If we remove E from \$, where E is the set of all points in which every face is different, it necessarily leaves $\not{E}$ the set of points in which at least one element is repeated. Therefore $\not{\mathscr{E}} = S - \mathscr{E}$ and

$$P[\not{E}] = \frac{S - \mathscr{E}}{S} = \frac{6^6 - 6!}{6^6} = 1 - \frac{6!}{6^6}$$

This exemplifies our rule for the probability that an event will not occur; that is, $P[\not{E}] = 1 - P[E]$.

2. An elevator leaving from the basement level with seven passengers has eight floors to traverse.

a. What is the probability the passengers will all be discharged on the fifth floor?

Solution. We can think of each passenger as distinctly identifiable and hence as a distinct trial in random selection of the population elements (floors) in

$$P = \{1, 2, 3, 4, 5, 6, 7, 8\}$$

We note that the first passenger can be discharged on any of eight different floors, as can the second, and each of the others. Since our trials (passengers) are *distinguishable* and sampling occurs with replacement (that is, there can be repetitions of elements in the sample points), application of Theorem 4.1.1 tells us that there are $S = 8^7$ distinguishable ways (ordered sample points containing repeated elements) in which the passengers may be discharged. Only one of these points, 5:5:5:5:5:5:5, meets the condition "all passengers discharged on the fifth floor"; that is, the element 5 was selected on all seven trials. Therefore $P[E] = 1/8^7 = 8^{-7}$.

b. What is the probability that all of the passengers will be discharged on the same *unspecified* floor?

Solution. Since there are eight floors, there are $\mathscr{E} = 8$ sample points in E and $P[E] = 8 \cdot 8^{-7} = 8^{-6}$.

c. What is the probability that exactly three passengers will be discharged on the second floor?

Solution. $\mathscr{S}$ and hence S remain as before. Every distinguishable way in which three passengers could be chosen to occupy the second floor is given by the number of distinct subpopulations of size three that could be formed from among seven passengers, or $\binom{7}{3}$, but this would not account for all of the sample points in E. For each of these $\binom{7}{3}$ subpopulations that might occupy the second floor and hence meet the condition required, any of the distributions of the four remaining passengers among the remaining seven floors would generate a distinct sample point. Hence for each of the $\binom{7}{3}$ ways in which a subpopulation of size three could be selected from among the seven passengers to occupy the second floor, the remaining four passengers could be distributed among the remaining seven floors in 7^4 ways. Hence $P[E] = \binom{7}{3}7^4/8^7$.

3. If r distinguishable balls are randomly distributed among n distinguishable cells, what is the probability that exactly k of them will occupy a specified cell, say the fifth?

Solution. Note that this is formally the same problem as the previous one. The r balls may be assigned to the n cells in n^r different ways to determine the size of $\mathbb{S}$. Furthermore, k balls may be selected from among the r to occupy the specified cell in $\binom{r}{k}$ ways. For each of these, the remaining $r - k$ balls may be distributed among the remaining $n - 1$ cells in $(n - 1)^{r-k}$ ways. Hence

$$P[E] = \binom{r}{k}(n - 1)^{r-k}n^{-r}$$

Notice that in a problem of this type a ball either goes into the specified cell or it does not. In meeting the conditions, any other cell it might occupy simply falls into the category of nonoccupancy of the specified cell. This dichotomous basis for judging an occurrence or nonoccurrence of the event places it in the category of a binomial model. This particular problem exemplifies a binomial model with a uniform sample space which is a special category. There are also binomial models for which the sample space is not uniform. The binomial model and its applications will be studied thoroughly in a later chapter.

4. Suppose a five-card poker hand is drawn from a standard deck.

a. What is the probability it will contain a flush in hearts—that is, every card in the hand will be a heart?

Solution. Since order is of no consequence for a poker hand, the sample space is defined as the set of all subpopulations of size 5 that may be formed from the 52-element population represented by the deck. Hence $S = \binom{52}{5}$. Thirteen cards in the deck are hearts. The size of the subset E of hands of five cards that are hearts is therefore $\mathscr{E} = \binom{13}{5}$. Thus

$$P[E] = \frac{\binom{13}{5}}{\binom{52}{5}} = \frac{(13)_5}{5!} \cdot \frac{5!}{(52)_5}$$

$$= \frac{13 \cdot 12 \cdot 11 \cdot 10 \cdot 9}{52 \cdot 51 \cdot 50 \cdot 49 \cdot 48} = .0005$$

In other words, this is an event that occurs only five times in 10,000 tries.

b. What is the probability that a flush of any kind will be drawn?

Solution. Here E is evidently four times the size of E for the previous problem, and $P[E] = 4\binom{13}{5}\binom{52}{5}^{-1}$.

c. What is the probability of drawing two kings and three queens?

Solution. Two kings may be drawn from the four available kings in $\binom{4}{2}$ ways. For each of these, three queens may be drawn from the four available in $\binom{4}{3}$ ways. Hence

$$P[2K, 3Q] = \frac{\binom{4}{2}\binom{4}{3}}{\binom{52}{5}}$$

d. What is the probability of drawing two kings?

Solution. As before, two kings may be drawn in $\binom{4}{2}$ ways, to meet the stipulated condition, but the number of points that would meet this condition includes every hand in which two kings could occur. For each of the $\binom{4}{2}$ ways in which two kings could be drawn, the 48 non-kings can form distinct subsets of size three in $\binom{48}{3}$ ways. Obviously, then,

$$P[E] = \frac{\binom{4}{2}\binom{48}{3}}{\binom{52}{5}}$$

e. What is the probability of drawing a full house—that is, three of any common face value and two of any other?

Solution. Three of a kind could be formed from some *particular* face value (say aces) in $\binom{4}{3}$ ways. Since there are 13 different face values, this condition could be met in $13\binom{4}{3}$ ways. For *each* of these, the remaining 12 face values could be formed into sets of two in $12\binom{4}{2}$ ways; thus

$$P[\text{full house}] = (13)_2\binom{4}{2}\binom{4}{3}\binom{52}{5}^{-1}$$

f. What is the probability of drawing at least three aces?

Solution. Drawing at least three aces means drawing either three or four aces. These are exclusive events since one cannot simultaneously have a total of three aces and a total of four. Call the events E_1 and E_2. Then

$$P[E_1 \cup E_2] = P[E_1] + P[E_2] = \frac{\binom{4}{3}\binom{48}{2} + \binom{4}{4}\binom{48}{1}}{\binom{52}{5}}$$

5. If there are three cars in a 10-slot parking lot, what is the probability they will occupy the last three slots if purely random forces determine the choices?

Solution. A slot can be occupied by only one car. Think of the cars as trials 1, 2, and 3. A place can be chosen for the first car in 10 different ways, for the second in nine ways, and the third in eight. Hence $S = (10)_3$. The three cars can occupy the three specified places in $\mathscr{E} = 3!$ ways. Hence $P[E] = 3!/(10)_3$.

There are many different ways to solve problems of probability. Note that the above solutions are stated in terms of a sample space $ and a subset E. That there may be shorter or more ingenious solutions for these particular problems is irrelevant; our concern has been to illustrate a powerful method of generality.

5.5 PARTITIONS

Suppose a class which meets for regular lectures twice a week is divided into smaller sections to meet as discussion groups for a third weekly session. Allocating the students into an exhaustive set of disjoint discussion groups would be called "partitioning" the population of students in the class, and the complete set of subpopulations constituting the discussion groups would be called a "partition." The same idea is stated more formally and rigorously in the following definition.

An ordered k-tuplet of exhaustive nonintersecting subpopulations of a population P is called a *partition* of P. The sizes of the subpopulations comprising a partition are fixed but need not be uniform. If r_i is the size of the ith subpopulation in a partition of P into k subpopulations and if n is the number of elements in P, then

$$\sum_{i=1}^{k} r_i = n$$

For any fixed set of values of r_i, the possible number of partitions of the population into k subpopulations is the number of distinct ways in which the elements of the population may be allocated among k such subpopulations.

Examples of partitions of $P = \{a, b, c, d, e, f, g, h\}$ into $k = 3$ subpopulations of sizes $r_1 = 2$, $r_2 = 3$, and $r_3 = 3$ are

(1) $(\{c, d\}, \{b, f, g\}, \{a, e, h\})$
(2) $(\{a, d\}, \{b, e, h\}, \{c, d, g\})$
(3) $(\{a, d\}, \{c, d, g\}, \{b, e, h\})$

Note that (2) and (3) differ only in the interchange of elements between the second and third positions. Also the elements within any subpopulation are, by definition of subpopulation, unordered, but the subpopulations themselves are ordered. We recall that "order" means not merely position but rather distinguishability, such as might be exemplified by position. For example, if a company had a sales staff of eight, that staff might be partitioned so that two are assigned to Washington, three to California, and three to Oregon. All distinct ways in which the staff could be so allocated would be the number of distinct partitionings.

5.6 THE MULTINOMIAL COEFFICIENT

THEOREM 5.6.1. Partitions of a population (set) of size n into k subpopulations (subsets) of sizes $r_1, r_2, r_3, \ldots, r_k$, respectively, may be formed in

$$\frac{n!}{r_1!r_2!\ldots r_k!} = \frac{\left[\sum_{i=1}^{k} r_i\right]!}{\prod_{i=1}^{k} r_i!}$$

distinguishable ways. This expression is called the multinomial coefficient and will be discussed in Section 10.2.

COMMENT. Recall that for a partition $\sum_{i=1}^{k} r_i = n$, then solving for r_k gives the following identity.

IDENTITY 5.6.1

$$n - r_1 - r_2 - \cdots - r_{k-1} = r_k$$

This identity is useful in our proof.

PROOF. A subpopulation of r_1 elements may be selected from the n elements in $\binom{n}{r_1}$ ways. For each of these a subpopulation of size r_2 may be selected from the remaining $n - r_1$ elements in $\binom{n-r_1}{r_2}$ ways, and so on, until finally r_{k-1} elements may be selected from the remaining $n - r_1 - r_2 - \cdots - r_{k-2}$ elements in

$$\binom{n - r_1 - r_2 - \cdots - r_{k-2}}{r_{k-1}} \quad \text{ways.}$$

It is not necessary to carry the process further, since, because of Identity 5.6.1, the last factor would be

$$\binom{r_k}{r_k} = 1$$

This is consistent with the fact that a residual subpopulation of size r_k could be formed from the last remaining r_k elements in only one way. Applying the general case of the fundamental principle of combinatorial analysis, we get

$$\binom{n}{r_1}\binom{n-r_1}{r_2}\binom{n-r_1-r_2}{r_3}\cdots\binom{n-r_1-r_2-\cdots-r_{k-2}}{r_{k-1}} \quad \text{ways.}$$

This product may be rewritten as

$$\frac{n!}{r_1!\cancel{(n-r_1)!}}\cdot\frac{\cancel{(n-r_1)!}}{r_2!\cancel{(n-r_1-r_2)!}}\cdot\frac{\cancel{(n-r_1-r_2)!}}{r_3!\cancel{(n-r_1-r_2-r_3)!}}$$

$$\cdots\frac{\cancel{(n-r_1-r_2-\cdots-r_{k-3})!}}{r_{k-2}!\cancel{(n-r_1-r_2-\cdots-r_{k-3}-r_{k-2})!}}$$

$$\cdot\frac{\cancel{(n-r_1-r_2-\cdots-r_{k-2})!}}{r_{k-1}!(n-r_1-r_2-\cdots-r_{k-1})!}$$

Since the factors cancel as indicated, then by again taking advantage of Identity 5.6.1 in the denominator of the last factor, we obtain

$$\frac{n!}{r_1!r_2!\ldots r_k!} = \frac{\left[\sum_{i=1}^{k} r_i\right]!}{\prod_{i=1}^{k} r_i!}$$

and the theorem is proved.

Examples

1. In how many ways may 15 students be partitioned into subcommittees of sizes 3, 5, and 7 that may meet simultaneously at different places?

Answer:

$$\frac{(3 + 5 + 7)!}{3!5!7!} = \frac{15!}{3!5!7!}$$

2. An elevator leaving the basement level with nine passengers has seven floors to traverse. What is the probability that exactly three passengers will be discharged on each of the second, fourth, and sixth floors?

Answer: As in previous elevator problems, $S = n^r = 7^9$. The number of sample points in E will be equal to the number of partitions consisting of ordered subpopulations, $r_1 = r_2 = r_3 = 3$, that may be formed from the nine passengers to occupy the second, fourth, and sixth floors. Thus

$$P[E] = \frac{9!}{(3!)^3} \cdot 7^{-9}$$

PROBLEMS

1. Given eight people:

a. How many ways can an ordered 8-tuple be formed with and without replacement?

b. How many ways can ordered groups of four be formed with and without replacement?

c. How many ways can unordered groups of four be formed with and without replacement?

d. How many different groups of four people can be formed from a group of eight?

e. Use a group of k people with $k < 8$, and answer parts a through d.

2. The children in a class choose a team of 10 out of their class of 30 to represent them. An educator is interested in "hierarchy" within the class and wishes to form a statistical model.

a. In how many possible ordered ways could this team be chosen from the class?

b. Give an example point using the digits 1 to 30 to identify class members. One may assume that these digits rank the students according to athletic ability.

c. The sample point will have 10 of the digits 1 to 30 in some order. Give two example points for each of the following teams: (1) the team that tends to have the best athletes, (2) the team that is "representative," and (3) the team that is weighted toward the poorer athletes.

d. Use other texts to find and describe briefly several tests that use this ordered-point or paired-ranks principle to formulate a statistical test.

3. Use the situation defined in Problem 2 to answer the following:

a. In how many unordered ways could the team be chosen from the class?

b. How many ways could the team be chosen

(1) So that 8 of the top 10 athletes are on the team?

(2) So that exactly 9 of the top 10 are on the team?

(3) So that exactly 10 of the top 10 are on the team?

c. What is the probability 8 or more of the top 10 athletes are on the team? (*Hint:* Review Section 4.3.)

d. If 8 of the top athletes are on the team, what could be reasonably concluded? Note the very limited use of order in this example.

4. Fourteen administrators are identified by the digits 1 to 14. Give three examples of partitions of these administrators to five offices so that the offices have 3, 4, 3, 2, 2 administrators, respectively.

5. Use the partition above to answer the following questions:

a. In how many unordered ways could the administrators be assigned to the branches?

b. If they had ranked positions within each office, in how many ways could they be assigned to offices?

c. An interesting administrative problem, fun to think about but rather advanced, is: Given an accepted hierarchy between the individuals and status associated with position and office, list the acceptable ways the individuals can be assigned to offices. Draw this in diagram form.

6. Given a sample of 300 people which results in N_i people from each of 10 exclusive groups so that

$$\sum_{i-1}^{k} N_i = 300$$

a. In how many ordered ways could this point be observed?
b. It is believed that there was bias in selecting the sample. The observations are broken into groups believed to be biased and believed to be unbiased. This division results in 20 bivariate categories with M_{ij} members in each. Explain how to interpret the expression

$$\frac{300!}{\prod_{i=1}^{10} \prod_{j=1}^{10} M_{ij}}$$

c. Suggest how the sample-space method might be used to determine the existence of bias. For example, how might the ratios M_{i1}/M_{i2} behave if there is no bias with respect to the categories i?

7. Given a composite event which has k trials from n elements.
a. How many points are there in the space for samples taken with replacement?
b. How many points are there in the sample space for samples taken without replacement?
c. How can the difference between the answers in parts a and b be interpreted and what happens when k is much, much less than n?
d. What is the probability of a "repeated element" in a point in the spaces in parts a and b above? What do these probabilities approach as n becomes large compared to k?

8. Given the population $P = \{a, b, c, d\}$:
a. Display the space $\$_u$ for unordered samples of size 3 drawn without replacement from P.
b. Calculate the number of elements in a space $\$_p$ consisting of all possible arrangements or orders of the elements in each of the points in $\$_u$.
c. Display spaces $\$_u$ and $\$_p$ in a manner that defines one as isomorphic to an exhaustive set of equal-sized subsets of the other.

d. Calculate the number of points in the space $\$_a$ for ordered samples of size 3 taken without replacement from *P*.
e. How does the size of $\$_a$ compare with the size of $\$_p$? What can be asserted about $\$_p$ and $\$_a$ that explains what you find?

CHAPTER 6

THE BALL-AND-CELL MODEL FOR THE ANALYSIS OF SAMPLE SPACES

THE BALL-AND-CELL model is a powerful adjunct of sample space analysis to use for problems of otherwise forbidding complexity. Much is owed to Feller* for demonstrating the ease and elegance of its use. Its understanding may require an initial reorientation of one's thought patterns, but the newly acquired power will compensate handsomely for the effort.

The ball-and-cell model consists of the conceptual random assignment of balls (thought of as trials) to cells (thought of as population elements). The conditions under which they are assigned correspond to the conditions under which sampling occurs, and each configuration of balls in cells corresponds to a unique point in the relevant sample space. In the terminology of set theory, the sample space and the space of all configurations of balls in cells are *isomorphic spaces*, since we have defined the conditions of distributing the balls so that the probability structures of the two spaces are inherently related. There is one and only one configuration of balls in cells corresponding to each point in the sample space; this ensures that the condition of equivalence is met for their respective sets of elements.

* See Feller, *An Introduction to Probability Theory and Its Applications*, *op. cit.*

6.1 ORDERED TRIALS

When we wish to regard the balls as *ordered* trials we shall conceive of them as being numbered; thus ball 1 corresponds to trial 1, and so forth. Consider the problem of determining the size of the space for ordered samples of size $r = 5$ drawn with replacement from the seven-element population

$$P = \{a, b, c, d, e, f, g\}$$

One point in such a sample space would be *ccafa*. This is uniquely represented by the ball-and-cell configuration shown below, where

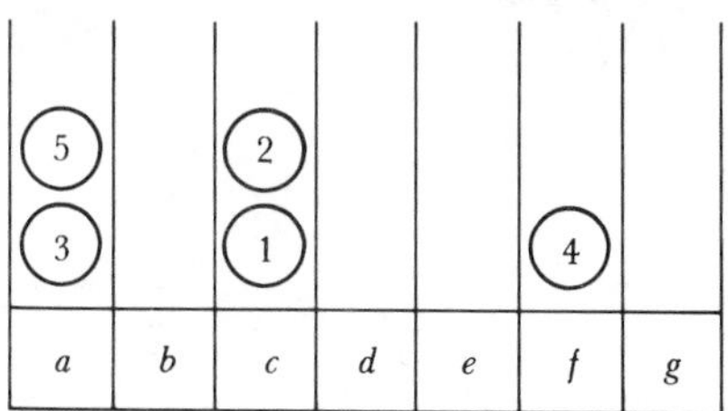

the positions of the elements in the point correspond to the numbers of the balls. If the cell configuration were as shown below, that would represent point *aaccf*.

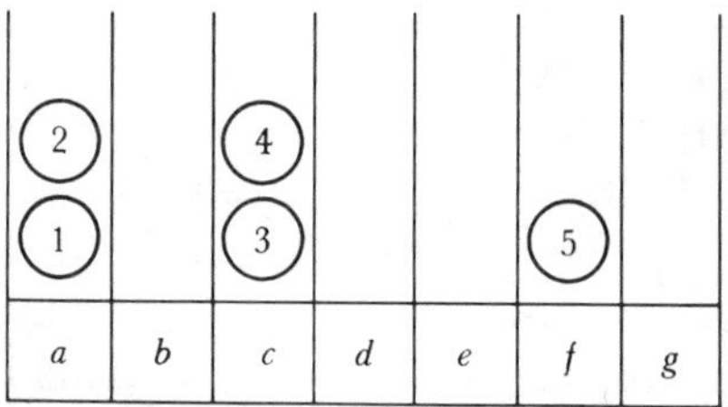

We may state, then, that the number of unique configurations of r distinguishable (numbered) balls distributed among n distinguishable cells is exactly equal to the number of points in the sample space corresponding to drawing ordered samples of size r with replacement from an n element population; that is, n^r. For the specific case of seven cells and five balls, we have 7^5.

A typical sample point for four tosses of a coin, say $TTTH$, would have the ball-and-cell representation shown below.

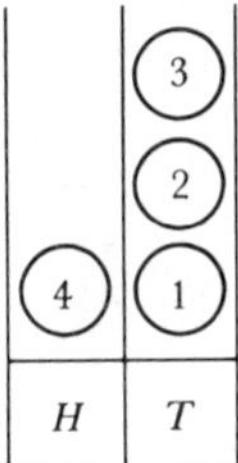

For three tosses of a die, the point 6:4:2 would be as illustrated below.

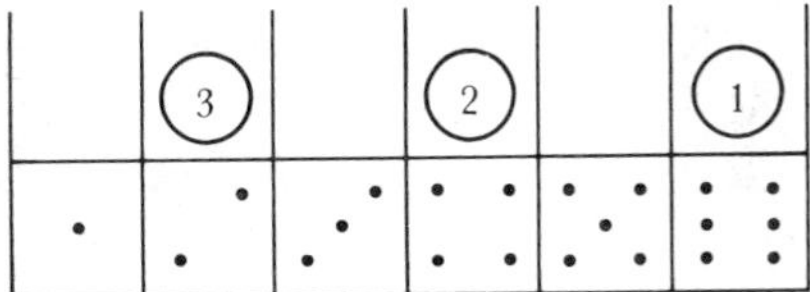

For elevator problems the relationship is too obvious to require illustration.

The ordered occurrence of four accidents according to days of the week (not necessarily in the same week) would show point *MMFW* as represented below. This would mean the first two

S	M	T_1	W	T_2	F	S
	2					
	1		4		3	

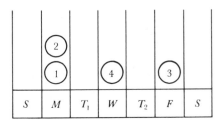

accidents occurred on a Monday (but not necessarily the same Monday), the third on a Friday, and the fourth on a Wednesday.

If we wish to impose the condition that no replacement occurs in the sampling, this, it will be recalled, implies that no elements will be repeated in the sample point. Correspondingly, the maximum number of balls occupying a cell is 1. Conversely, multiple occupancy of cells implies sampling with replacement. A typical ball-and-cell configuration for ordered samples of size 5 drawn without replacement would be as shown below, which is point *fbdac*.

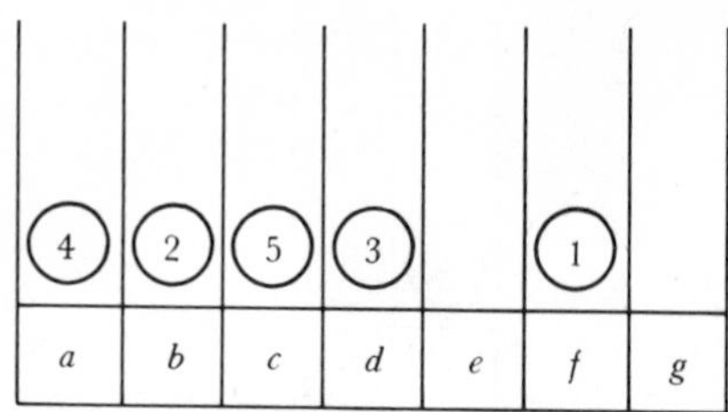

The number of distinguishable ways in which r distinguishable balls may be distributed among n distinguishable cells without multiple occupancy is exactly equal to the number of ways in which ordered samples of size r may be drawn without replacement from an n-element population, that is, $(n)_r$. We may repeat for emphasis that "ordered samples" and sample points that are "arrangements" are corresponding elements in isomorphic spaces.

6.2 UNORDERED TRIALS

It will be recalled that the number of points in the space for *unordered* samples of size r taken without replacement from an n-element population is $\binom{n}{r}$. These points could, of course, be decomposed into $r!\binom{n}{r}$ sample points, which is a larger number, but since the nonprimitive space of compound points is uniform and the size of such a space is smaller, it may be used more conveniently.

All $\binom{n}{r}$ possible points in such a space may be represented by a ball-and-cell model that excludes multiple occupancy and represents the balls without numbers. For example, point $[a, b, e, g]$ is as represented below. The single occupancy meets the condition that no

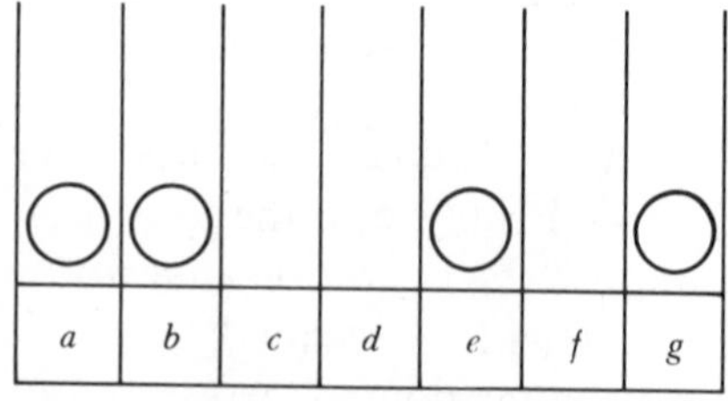

elements may be repeated and the indistinguishable balls represent the irrelevance of order in the trials. If the balls in the cells were numbered, we would require 4! different cell configurations to represent the 4! orders of the elements a, b, e, and g.

We may then state that the number of distinguishable distributions of r indistinguishable balls among n distinguishable cells with multiple occupancy excluded is exactly equal to the number of distinct subpopulations of size r that may be formed from the elements in a population of size n, or, what is the same thing, the number of unordered samples of size r that may be drawn without replacement from an n-element population, that is, $\binom{n}{r}$.

6.3 ARRANGEMENTS OF INDISTINGUISHABLE ELEMENTS

We may make immediate use of the ball-and-cell concept in deriving an important theorem. It is concerned with the number of distinguishable arrangements that can be made from two groups of objects which have intergroup but not intragroup distinguishability.

THEOREM 6.3.1. The number of distinguishable linear arrangements of a α-elements and b β-elements is

$$\binom{a+b}{a} = \binom{a+b}{b}$$

Example

Five indistinguishable red books and three indistinguishable yellow books may be arranged on a bookshelf in

$$\binom{5+3}{3} = \binom{8}{3}$$

distinguishable ways. If we call the red books α's and the yellow books β's, one such arrangement might be $\alpha\alpha\alpha\beta\beta\alpha\beta\alpha$.

PROOF. If we have a α's and b β's to arrange, this implies that there is a total of $(a + b)$ positions to be filled with these elements. These positions may be thought of as $(a + b)$ cells.

Consider first the possible distributions of the α's only. Distributing a indistinguishable α's among $(a + b)$ cells could be done in as many ways as a indistinguishable balls could be so distributed. Since the set of subpopulations of size a that may be formed from an $(a + b)$ element population is isomorphic with the set of configurations of a indistinguishable balls with single occupancy among $(a + b)$ cells, then the α's may be distributed in

$$\binom{a+b}{a} = \binom{a+b}{b}$$

ways. Once the a α's are placed, the β's can only go into the remaining b slots; thus the number of ways is completely determined by the distributions of the α's, and the theorem is proved.

A generalization of this theorem follows:

THEOREM 6.3.2. Given r_1 elements of one sort, r_2 of another, through r_k elements of a final sort such that

$$\sum_{i=1}^{k} r_i = n$$

then the number of distinct linear arrangements of these elements is

$$\frac{n!}{r_1!r_2!\cdots r_k!} = \frac{\left[\sum_{r=1}^{k} r_i\right]!}{\prod_{i=1}^{k} r_i!}$$

This will be recognized as the multinomial coefficient of Theorem 5.6.1 that deals with the number of ordered subpopulations of sizes $r_1, r_2, \ldots, r_k$ that may be formed from a population of size

$$n = \sum_{i=1}^{k} r_i$$

However, the interpretations of the meanings in the two cases should be kept distinct.

PROOF. In a manner directly analogous to the previous theorem, the number of distinguishable arrangements of the r_i elements of k various sorts will be equal to the number of ways in which

r_1 balls of one sort, r_2 of another, through r_k of a final sort may be distributed with single occupancy among a set of linearly adjacent cells whose number is equal to that of the total number of elements, that is,

$$\sum_{i=1}^{k} r_i \quad \text{cells}$$

The n cells may be partitioned into k subpopulations such that the first subpopulation may contain r_1 balls of the first sort, the second, r_2 of the second sort, and the kth, r_k of the final sort, in

$$\frac{\left[\sum_{i=1}^{k} r_i\right]!}{\prod_{i=1}^{k} r_i!} = \frac{n!}{\prod_{i=1}^{k} r_i!} \quad \text{ways}$$

and the theorem is proved.

Example

In how many ways may three Orientals, four Caucasians, and two Polynesians be seated at a lunch counter?

Answer:

$$\frac{(3+4+2)!}{3!4!2!} = \frac{9!}{3!4!2!} = 1260 \text{ ways}$$

PROBLEMS

1. Trials 1 to 10 are persons ranked 1 to 10 on a general knowledge test. They are given a second test of reaction speed marked on a five-point scale. The results are as follows:

Person	1	2	3	4	5	6	7	8	9	10
Score	2	1	2	3	1	3	4	5	4	5

a. Draw a ball-and-cell model for this experiment.
b. What hypothesis would be appropriate for investigation?

c. How many points are in this space?

d. Give an example of a typical point.

e. What are some of the implications of assuming that this space is primitive?

2. Thirty people are given the reaction speed test suggested in Problem 1.

a. Construct a table giving a possible outcome and then answer parts a to e in Problem 1 for this sequence of unordered trials.

b. How does the "lack of order" affect the hypothesis we might wish to investigate?

3. Eight abstract pictures of the same physical size and by unknown artists were chosen so that each picture had a higher price than the one chosen before it. A group of experts was asked to price the pictures as low (*l*), medium (*m*), and high (*h*). One expert gave these prices:

Picture	1	2	3	4	5	6	7	8
Price	*l*	*m*	*h*	*l*	*m*	*h*	*l*	*m*

Answer parts a through e of Problem 1 for this example.

4. Twelve people were available for employment. These people were either white or nonwhite. They were assigned to labor or office positions, or they were refused employment. According to the authorities, treatment and racial background were independent factors. Draw a ball-and-cell model for this example and give a typical resulting distribution in the six categories. Then answer all parts of Problem 1.

5. Set up ball-and-cell models for Problems 1 and 3 in Chapter 4 and Problem 4 in Chapter 5.

CHAPTER 7

A STATISTICAL PROBLEM

IN THIS CHAPTER, we shall make the transition from the mathematics of probability to statistical inference, an area of primary interest in our study. Statistical inference and related fields such as descriptive statistics and statistical estimation constitute an inclusive field called statistics.

7.1 A METHODOLOGICAL NOTE

In considering the application of statistics to substantive scientific investigation, it is important to be aware that statistical theory is a branch of mathematics and, as such, its concepts refer only to mathematical relationships. No amount of observation could prove a single mathematical proposition. Substantive phenomena, on the other hand, are nonmathematical, but their analysis is possible if one can find mathematical expressions that will facilitate reasonably correct inferences about the relationships of conditions or attributes. Within certain theoretical frames of reference of *substantive* theory, one may use such terms as "cause" and "effect."*

* Although these terms have fallen into disfavor owing to naïve use of them, they can be very valuable when properly defined and carefully used.

However, there are no such terms in the vocabulary of mathematics. Their closest equivalents, in mathematics, are "independent variable" and "dependent variable," but these by no means automatically imply cause and effect. In statistics, one frequently deals with the relationships of variables in terms of statistical independence. If a statistical expression is an adequate conceptual representation of a set of substantive conditions under investigation, then finding that their counterpart mathematical variables are statistically *independent* could constitute a sufficient basis for discrediting the hypothesis that they are causally related, at least in the manner described by the function implicit in the statistical expression. But a finding of statistical dependence establishes only that the observed data are not inconsistent with the possibility of a causal relationship. Independently of substantive theoretical considerations, statistical dependence provides no basis for deciding which factor might be a cause and which an effect, and also gives no basis for determining whether the factors are even causally related to each other rather than common consequences of the same causal factors. The determination of such matters is the concern of substantive theories, and the rationale of the validity of substantive theoretical inference is known as *methodology.* The erroneous identification of statistics with methodology is widely prevalent—indeed these two areas are synonymous in many minds.

Since this book is oriented to application, avoidance of terminology that is essentially substantive in its denotation would be unnecessarily restrictive. We shall frequently take the liberty of assuming that methodological considerations justify the translation of statistical hypotheses into substantive terminology, but as a compromise to mathematical readers we shall endeavor to restrict claims based on the finding of statistical dependence to such expressions as "the evidence is consistent with" or "tends to support" a specified substantive hypothesis.

The critically important concepts of "random" and "accidental" are essential to the application of statistics to substantive investigation; however, statistical theory does not delineate useful meanings to these concepts within its context because in practice they are used intuitively. Such solipsistic concepts as "equally probable" are characteristically employed in definitions of these concepts. Probability in relation to substantive investigation provides a measure of the degree of justified confidence of the occurrence of a specified substantive event. Random and accidental are highly relative concepts and will always be conceived as specific to a particular frame of reference. For instance, to say that an event is "accidental" means that the frame of reference in which a person conceptualizes it does not provide any basis for a foreknowledge of its occurrence. Or if one "randomly" draws a card from a deck, he should not suppose that this implies some suspension of the laws of nature; in fact, he might very well believe that which card he shall draw is rigidly determined. In such a context, the probability for the card one actually draws is 1 and for those which he does not draw it is 0. Probability becomes relevant only as a measure of the limits of one's ignorance of the outcome of an experiment or investigation when his frame of reference fails to provide for all of the information that is required to be certain of the outcome. An event that might be highly predictable in one frame of reference could be completely random in another. For example, there is nothing random in any absolute sense in selecting sample specimens with the aid of random numbers. We might make accurate predictions of which specimens you would choose if we had precise information about the function you would employ to generate the "random" numbers. Similarly, when we talk about an "accident" we do not mean that a miracle has occurred, but only an event that we would have been unlikely to predict within the framework of our available knowledge. A driver at a traffic intersection might be killed owing to the "unlikely" event that the driver of a second vehicle ignored the red light. This does not mean that the accident had no "causes." Had the first driver known that the other was inebriated, for instance, it might have meant his own survival, but this is a difference in knowledge, not a difference in the substantive conditions that led the culpable party to violate the traffic signal.

Although statistical inference is entirely dependent upon the mathematics of probability, it requires a subtle but important shift in perspective. The following problem is presented to serve as a vehicle for the transition.

7.2 A FISH STORY

In a fishing party of five, I. Walton caught seven of the fish in the party's total catch of eight. The other members said he was just lucky, but he imputed his accomplishment to superior skill. If we interpret "luck" to mean benefiting from a random event (like winning a raffle), was Walton justified in rebuking the other members of the party for a "sour grapes" attitude? Finding the answer to this problem will involve more than just the computation of probabilities.

First, our concepts must be put in operational form. For instance, "luck" has to be further defined before we can resolve the key issue, or our problem will be ambiguous. Are we seeking to determine whether the evidence supports the general proposition that fishing depends on luck rather than skill, or are we starting out with that as an assumption and seeking to determine whether Walton in particular just happened to be the lucky one? Since the first of these alternatives coincides more closely to the objectives of social statistical models, we shall make it our primary concern.

Second, we must set up the problem in such a way that empirical facts—that is, the number and distribution of the fish caught—play a decisive part in our conclusion. We are not just asking what the probability is that seven of the eight fish will be caught by someone; we are also asserting that they have been caught and we are requiring an evaluation of this occurrence. In the case of an event that has occurred, the probability of its occurrence is assigned the value 1, which is certainty. Statistically we are interested in the probability that it would have occurred under the condition that it was "random" relative to a particular frame of reference. However, the "point probability"—or the probability of the specific event by itself—is seldom an object of sufficient statistical interest. If the size of a sample space is even moderately large, any point in it will be improbable. Our problem is to determine whether the observed event belongs to a *set* of events comprising a compound event of infrequent occurrence, or, more accurately, that would be of infrequent occurrence if the hypothesis that the event was a random one is correct. This hypothesis has a special name; it is called the *null hypothesis* and is conventionally abbreviated with the symbol H_0.

Stated slightly different, one may define a certain compound event as the set of all points whose observed occurrence calls for the rejection of the null hypothesis on the grounds that if that hypothesis were correct, such an event would be unlikely—that is, improbable. This compound event is known as the *region of rejection*, and its probability is known as the *confidence level.* It will be convenient for subsequent discussion to refer to a point or subset of points in the region of rejection as a "rare event."

Rejection of the null hypothesis implies the acceptance of an alternative hypothesis or of an exhaustive set of alternative hypotheses. It is desirable, where possible, to define the null and alternative hypotheses as "contradictories" so that rejection of the null hypothesis logically compels acceptance of a single alternative. We shall try to adhere to this and we shall designate such an alternative to the null hypothesis as H_1. When this condition is met, then we accept H_1 if, under H_0, the observed outcome would be a rare event.

The conventional letter representation of the confidence level or probability associated with the region of rejection is α. It is evident that α is the risk one is willing to take of being wrong if it should happen to be true that the null hypothesis is in fact correct.

We may now illustrate a number of the things we have said by developing a solution to our fish problem. First, we formulate our null hypothesis.

> H_0: The observed distribution of the 8 fish among the 5 fishermen was random

In substantive language, the observed distribution of the fish is owed to forces that bear no determinate relationship to individual differences among the fishermen. We shall assume that experimental conditions rule out all possible alternatives except "luck" and differential skill. Without control of the experimental conditions, alternatives like "a scuba diver secretly attached the fish to Walton's hook" would be logically possible. Technically, the alternative hypothesis is

> H_1: The observed distribution of the fish among the fishermen was not random

But by our assumption, the substantive interpretation of H_1 would be that differential skill accounts for the observed distribution of the catch among the fishermen, and hence its acceptance would constitute evidence that "fishing is a matter of skill." Note that the *statistical* variables are "distribution pattern of the catch" and "individual fishermen," while the substantive variables are "distribution pattern of the catch" and "differential skill of the fishermen." We shall define our region of rejection as the set of points formed by starting with that representing the maximum number of the fish that could be caught by a single fisherman (that is, eight), then adding the point representing the second largest number (seven), and so on, in descending order, terminating with the last point whose inclusion in the set would not carry the value of the probability of their union beyond .01. This, of course, ensures that the probability of rejecting the null hypothesis will be equal to or less than .01. Hence $\alpha = .01$. This is an arbitrary choice of the investigator. If we were willing to run the risk of making a wrong decision when the null hypothesis is in fact true five times out of every 100 times rather than once every 100 times, we would set $\alpha = .05$. To reject the null hypothesis when it is true is generally called a Type I error. Hence α is the risk of committing a Type I error.

One might ask, "Why not be conservative and set α at an extremely small level?" The answer is that, the lower the value we assign to α, the more we increase another type of risk—the risk that we will accept the null hypothesis when it is in fact false. This is known as a Type II error, and the risk associated with it is commonly designated as β. There is no general procedure for determining β. It varies according to a variety of conditions that would be too diversionary to go into here. It should be noted that, in general, $\beta \neq 1 - \alpha$ contrary to what one might be tempted to think. Most often, the value of α is the controlling decision, with no attempt to determine β in the specific case. β is of concern to statistical specialists in determining the relative "power" of alternative tests. One type of test is defined to be more powerful than another if its β is optimal for any given α. The power of a test is defined as $1 - \beta$, which for evident reasons is the probability of rejecting H_0 when it is in fact false. Table 7.2.1 summarizes this information.

Rejecting H_0 is a much more decisive action for small samples than accepting H_0. It would be far more accurate to say that we cannot reject H_0, which is not quite the same thing as saying we accept it. The rejection of H_0 for any given α is just as valid with a small sample as with a large one, whereas the greater the sample size, the greater the validity of accepting H_0 if the test indicates its nonrejection. If we reject H_0, then the valid measure of justifiable confidence in our decision is α, whose value we know because we ourselves have chosen it. However, we would generally not know β, whose value is required to measure the confidence that is justified in accepting H_0. It is perhaps astonishing but nevertheless true that if the results

TABLE 7.2.1 / Four Alternative Outcomes in Testing a Hypothesis

	TERM	PROBABILITY
1. Rejecting null hypothesis when it is in fact true	Type I error	α
2. Accepting null hypothesis when it is in fact true	Correct decision	$1 - \alpha$
3. Accepting null hypothesis when it is in fact false	Type II error	β
4. Rejecting null hypothesis when it is in fact false	Power of a test* (correct decision)	$1 - \beta$

* In general, the power of a test can be increased by increasing the size of the sample.

indicate rejection of H_0, then a small sample is just as good as a large one for any given value of α. In this case, the only significance of the size of the sample is the freedom one has to select a smaller value of α for a larger sample. A value of α that is set too low for the sample size would make rejection of H_0 mathematically impossible, and conducting the investigation would be pointless.

We complete our statistical investigation when we determine whether the event that a single fisherman from a party of five would catch at least seven out of a total of eight fish, would occur less than 1 percent of the time if the null hypothesis were true. In such a case, catching at least seven of the eight fish would be a rare event.

First, consider the event that one fisherman in particular (in this case Walton) would catch exactly seven of the fish.

Think of the fish as balls (trials) to be distributed among five cells (the fishermen). Subpopulations of seven from the eight fish to occupy Walton's cell could be formed in $\binom{8}{7}$ ways. For each of these, the remaining single fish could be distributed among the four remaining fishermen in four ways. We thus have a total of $4\binom{8}{7}$ sample points. But our problem was to find the probability that *any* single fisherman would catch seven fish. Since there are five fishermen, we have an event set of $5 \cdot 4\binom{8}{7}$ points.

The size of the sample space is equal to the number of ways eight fish could have been distributed among five fishermen (eight balls among five cells). Since multiple occupancy is implied by the substantive conditions of the problem, then $S = n^r = 5^8$. If we let

E_i be the event that i fish are caught by some single, unspecified fisherman, then,

$$P[E_7] = \frac{(5)_2\binom{8}{7}}{5^8}$$

This is the probability for exactly seven fish, but we require the probability for "at least seven" (that is, seven or more) fish. The only number greater than seven that could have been caught, given a *total* of eight, is eight fish, which we may call E_8.

Some single fisherman could have caught all eight in five ways, so that $E_8 = 5$ and

$$P[E_8] = \frac{5}{5^8}$$

The probability, then, that some single unspecified fisherman would have caught at least seven fish by "luck" is

$$P[E_7 \cup E_8] = P[E_7] + P[E_8] = \frac{(5)_2\binom{8}{7}}{5^8} + \frac{5}{5^8}$$

$$= \frac{(5 \cdot 4 \cdot 8) + 5}{5^8} = \frac{165}{390625} = .0004$$

In other words, such an event would have occurred by "luck" or "chance" only four times in 10,000 tries. Since clearly $.0004 < .01 = \alpha$, Walton's achievement is a rare event, under the hypothesis that it is due to random forces. We therefore reject H_0 that it was due to chance and accept H_1 that fishing is indeed a matter of skill, since by our assumptions $\{H_0, H_1\}$ and {"luck," "skill"} are isomorphic sets whose equivalence is defined by $(H_0, H_1) =$ ("luck," "skill").

7.3 PROBABILITY DISTRIBUTIONS AND DIRECTIONAL TESTS

When a function is defined so as to pair each and every point in a sample space with its corresponding probability, that function is called a *probability distribution.* A primitive space or any other uniform space will always have a so called "square distribution," meaning that the probability will be uniformly the same in every ordered pair in the function.

If the S points in a sample space \$ have numerical values such that, for any two of those values i and j, it is always possible to determine either that $i < j$ or $j < i$, then the ordered pairs in the probability distribution can be ranked to correspond to the order of magnitude of their respective sample point values. When so ranked, the sample points in the pairs would form an increasing sequence of values, but generally the probabilities would not. If there is some positive integer k for which the first k probabilities in the probability distribution thus ranked form a nondecreasing sequence, and the last $S - k$ values form a nonincreasing sequence, then that distribution is said to be *two tailed.* The sample points with the nondecreasing probabilities are said to fall on the *left tail* of the distribution, and those with the nonincreasing probabilities are said to fall on the *right tail.* Table 7.3.1 displays a two-tailed probability distribution which only coincidentally happens to be symmetrical.

TABLE 7.3.1 / Example of a Two-Tailed Probability Distribution

Rank of sample point	1	2	3	4	5	6	7	8
Value of sample point	0	1	2	3	4	5	6	7
Probability	.008	.055	.164	.273	.273	.164	.055	.008

In this example, the condition for a two-tailed distribution is satisfied if $k = 4$ or $k = 5$, since $P[E_4 = 3]$ in the fourth position of the distribution and $P[E_5 = 4]$ in the fifth position both equal .273. In this particular case, then, there happens to be a "plateau" rather than a unique maximum value in the probability sequence, but a unique maximum does occur in many two-tailed distributions. At the other extreme, the whole probability sequence in a square distribution is a plateau.

A statistical test for which the region of rejection comprises a set of say, m points of ranks 1 through m, is called a *left-tailed test.* If the region of rejection comprises the set of points with the ranks

$(S - m + 1)$ through S, it is called a *right-tailed test.* The test for our "fish story" of Section 7.2 was right tailed.

Sometimes the region of rejection is defined as a union of sets of points at both extremities of the distribution. In this case, the test is referred to as a *two-tailed test.* For two-tailed tests it is common practice to define the left tail segment and the right tail segment of the region of rejection so that the probability of each is $\alpha/2$. It will be recalled that α is the probability of the whole region of rejection however it is defined.

A test for which the region of rejection is defined on a single tail is called *directional.* Since it is not always obvious on which tail one has defined the region of rejection, this has to be determined to avoid gross misinterpretation of the results. This problem will be discussed when it arises.

There is a certain incongruity in speaking of "tails" of distributions in conjunction with nonparametric statistical distributions and perhaps more generally within the context of a set theoretical approach because the term carries geometrical implications. However, the manner in which we have defined the concept would appear to be compatible, thus shifting the issue to a terminological rather than a conceptual one. The term has been used here because of a certain carry-over value it might have for the reader whose interests are not confined to nonparametric statistics.

Nothing in the foregoing discussion should be construed to imply that nonparametric distributions are in general "tailed" distributions. These constitute, in fact, a very special case that could logically be handled under a more general set of procedures. We have chosen to single these distributions out with a special label because of the convenience this affords in the proper reading of certain tabulated values of probabilities used with some models. For distributions to be "tailed," their random variables must take on numerical values that may logically be ranked in a single sequence whose corresponding sequence of probabilities must meet an additional restrictive condition as has been indicated. One of the most valuable features of nonparametric tests is their general freedom from such restrictions. Particularly valuable is their capability of handling variables which have *qualitative* values which, by definition, imply no numerical hierarchy—variables like "race," "religion," or "geographical region." For instance, the range of values that the variable "race" might take on in some particular model might be {Caucasian, Negro, Oriental, other}. The restrictions required for tailed distributions would eliminate many of the most unique and valuable nonparametric models—for instance, certain multidimensional models. These special capabilities of nonparametric models should be increasingly appreciated as they are encountered in subsequent discussion.

PROBLEMS

1. Persons in an urban renewal area are allowed to choose alternative accommodation in any of five projects which are built identically "architecturally" but are in different geographical areas of the city. A sample size of 10 indicates none go to area 1, one goes to area 2, two go to area 3, three to area 4, and four moves to area 5.

a. Give a sample point that would be a "typically" random pattern.

b. Given H_0: The persons will show no preference for any area. State H_1, the alternative hypothesis, and test H_0.

c. Given H_0: The persons will show no preference for area 5. State H_1 and verify that it includes *all* alternatives to H_0. Then test it.

Hint: In both b and c, determine an "alpha level" and start to accumulate probabilities of points as extreme or more extreme than the one observed.

2. Review the problems in Chapters 4, 5, and 6 and explain ways regions of rejection can be determined.

3. Assume a coin is to be tossed 10 times. Determine the .01 levels for the three possible hypotheses given below. Also give the alternative hypotheses for parts c and d.

a. H_0: The coin has a bias to heads.
H_1: The coin has no bias towards heads.

b. Why would the following H_1 be invalid for part a? H_1: The coin has no bias.

c. H_0: the coin has no bias towards tails.

d. H_0: The coin has no bias.

e. How likely is $HTHTHTHTHT$ compared to the "rare events" you have defined?

4. Note that since H_0 and H_1 are mutually exclusive and exhaustive events $P(H_0) + P(H_1) = 1$ is a condition that must be satisfied.

a. Why is the above true?

b. Which results from Chapter 4 can be used to prove this?

CHAPTER 8

THE HYPERGEOMETRIC DISTRIBUTION AND ITS APPLICATIONS

WE SHALL NOW derive an important probability distribution which incorporates the assumptions that samples are unordered and are drawn without replacement. We shall then demonstrate how this distribution serves as the mathematical basis of a deservedly famous statistical model, named the *Fisher exact probability test* for the eminent statistician who devised it. We shall demonstrate its practical application and show how its usefulness can be extended by increasing the size of the table in which the "exact probability" method is used.

8.1 THE HYPERGEOMETRIC DISTRIBUTION

Consider the following problem. A sample of size $n = 7$ is taken *without replacement* from a population of $N = 15$ balls of which $k = 5$ are red. What is the probability that the sample will contain exactly $r = 3$ red balls?

A sample of size 7 can be made from a population of 15 elements in $S = \binom{N}{n} = \binom{15}{7}$ ways. A group of three red balls can be formed from five in $\binom{k}{r} = \binom{5}{3}$ ways. For each of these, a group of size $n - r = 7 - 3 = 4$ can be formed from the remaining $N - k = 15 - 5 = 10$ nonred balls in $\binom{N-k}{n-r} = \binom{15-5}{7-3} = \binom{10}{4}$ ways. Hence

$$P[N, n, k, r] = P[15, 7, 5, 3] = \frac{\mathscr{E}}{S} = \frac{\binom{k}{r}\binom{N-k}{n-r}}{\binom{N}{n}} = \frac{\binom{5}{3}\binom{10}{4}}{\binom{15}{7}}$$

$$= \frac{(5)_2}{2!} \cdot \frac{(10)_4}{4!} \cdot \frac{7!}{(15)_7} = \frac{140}{429} = .32634$$

Now consider the following generalized problem: What is the probability that a random sample of size n drawn without replacement from a population of size N, k of whose elements are red, will contain exactly r red elements?

$$P[N, n, k, r] = \frac{\binom{k}{r}\binom{N-k}{n-r}}{\binom{N}{n}}$$

If we asked for the probability that a sample of size k, drawn from a population of size N of which n elements were red, would contain exactly r red elements, we would have

$$P[N, k, n, r] = \frac{\binom{n}{r}\binom{N-n}{k-r}}{\binom{N}{k}}$$

We will now show that $P[N, n, k, r] = P[N, k, n, r]$—that is, the n and the k interchanged will yield exactly the same probability. This is a useful identity.

PROOF

$$P[N, k, n, r] = \frac{\binom{n}{r}\binom{N-n}{k-r}}{\binom{N}{k}}$$

$$= \frac{n!}{r!(n-r)!} \cdot \frac{(N-n)!}{(k-r)!(N-n-k+r)!} \cdot \frac{k!(N-k)!}{N!}$$

which by commutativity of factors can be written

$$\frac{k!}{r!(k-r)!} \cdot \frac{(N-k)!}{(n-r)!(N-k-n+r)!}$$

$$\cdot \frac{n!(N-n)!}{N!} = \frac{\binom{k}{r}\binom{N-k}{n-r}}{\binom{N}{n}} = P[N, n, k, r]$$

Q.E.D.

If we substitute a variable x for r,

$$P[N, n, k, r] = P[N, n, k, x(= r)]$$

whereas for statistical purposes we are interested in the probability of ranges of values of the variable, as in

$$P[N, n, k, 0 \leq x \leq r] = \sum_{x=0}^{r} \frac{\binom{k}{x}\binom{N-k}{n-x}}{\binom{N}{n}} = \binom{N}{n}^{-1} \sum_{x=0}^{r} \binom{k}{x}\binom{N-k}{n-x}$$

where $r \leq n \leq k$, or

$$P[N, n, k, r \leq x \leq n] = \binom{N}{n}^{-1} \sum_{x=r}^{n} \binom{k}{x}\binom{N-k}{n-x}$$

For example, we might wish to know the probability that the sample would contain r or fewer red elements, rather than exactly r of them in a sample of size n.

From our basic information N, n, k, r, we might find our other factors simply with the aid of a table.

DEPENDENT CHARACTERISTIC	GROUP I (SAMPLE)	GROUP II (BALANCE)	POPULATION
Has	r		k
Has not			
Population	n		N

All other entries are thus completely determined.

DEPENDENT CHARACTERISTIC	GROUP I	GROUP II	TOTALS
Has	r	$k - r$	k
Has not	$n - r$	$N - n - k + r$	$N - k$
Totals	n	$N - n$	N

Suppose we went in the opposite direction and selected the groups in terms of their distinguishing attributes. If we recorded from observation their characteristic compositions, however these happen to occur, we would then have the following:

DEPENDENT CHARACTERISTIC	GROUP I	GROUP II	TOTALS
Has	r	$k - r$	
Has not	$n - r$	$N - n - k + r$	
Totals			

From this we would be able to fill in the marginal values by simple addition.

This would strongly suggest using the hypergeometric distribution to find the probability that the observed composition [that is, $r/(n-r)$] of the dependent group (sample) would occur under the hypothesis that the composition of the whole (independent) group with respect to the same attribute be in the proportion $k/(N-k)$. That is,

$$P[E] = \frac{\binom{k}{r}\binom{N-k}{n-r}}{\binom{N}{n}}$$

which is our original hypergeometric term. However, from a statistical point of view, we ask the probability of a distribution as extreme or more extreme than that observed—that is, either

$$P[x \mid 0 \leq x \leq r] = \binom{N}{n}^{-1} \sum_{x=0}^{r} \binom{k}{x}\binom{N-k}{n-x}$$

or

$$P[x \mid r \leq x \leq n] = \binom{N}{n}^{-1} \sum_{x=r}^{n} \binom{k}{x}\binom{N-k}{n-x}$$

or both, depending upon which alternatives relevant to the case are being studied. Note then that the hypergeometric term

$$P[r] = \frac{\binom{k}{r}\binom{N-k}{n-r}}{\binom{N}{n}}$$

implies the following question. If two exclusive and jointly exhaustive sets of elements occur in the population of size N in the ratio of k to $N-k$, what is the probability of drawing them in the ratio of r to $n-r$ in a sample of size n drawn without replacement?

If $n \leq k$, the sum of the whole hypergeometric distribution is

$$\binom{N}{n}^{-1} \sum_{x=0}^{n} \binom{k}{x}\binom{N-k}{n-x} = 1$$

If $k \leq n$, it is

$$\binom{N}{k}^{-1} \sum_{x=0}^{k} \binom{n}{x}\binom{N-n}{k-x} = 1$$

If these sums were not equal to 1, their terms could not be probabilities. We can show that the sum of the terms is 1.

We know that

$$\sum_{x=0}^{n} \binom{k}{x}\binom{N-k}{n-x}$$

accounts for every point in the sample space; that is, every outcome from no red elements to the case where all elements in the sample are red, given that $n \leq k$, because it exhausts all the possibilities. We also know that this number is $\binom{N}{n}$. Therefore

$$\binom{N}{n} = \sum_{x=0}^{n} \binom{k}{x}\binom{N-k}{n-x}$$

and

$$\sum_{x=0}^{n} \binom{k}{x}\binom{N-k}{n-x}\binom{N}{n}^{-1} = 1$$

This is also true for the case in which $k \leq n$.

The next section concerns an important application of the hypergeometric model.

8.2 THE FISHER EXACT PROBABILITY TEST

Suppose on a certain day five appointments are to be made to a metropolitan police department. Out of 15 qualified applicants to appear, nine are Negro and six Caucasian. One Negro and four Caucasians are appointed. Using a confidence level of $\alpha = .05$, can we determine that the protests of discrimination voiced by the NAACP are plausible?

We may tabulate our information as follows:

RACE	APPOINTED	NOT APPOINTED	MARGINAL TOTAL
Negro	$1 = r$	8	$9 = k$
Caucasian	4	2	6
Marginal total	$5 = n$	10	$15 = N$

We are asking whether a pattern of this sort would be a rare event if the factor of race played no part in the decisions. Our hypotheses are:

H_0: The relationship of the variables "race" and "appointment status" is either random, or Negroes are favored

H_1: Negro applicants are disproportionately underrepresented in the category of "appointed"

Our stochastic problem may be stated as follows: If a random sample of five (successful job applicants) were drawn from a population of nine Negroes and six Caucasians, what is the probability that it would contain fewer than two Negroes? If this probability should turn out to be less than .05, we will conclude that a rare event would have occurred under the null hypothesis H_0 and reject it in favor of H_1.

Call E_0 the event "no Negroes are appointed" and E_1 the event "one Negro is appointed." These are obviously exclusive events, since they could not be true simultaneously.

$$P[E_1] = \frac{\binom{9}{1}\binom{6}{4}}{\binom{15}{5}} = \frac{9}{1} \cdot \frac{6 \cdot 5}{2} \cdot \frac{5 \cdot 4 \cdot 3 \cdot 2 \cdot 1}{15 \cdot 14 \cdot 13 \cdot 12 \cdot 11} = \frac{45}{1001}$$

$$P[E_0] = \frac{\binom{9}{0}\binom{6}{5}}{\binom{15}{5}} = \frac{1 \cdot 6 \cdot 5!}{(15)_5} = \frac{2}{1001}$$

$$P[0 \le x \le r = 1] = P[E_1 \cup E_0] = P[E_1] + P[E_0]$$

$$= \frac{45}{1001} + \frac{2}{1001} = \frac{47}{1001} = .0469 < .05 = \alpha$$

From these data, we would conclude that the observed pattern of appointments would be a rare event under the null hypothesis. We would therefore reject H_0 in favor of H_1 and conclude that the NAACP's protests had validity. Notice that this was a one-tailed test, since we tested not the unqualified assertion that the appointments were disproportionate but specifically that they were unfavorable to the Negroes.

A two-tailed test would generally not be used with investigations of known outcome. For a two-tailed test, we would reject the null hypothesis if the proportion of *either* group were so low as to constitute a rare event. Moreover, we would have to test the outcome against $\alpha/2 = .025$ instead of $\alpha = .05$ because α is the sum of probabilities of the region of rejection. For a two-tailed test sample points from both tails would contribute to the sum of probabilities represented by α. One-half the probabilities would be from one tail and one-half from the other. Had our test been a two-tailed one, we would have accepted H_0 and rejected H_1 because $.0469 > .025 = \alpha/2$.

We purposely chose an arithmetically simple problem as our first illustration. With $r = 1$, we had only two probabilities to compute. It may well be imagined that with an r of, say, 33 (and correspondingly larger values of the other variables N, n, and k) the arithmetic could be formidable. For this reason, the Fisher exact test has been less popular than might otherwise have been the case. It is much easier to find the tabulated values for the chi-square (χ^2) contingency table (to be discussed in a later chapter). However, the tables of probabilities associated with χ^2 are computed under the assumption that sampling was made *with replacement*—an assumption that for many sociological samples does not agree with the facts, and unless the size of the sample n is quite small relative to the population N, the results could be quite invalid. The χ^2 test has other disadvantages. The tabulated probabilities are only approximate because they are obtained from a continuous approximating function, whereas the data are actually discrete and finite. Suggested "continuity corrections" for this have been largely discredited. Moreover, one has to be concerned with minimum numbers per cell, which is of no concern at all in the use of the Fisher exact test.

In any event, the computational convenience of the χ^2 model is no longer a plausible excuse for the 2×2 case ($= 2$ columns $\times$ 2 rows $= 4$ cells). With the use of Lieberman and Owen's *Tables of the Hypergeometric Probability Distribution*,* the exact probabilities may be conveniently obtained with little or no computation.

The reader will recall from the last section that once N, n, k, and r are given, all other relevant parameters are completely determined. Hence the Lieberman and Owen probabilities are identified as

$$P[N, n, k, x \leq r]$$

In the illustrative example we have just presented,

$$P[N, n, k, r] = P[15, 5, 9, 1] = P[15, 9, 5, 1]$$

* G. J. Lieberman and D. B. Owen, *Tables of the Hypergeometric Probability Distribution* (Stanford, Calif.: Stanford University Press, 1961).

since, as we have previously shown, n and k are always interchangeable. If we consult page 41 of the Lieberman and Owen tables (reproduced on the next page), we see

$$P[15, 9, 5, x \leq 1] = .046953$$

This agrees with our own computation. As may be seen, the point probabilities in Lieberman and Owen are tabulated under $p(x)$ and the cumulatives, which are of more general statistical interest, are under $P(x)$.

More detailed instructions for use of the Lieberman and Owen tables will be given later; however, some additional theoretical matters must be considered first.

8.3 THE HYPOTHESIS OF THE MARGINAL POPULATION AS A RANDOM SAMPLE

In our first illustration, the size of the relevant population was clearly $N = 15$. The question naturally arises as to the feasibility of the Fisher exact test when the groups to be compared are thought of as samples drawn from larger populations. For instance, suppose that random samples of 18 West Germans and 15 Frenchmen are polled to determine their attitude toward NATO, with the following results:

	ATTITUDE TOWARD NATO		MARGINAL
	FAVOR	OPPOSED	TOTALS
West Germans	11	7	18
Frenchmen	3	12	15
Marginal totals	14	19	33

In this case, we are interested in the following question. If the 33 respondents were a sample that had been drawn at random from a population in which Frenchmen and West Germans had attitude distributions in identical proportions, would the distribution observed in the sample be a rare event?

To make such a judgment, we must have reasonably valid knowledge of the composition of the common population from

Sample Page from *Tables of the Hypergeometric Probability Distribution**

Table for $N = 2$, $n = 1$, through $N = 100$, $n = 50$

N	n	k	x	P(x)	p(x)
15	7	7	5	0.991142	0.091375
15	7	7	6	0.999845	0.008702
15	7	7	7	1.000000	0.000155
15	8	1	0	0.466667	0.466667
15	8	1	1	1.000000	0.533333
15	8	2	0	0.200000	0.200000
15	8	2	1	0.733333	0.533333
15	8	2	2	1.000000	0.266667
15	8	3	0	0.076923	0.076923
15	8	3	1	0.446154	0.369231
15	8	3	2	0.876923	0.430769
15	8	3	3	1.000000	0.123077
15	8	4	0	0.025641	0.025641
15	8	4	1	0.230769	0.205128
15	8	4	2	0.661538	0.430769
15	8	4	3	0.948718	0.287179
15	8	4	4	1.000000	0.051282
15	8	5	0	0.006993	0.006993
15	8	5	1	0.100233	0.093240
15	8	5	2	0.426573	0.326340
15	8	5	3	0.818182	0.391608
15	8	5	4	0.981352	0.163170
15	8	5	5	1.000000	0.018648
15	8	6	0	0.001399	0.001399
15	8	6	1	0.034965	0.033566
15	8	6	2	0.230769	0.195804
15	8	6	3	0.622378	0.391608
15	8	6	4	0.916084	0.293706
15	8	6	5	0.994406	0.078322
15	8	6	6	1.000000	0.005594
15	8	7	0	0.000155	0.000155
15	8	7	1	0.008858	0.008702
15	8	7	2	0.100233	0.091375
15	8	7	3	0.404817	0.304584
15	8	7	4	0.785548	0.380730
15	8	7	5	0.968298	0.182751
15	8	7	6	0.998757	0.030458
15	8	7	7	1.000000	0.001243
15	8	8	1	0.001243	0.001243
15	8	8	2	0.031702	0.030458
15	8	8	3	0.214452	0.182751
15	8	8	4	0.595183	0.380730
15	8	8	5	0.899767	0.304584
15	8	8	6	0.991142	0.091375
15	8	8	7	0.999845	0.008702
15	8	8	8	1.000000	0.000155
15	9	1	0	0.400000	0.400000
15	9	1	1	1.000000	0.600000
15	9	2	0	0.142857	0.142857
15	9	2	1	0.657143	0.514286

N	n	k	x	P(x)	p(x)
15	9	2	2	1.000000	0.342857
15	9	3	0	0.043956	0.043956
15	9	3	1	0.340659	0.296703
15	9	3	2	0.815385	0.474725
15	9	3	3	1.000000	0.184615
15	9	4	0	0.010989	0.010989
15	9	4	1	0.142857	0.131868
15	9	4	2	0.538461	0.395604
15	9	4	3	0.907692	0.369231
15	9	4	4	1.000000	0.092308
15	9	5	0	0.001998	0.001998
15	9	5	1	0.046953	0.044955
15	9	5	2	0.286713	0.239760
15	9	5	3	0.706294	0.419580
15	9	5	4	0.958042	0.251748
15	9	5	5	1.000000	0.041958
15	9	6	0	0.000200	0.000200
15	9	6	1	0.010989	0.010789
15	9	6	2	0.118881	0.107892
15	9	6	3	0.454545	0.335664
15	9	6	4	0.832168	0.377622
15	9	6	5	0.983217	0.151049
15	9	6	6	1.000000	0.016783
15	9	7	1	0.001399	0.001399
15	9	7	2	0.034965	0.033566
15	9	7	3	0.230769	0.195804
15	9	7	4	0.622378	0.391608
15	9	7	5	0.916084	0.293706
15	9	7	6	0.994406	0.078322
15	9	7	7	1.000000	0.005594
15	9	8	2	0.005594	0.005594
15	9	8	3	0.083916	0.078322
15	9	8	4	0.377622	0.293706
15	9	8	5	0.769231	0.391608
15	9	8	6	0.965035	0.195804
15	9	8	7	0.998601	0.033566
15	9	8	8	1.000000	0.001399
15	9	9	3	0.016783	0.016783
15	9	9	4	0.167832	0.151049
15	9	9	5	0.545455	0.377622
15	9	9	6	0.881119	0.335664
15	9	9	7	0.989011	0.107892
15	9	9	8	0.999800	0.010789
15	9	9	9	1.000000	0.000200
15	10	1	0	0.333333	0.333333
15	10	1	1	1.000000	0.666667
15	10	2	0	0.095238	0.095238
15	10	2	1	0.571429	0.476190
15	10	2	2	1.000000	0.428571
15	10	3	0	0.021978	0.021978

N	n	k	x	P(x)	p(x)
15	10	3	1	0.241758	0.219780
15	10	3	2	0.736264	0.494505
15	10	3	3	1.000000	0.263736
15	10	4	0	0.003663	0.003663
15	10	4	1	0.076923	0.073260
15	10	4	2	0.406593	0.329670
15	10	4	3	0.846154	0.439560
15	10	4	4	1.000000	0.153846
15	10	5	0	0.000333	0.000333
15	10	5	1	0.016983	0.016650
15	10	5	2	0.166833	0.149850
15	10	5	3	0.566434	0.399600
15	10	5	4	0.916084	0.349650
15	10	5	5	1.000000	0.083916
15	10	6	1	0.001998	0.001998
15	10	6	2	0.046953	0.044955
15	10	6	3	0.286713	0.239760
15	10	6	4	0.706294	0.419580
15	10	6	5	0.958042	0.251748
15	10	6	6	1.000000	0.041958
15	10	7	2	0.006993	0.006993
15	10	7	3	0.100233	0.093240
15	10	7	4	0.426573	0.326340
15	10	7	5	0.818182	0.391608
15	10	7	6	0.981352	0.163170
15	10	7	7	1.000000	0.018648
15	10	8	3	0.018648	0.018648
15	10	8	4	0.181818	0.163170
15	10	8	5	0.573427	0.391608
15	10	8	6	0.899767	0.326340
15	10	8	7	0.993007	0.093240
15	10	8	8	1.000000	0.006993
15	10	9	4	0.041958	0.041958
15	10	9	5	0.293706	0.251748
15	10	9	6	0.713287	0.419580
15	10	9	7	0.953047	0.239760
15	10	9	8	0.998002	0.044955
15	10	9	9	1.000000	0.001998
15	10	10	5	0.083916	0.083916
15	10	10	6	0.433566	0.349650
15	10	10	7	0.833167	0.399600
15	10	10	8	0.983017	0.149850
15	10	10	9	0.999667	0.016650
15	10	10	10	1.000000	0.000333
15	11	1	0	0.266667	0.266667
15	11	1	1	1.000000	0.733333
15	11	2	0	0.057143	0.057143
15	11	2	1	0.476190	0.419048
15	11	2	2	1.000000	0.523810
15	11	3	0	0.008791	0.008791

N	n	k	x	P(x)	p(x)
15	11	3	1	0.153846	0.145055
15	11	3	2	0.637363	0.483516
15	11	3	3	1.000000	0.362637
15	11	4	0	0.000733	0.000733
15	11	4	1	0.032967	0.032234
15	11	4	2	0.274725	0.241758
15	11	4	3	0.758242	0.483516
15	11	4	4	1.000000	0.241758
15	11	5	1	0.003663	0.003663
15	11	5	2	0.076923	0.073260
15	11	5	3	0.406593	0.329670
15	11	5	4	0.846154	0.439560
15	11	5	5	1.000000	0.153846
15	11	6	2	0.010989	0.010989
15	11	6	3	0.142857	0.131868
15	11	6	4	0.538461	0.395604
15	11	6	5	0.907692	0.369231
15	11	6	6	1.000000	0.092308
15	11	7	3	0.025641	0.025641
15	11	7	4	0.230769	0.205128
15	11	7	5	0.661538	0.430769
15	11	7	6	0.948718	0.287179
15	11	7	7	1.000000	0.051282
15	11	8	4	0.051282	0.051282
15	11	8	5	0.338462	0.287179
15	11	8	6	0.769231	0.430769
15	11	8	7	0.974359	0.205128
15	11	8	8	1.000000	0.025641
15	11	9	5	0.092308	0.092308
15	11	9	6	0.461538	0.369231
15	11	9	7	0.857143	0.395604
15	11	9	8	0.989011	0.131868
15	11	9	9	1.000000	0.010989
15	11	10	6	0.153846	0.153846
15	11	10	7	0.593407	0.439560
15	11	10	8	0.923077	0.329670
15	11	10	9	0.996337	0.073260
15	11	10	10	1.000000	0.003663
15	11	11	7	0.241758	0.241758
15	11	11	8	0.725275	0.483516
15	11	11	9	0.967033	0.241758
15	11	11	10	0.999267	0.032234
15	11	11	11	1.000000	0.000733
15	12	1	0	0.200000	0.200000
15	12	1	1	1.000000	0.800000
15	12	2	0	0.028571	0.028571
15	12	2	1	0.371429	0.342857
15	12	2	2	1.000000	0.628571
15	12	3	0	0.002198	0.002198
15	12	3	1	0.081319	0.079121

$N = 15$ $n = 7$–12

* G. J. Lieberman and D. B. Owen (Stanford, Calif.: Stanford University Press, 1961), p. 41. Copyright 1961 by the Board of Trustees of the Leland Stanford Junior University. Reproduced with the kind permission of the publishers.

which the samples were drawn, if indeed they were drawn from a common (that is, homogeneous) population. Without additional information, the *maximum likelihood estimate* of the composition of such a common population is that given in the marginal totals column—that is, $\frac{18}{33}$ West Germans and $\frac{15}{33}$ French. Correspondingly, if the French and West Germans do not differ in their attitudes toward NATO, the expected number of West Germans favorable would be $(\frac{18}{33})14 \doteq 8$, and the expected number of Frenchmen favorable would be $(\frac{15}{33})14 \doteq 6$. These are obviously not the observed values, but the question naturally arises as to whether the discrepancies between the observed and expected values are chance differences that would be occasioned by the vicissitudes of random sampling.

We shall not attempt a rigorous investigation of why the marginal total is a "maximum likelihood estimate" of a postulated common population.* We shall settle here for the intuitive notion that combining the data from the two samples utilizes the maximum information available.

This notion of "maximum likelihood estimate" implies two things. First, *if* the two samples are drawn from a common population, it is more probable that it has the composition of the marginal totals than that it has any other composition. Second, the converse of this, *if* the two samples were not drawn from a common population with the composition of the marginal totals, it is even less likely that they were both drawn from a common population with any other *specified* composition. This implies then that if we reject the hypothesis that they were drawn from a population with the observed marginal total composition, we automatically reject even more decisively the hypothesis that they were drawn from a population of any specified alternative composition.

Because the implicit relationship of the samples to the composite sample represented by the marginal totals is that their elements under the null hypothesis were drawn from it *without replacement*, it is not true that the probabilities under this hypothesis are the same as though the elements were drawn from a different-sized population of the same composition. For instance, in $P = \mathscr{E}/S$, S would be far less affected by each successive draw from a large population than would be the case for a small population of, say, size 15. However, it *is* true that the two samples can be like each

* The interested reader may pursue the matter further in Feller, *An Introduction to Probability Theory and Its Application, op. cit.*, pp. 43–45.

other only in measure as they approach the marginal total in composition. This can be seen from the theorems presented below. The ratios x/n and $(k - x)/(N - n)$ represent the proportions in which the dependent variable occurs, respectively, in each of the two samples, and k/N is the corresponding proportion for the composite marginal sample. N, n, and k are positive constant integers and x is a nonnegative variable integer less than n or k, whichever is the smaller; symbolically, $0 \leq x \leq \min[n, k]$.

THEOREM 8.3.1. Given that any two of the ratios x/n, $(k - x)/(N - n)$, and k/N are equal, then all three are equal.

PROOF. Suppose $x/n = (k - x)/(N - n)$. Then $Nx - nx = nk - nx$. Hence $Nx = nk$ and $x/n = k/N$. It follows by transitivity that $(k - x)/(N - n) = k/N$.

We may regard the theorem as proved without going through the roster of possible starting points.

THEOREM 8.3.2. If $x/n \neq k/N$, then either

(a) $$\frac{x}{n} < \frac{k}{N} < \frac{k - x}{N - n}$$

or

(b) $$\frac{x}{n} > \frac{k}{N} > \frac{k - x}{N - n}$$

PROOF. For (a) if $x/n < k/N$, then $Nx < nk$ and $-Nx > -nk$. Adding Nk to both sides gives $Nk - Nx > Nk - nk$. Factoring gives $N(k - x) > k(N - n)$; hence $(k - x)/(N - n) > k/N$, since all factors are positive. Proof of (b) is similar except that the inequality signs are reversed. The theorem is proved.

We may summarize both theorems as either

(1) $$\frac{x}{n} \leq \frac{k}{N} \leq \frac{k - x}{N - n}$$

or

(2) $$\frac{x}{n} > \frac{k}{N} > \frac{k - x}{N - n}$$

The implications of (1) show that (2) could be analyzed similarly. Recalling that $0 \leq x \leq \min[n, k]$, then as x increases to either n or k, whichever is the smaller, $k - x$ decreases to either $k - n$ or $k - k = 0$, respectively. It follows that the larger the value of x, the greater the value of x/n and, correspondingly, the smaller the values of $k - x$ and hence of $(k - x)/(N - n)$. We may now state that the proportions of the two samples are inversely associated and that they approach each other in similarity of composition only to the degree that they approach the composition of the composite sample represented by the marginal total.

To summarize, if we reject the hypothesis that either of the two samples was drawn from the marginal population, we simultaneously reject the hypothesis that they were both drawn from a common homogeneous population.

Use of the Fisher exact test with the NATO attitude problem implies that under the null hypothesis a random sample of size $N = 33$ was drawn from a population of, say, size N' in which N is small relative to N', and the question of replacement is therefore a matter of indifference. The proportions in this sample represent a maximum likelihood estimate. If this sample divides into two exclusive and exhaustive groups of 18 West Germans and 15 Frenchmen, the occurrence of three or fewer Frenchmen in a random sample of size 14 drawn without replacement from the sample of size 33 either is or is not a rare event. If it is not a rare event, we may not reject the hypothesis that the West Germans and French are alike with respect to the dependent attribute. Our hypotheses may be stated as follows:

H_0: The proportion of West Germans favoring NATO does not exceed the proportion of French favoring it

H_1: The proportion of West Germans favoring NATO is greater than the proportion of Frenchmen favoring NATO

On page 122 of the Lieberman and Owen tables, it may be determined that $P[33, 15, 14, x \leq 3] = .020225$. If $\alpha = .05$, we reject H_0 that the two samples were drawn from a homogeneous population and accept H_1 that the West Germans are more favorably disposed toward NATO than the French.

8.4 PROCEDURES FOR USING THE LIEBERMAN AND OWEN TABLES

In our previous examples, we were able to use the Lieberman and Owen tables in a fairly straightforward manner. It happens, however, that a number of so-called "symmetry relationships" exist that reduce the number of entries that need to be made in the tables. We already have seen, for instance, that values for n and k are completely interchangeable. We can also see from the formula that the probability is the same whether we use the hypergeometric term for r occurrences in a sample of size n, or $k - r$ occurrences in a sample of size $N - n$, or for $n - r$ in a sample of size n, or $(N - n - k + r)$ in a sample of size $N - n$, and so forth. This is almost apparent by inspection of the schematic tables at the beginning of the chapter. We also know that, in general, $P[\not{E}] = 1 - P[E]$. Where cumulative values are concerned, then

$$P[x \mid r \leq x \leq n] = \sum_{x=r}^{n} P[N, n, k, x] = 1 - \sum_{x=0}^{r-1} P[N, n, k, x]$$

$$= 1 - \sum_{x=1}^{r} P[N, n, k, x - 1]$$

For these reasons, all values are, in effect, available even if only the values for $P[N, n, k, r]$ are printed with $(N/2) \geq n \geq k \geq r$. If, for instance, $n > (N/2)$ then $N - n < (N/2)$ and $N - n$ may be used in place of n, and so forth. This procedure results in a simpler table somewhat inconvenient to use, but the following procedures make the effort painless.

Symmetry Relationships for Use with Lieberman and Owen Tables of the Hypergeometric Probability Distribution

Use of the symmetry instructions on pp. 4–6 of Lieberman and Owen or on pp. 458–59 of Owen's *Handbook of Statistical Tables* can lead to incorrect results. The following procedure is recommended as being somewhat more foolproof when these tables are used for contingency table problems requiring Fisher exact probabilities.

Lieberman and Owen use the following tabular notation; it is also consistently adhered to in their tabulated probability values.

CHARACTERISTIC II	CHARACTERISTIC I		TOTALS
	HAS	DOES NOT HAVE	
Has	x	$k - x$	k
Does not have	$n - x$	$N - n - k + x$	$N - k$
Totals	n	$N - n$	N

Considerable flexibility can be exercised in interchanging the cell designations with each other and in exchanging the marginal designations with each other as long as overall consistency is maintained. The procedures below provide for this automatically.

Assign the symbol n to the largest marginal entry (row or column) such that $n \leq N/2$. Select k on the other margin and x at the intersection of k and n in such a way that $x \leq k \leq n$. This is much easier than it sounds since only two choices are possible, and one of these will automatically meet the condition. All other entries are, of course, now completely determined.

Depending on the choice made, either x, $n - x$, or $k - x$ will be the smallest entry in the table.

If x is the smallest entry, you may read your answer directly from the table of probabilities as $P(N, n, k, x)$. Otherwise your answer is obtained as $1 - P(N, n, k, x - 1)$.

No interpolation will be needed for cases in which $N \leq 50$. For values of $N > 50$ which lie between those given in the tables, interpolation procedures are given on pp. 23–24 of Lieberman and Owen.

8.5 INTERPOLATION OF THE LIEBERMAN AND OWEN TABLE VALUES

Where $50 < N$, the Lieberman and Owen tables give values for N in increments of 10 so that intermediate values must be interpolated. We shall use a problem that will illustrate both the use of the symmetry instructions and interpolation procedures. Our illustration will use results from an actual experiment in social perception.

Two sets of respondents, one set drawn from a metropolitan police force and another drawn from the student body of an ordinary public high school, were asked to report what they observed when shown a news photograph of a crowd. Photographed in the crowd action was a person committing a delinquent act. The respondents were classified as to whether or not they reported the delinquent act. The following results were obtained.

TYPES OF RESPONDENTS	REPORTED THE DELINQUENT ACT		MARGINAL TOTAL
	YES	NO	
Policemen	$11 = x$	10	$21 = n$
High school students	3	39	42
Marginal total	$14 = k$	49	$63 = N$

In accordance with the instructions, variables were assigned as indicated in the table. N is always the grand total of the respondents. $n = 21$ is the largest marginal total not exceeding $(N/2)$. That is, $(N/2) = (63/2) = 31.5 > n = 21$. $k = 14$ is a marginal total not greater than $n = 21$ and x is at the intersection of the n row and the k column. Since x is not the smallest cell entry, we seek

$$1 - P[N, n, k, x - 1] = 1 - P[63, 21, 14, 10]$$

H_0: The category "policemen" implies no greater tendency to perceive the delinquent act than does the category "student"

H_1: The number of policemen perceiving the delinquent act is disproportionately greater than their number in the population of policemen and high school students.

We will choose $\alpha = .01$.

There are no values for $N = 63$ in the Lieberman and Owen tables. We must therefore interpolate between the values for $N = 60$ and $N = 70$. However, we must also expect under such circumstances that n would be smaller where N is 60 and larger where N is 70. We make the assumption that the ns vary in direct proportion to the Ns. That is,

$$\frac{n_i}{n} = \frac{N_i}{N}$$

hence

$$n_i = \frac{nN_i}{N} = \left(\frac{n}{N}\right)N_i$$

For $N_1 = 60$ and $N_2 = 70$,

$$n_1 = \frac{21(60)}{63} = 20$$

$$n_2 = \frac{21(70)}{63} \doteq 23$$

$$P[N_1, n_1, k, x] = P[60, 20, 14, 10] = .999898$$

$$P[N_2, n_2, k, x] = P[70, 23, 14, 10] = .999879$$

$$P_{60} - P_{70} = .999898 - .999879 = .000019$$

Since 63 is about .3 of the way through the interval 60 to 70,

$$.000019(.3) = .000006$$

and

$$.999898 - .000006 = .999892 = P[63, 21, 14, 10]$$

But we need

$$1 - P[E] = 1 - .999892 = .000108 < .01 = \alpha$$

This is a significant result, and we conclude that the police are much more prone to perceive the delinquent act than are the high school students.

It was, of course, not necessary to carry out the interpolation in this instance because the value fell between two probabilities either of which was highly significant. This will often be the case. However, the procedure for interpolation was completed to illustrate the technique for a case where it might be needed.

8.6 A MEDIAN TEST

Once the fundamental principles of a technique are understood, their creative use depends upon the imaginativeness of the investigator. There are no formulas into which data may be mechanically fed to produce science. An interesting use of the Fisher exact model is its adaptation as a *median test.* This involves finding the median value of an attribute and classifying the cases as "above the median" and "below the median" for column or row categories. If there are an odd number of cases, the median does not split into "above" and "below," but this difficulty can be surmounted by defining one of the categories as "$\leq$ the median" and the other as "$>$ the median," or the converse can be used.

The following experiment illustrates this use. A political scientist wishes to test the hypothesis that those with less education are more prone to endorse the House Un-American Activities Committee than are the better educated element in the population. By polling a sample controlled for such obvious factors as age, sex, and so forth, and by finding the median number of years of education, the data were tabulated as follows:

YEARS OF EDUCATION	ATTITUDE TOWARD HUAC		MARGINAL TOTAL
	FOR	AGAINST	
Above median	1	9	10
Below median	8	2	10
Marginal total	9	11	20

It is suggested that the reader set $\alpha = .01$ and complete the analysis by setting up H_0, H_1, and so forth. Computation should be done with the formula and the answer checked in the Lieberman and Owen tables if they are available.

The same general model may be used in a variety of ways such as for "treatment" and "control" groups. In "treatment" experiments (for example, exposed to a propaganda film or not exposed) the respondents should be assigned randomly to the treatment and control groups.

8.7 A ONE-SAMPLE PROBLEM

Although our illustrations with the 2×2 table have essentially involved deciding whether two samples might have been drawn randomly from a population that was homogenous with respect to the dependent factor, it can also be of instrumental use in deciding whether a single sample drawn from a population of known size supports an hypothesis as to the proportion of population elements possessing some specified attribute.

The following problem illustrates this. A journalist wishes to have available, for whenever it might be useful, the minimum number in a random sample of 35 United States Senators who would have to favor cloture to justify the prediction that a filibuster will be broken by a Senate motion to close debate. He is willing to take a 1 percent risk of predicting passage of the motion when, in fact, there are enough votes to defeat it.

The population is the U.S. Senate, whose size is known to be 100. Since a two-thirds majority is necessary to close debate, 67 votes would be required. However, because of the fact that our hypergeometric probability distributions are tabulated only for $(N/2) \geq n \geq k \geq x$, and since $\frac{100}{2} = 50 \leq 67 = k$, it is better to define our solution in terms of the size of the minority needed to defeat cloture.

The motion will be carried if the number of "nay" elements in the population does not exceed $k = 33$. Our hypotheses may be set up as follows:

H_0: The population from which the sample was drawn contains $k = 34$ or more votes against the motion to close debate.

H_1: $k < 34$.

By stipulation, $\alpha = .01$.

If the number of nay votes r in the sample should be greater than one-third of the sample size, then H_0 would be accepted without further consideration, and one would have no basis for expecting the motion for cloture to pass. If the number of nay votes in the sample should be equal to or less than one-third of the totals, then one must investigate further to see whether such a number would be a rare event under the null hypothesis. Since $\frac{1}{3}(35) = 11.7$, we would continue the investigation only if $r < 12$. We may set up a table as follows (the circumflex over the k indicates that it is the quantity in question).

	SAMPLE	RESIDUAL SAMPLE	POPULATION
Against motion	$r < 12$	$(\hat{k} - r) > 22$	$34 = \hat{k}$
Favor motion	$(n - r) > 23$	$(n - n - \hat{k} + r) < 43$	$66 = N - \hat{k}$
	$n = 35$	$(N - n) = 65$	$100 = N$

Since 12 is the smallest entry in the table, we look for the maximum value of r such that

$$P[100, 35, 34, 0 \leq x \leq r] \leq .01$$

On page 552 of the Lieberman and Owen tables, we see that for the relevant parameters

$$P[0 \leq x \leq r = 5] = .001715 < .01 = \alpha$$

$$P[0 \leq x \leq r = 6] = .007209 < .01 = \alpha$$

$$P[0 \leq x \leq r = 7] = .023978 > .01 = \alpha$$

Hence $r = 6$ is the maximum value of r that will permit rejection of H_0 and lead the journalist to accept H_1 and its substantive implication that debate will be closed. Conversely, $35 - 6 = 29$ is the minimum number of "aye" votes in the sample required to justify the prediction that cloture will be carried and the filibuster will be defeated.

Stated differently, if there are 34 negative votes in the population (H_0), then the occurrence of six or fewer negative votes in a sample of size 35 would have a probability of $.007 \leq .01$ and hence would be a rare event. The region of rejection would thus be $0 \leq x \leq 6$ negative votes.

8.8 EXTENSION OF THE FISHER TABLE BEYOND THE 2 × 2 CELL CASE

Insofar as the *point* probabilities are concerned, extension of the hypergeometric model to include more subclasses of population elements presents no special difficulty. The defining problem would be:

> Given a population containing k_1 elements of one sort, k_2 of another, . . . , and finally k_v of a final sort, what is the probability that a sample of size n drawn without replacement would contain r_1 elements of the first sort, r_2 of the second, . . . , and r_v of a final sort?

It is evident that

$$\sum_{i=1}^{v} k_i = N \quad \text{and} \quad \sum_{i=1}^{v} r_i = n$$

As stated before, samples of size n without repeated elements and without regard to order may be formed in $S = \binom{N}{n}$ distinct ways. Subpopulations of size r_1 may be formed from k_1 population elements of the first sort in $\binom{k_1}{r_1}$ different ways. For each of these, subpopulations of size r_2 may be formed from k_2 elements of the second sort in $\binom{k_2}{r_2}$ ways, . . . , and finally the

$$k_v\left(= N - \sum_{i=1}^{v-1} k_i\right)$$

residual population elements may be formed into subpopulations of size

$$r_v\left(= n - \sum_{i=1}^{v-1} r_i\right) \quad \text{in} \quad \binom{k_v}{r_v} \quad \text{ways}$$

Hence

$$P\left[\bigcap_{i=1}^{v} E_i\right] = \frac{\binom{k_1}{r_1}\binom{k_2}{r_2}\cdots\binom{N-k_1-k_2-\cdots-k_{v-1}}{n-r_1-r_2-\cdots-r_{v-1}}}{\binom{N}{n}}$$

Consideration of the 2×3 case will serve to illustrate both the possibilities and the difficulties of the $2 \times v$ case. The point probability for the 2×3 case is

$$P[r_1 \cap r_2] = \frac{\binom{k_1}{r_1}\binom{k_2}{r_2}\binom{N-k_1-k_2}{n-r_1-r_2}}{\binom{N}{n}}$$

This is translated into a 2×3 contingency table.

CHARACTERISTIC A	CHARACTERISTIC B		MARGINAL TOTAL
	I	II	
+	r_1	$k_1 - r_1$	k_1
−	r_2	$k_2 - r_2$	k_2
0	$n - r_1 - r_2$	$N - k_1 - k_2 - n + r_1 + r_2$	$N - k_1 - k_2$
Marginal total	n	$N - n$	N

The advantages of this extension by just this one row should be readily apparent. No longer is the investigator confined to dichotomous classifications. For instance, instead of just "yes" or "no," there is also provision for "no response." Instead of "above average income" and "below average income," there is "upper," "middle," and "lower." A little exercise of the imagination will provide many more examples.

This extended form has, until recently at least, been virtually ignored. Foremost among the reasons has been that the computations required to find the cumulative probabilities for even a relatively small number of cases were prohibitively time consuming. With the development of the high-speed electronic computer, this problem reduces to a simple matter of the cost of machine time. There was also a theoretical problem to solve, that is, the definition of a "rare event" for this particular distribution. In the 2×2 case, we obtain all of the probabilities necessary to assess a directional "rare event" when x assumes the values from r through 0. With an additional dimension involved, we may want to terminate the computations by letting two of the cells go to 0, but which two cells? The simplest solution is to define the region of rejection as the set of points with the least probable values and encompass as many points as are required to insure that their union will have the highest probability not exceeding α. The test is nondirectional. The author has written and tested a computer program for the 2×3 case. This program, written in the computer language ALGOL,* is reproduced in Appendix B. It finds cumulative

$$P[N, n, k_1, k_2, x_1, x_2]$$

The reader with the knowledge to do so may wish to write his own program in some other language, say, FORTRAN. If so, he will reduce considerably the amount of computation and hence the amount of machine time, as well as solve a number of problems of machine capacity, by using the following iterative formula:

$$P[x_1, x_2] = \frac{P[x_1, x_2 - 1](k_2 + 1 - x_2)(n + 1 - x_1 - x_2)}{x_2(N - k_1 - k_2 - n + x_1 + x_2)}$$

The time saving results primarily from the fact that all factorial expressions have been eliminated, and partly through the opportunity to combine groups of constants for storage in the computer memory.

An iterative formula requires a starting point, which in this case may be obtained as

$$P[x_1, 0] = \frac{\binom{k_1}{x_1}\binom{N - k_1 - k_2}{n - x_1}}{\binom{N}{n}}$$

* Only the most trivial changes would be required to convert ALGOL into a PL/1 program.

The iterative formula was obtained by setting the ratio

$$\frac{P[x_1, x_2]}{P[x_1, x_2 - 1]}$$

equal to the ratio of their corresponding hypergeometric expressions, making the necessary algebraic simplifications, and then multiplying both sides of the equality by $P[x_1, x_2 - 1]$. The reader may wish to verify this for himself and is encouraged to do so.

PROBLEMS

1. A statistical model for inmarriage patterns can be formulated by using the hypergeometric distribution. Use the following data to formulate such a model. A group of 50 German grooms marry brides from an "available bride population" of 200 brides. Sixty of these brides are German. Because the grooms are all German, each marriage where the bride is a German is an inmarriage.

- **a.** What is the probability of 10 inmarriages? What is the probability of 10 or fewer inmarriages?
- **b.** Give an expression for the probability of n inmarriages?
- **c.** How could the term "available bride population" be represented in the model?
- **d.** How many inmarriages must occur before you would conclude (at the 5 percent level) that chance was not the only factor in ethnic marriage patterns?

2. Office positions can usually be classified as "female" or "male." An enlightened employer claims that he does not respect these "rigid ideas of role." He claims he places the "best person for the job" in that job. The following results were observed.

POSITIONS FILLED BY	POSITIONS USUALLY CLASSIFIED AS		TOTAL
	MALE	FEMALE	
Male	5	5	10
Female	5	5	10
Total	10	10	20

a. Test H_0: the two factors are independent.
b. If we accept H_0, does this show that this employer is unique?
c. If H_0 is that male positions are filled by males and female positions are filled by females and we accept this, explain why the following can or cannot be concluded.

H_1: The best person is not always put in the best job.

Hint: If H_0 and H_1 are as given above, $P(H_0) + P(H_1)$ need not equal 1 since H_0 and H_1 are not exclusive. Why?
d. Set up a "better" design for this study. Explain why you think your design is better.

3. In a city parks and recreation department there were two groups of people—the "local boys" and the "outsiders." A consultant felt there was discrimination against the "outsiders" which resulted in an inbreeding within the department. The records of advancement were studied for the staff and the following results were obtained:

	ADVANCEMENT		
	RAPID	SLOW	TOTAL
Outsiders	5	9	14
Local boys	10	7	17
Total	15	16	31

a. Was the consultant's conjecture supported by the above data?
b. Explain at least three methodological problems that could cause the observed distribution—for example, the possibilities resulting if outsiders are brought in at a higher rank, thus having less scope for advancement.

4. A researcher believes a high I.Q. and good coordination are related. He tests 10 children and compiles the results shown on next page.

Child	1	2	3	4	5	6	7	8	9	10
I.Q.	148	130	125	120	115	110	105	95	90	86
Reaction speed only	10	20	15	9	14	10	8	14	11	7

a. Formulate an hypothesis and use the median test to test it.
b. Explain why the median test is "more valid" than a parametric test.
c. Why is it likely that a test making more use of order would give better results?
d. What is meant by better results?

5. In a study of the use of parks, they are divided into areas according to function. The parks are also classified as being in areas of high or average residential density. In this study the following usage was found.

RESIDENTIAL DENSITY	USE		TOTAL
	HIGH	AVERAGE	
High	5	12	17
Average	5	2	7
Total	10	14	24

a. Given H_0: The higher the density, the higher the use. State H_1.
b. Given H_0: There is no relation between density and use. State H_1.
c. Given H_0: There is higher use in lower density areas. State H_1.
d. Test parts a, b, and c above, and draw conclusions as if only one of these were being tested. Note that if one is tested, tests of the others are not valid unless the dependence is taken into account—for example, by using Boole's inequality (explained in later problem sets).

e. State the reasons that each of the hypotheses a, b, and c could be valid. For example, in many cities high-density areas tend to have fewer children. In this case, which hypotheses above would be most reasonable to test?

CHAPTER 9

THE BINOMIAL DISTRIBUTION AND ITS APPLICATIONS

ALTHOUGH IT IS relatively simple, the binomial distribution has found an amazing variety of applications—from deciding whether epidemics exist to assessing the vote-pulling power of political candidates. Easy to use, it can yield decisive information with very small samples. It is frequently listed as one of the three most important probability distributions—along with the normal and Poisson distributions.

9.1 THEORETICAL CONSIDERATIONS—BERNOULLI TRIALS

Suppose we have a population P consisting of N elements of which exactly k share some common attribute. If a sample of size n is drawn with replacement after each trial, then any point in the sample space for the experiment will be a composite outcome of n independent trials, each with the same probability of drawing an element having the specified attribute. That constant trial-to-trial probability will be $p = k/N$. The constant trial-to-trial probability of drawing an element that does not have the attribute is $q = 1 - p = (N - k)/N$.*

* p and q need not be rational for the binomial probability distribution, but they happen to be rational here because of our definition of probability.

We have here an experiment in which, for any trial, a determination is made that an element either has the specified attribute or it does not. The model is that there is an elementary event set E for each trial such that $P[E] = p$, and another for its complement $\not E$ such that $P[\not E] = q$. Each point in the sample space will contain some number x, of Es, varying from 0 to n, and a balance of $(n - x)$ $\not E$s. The two outcomes of elementary events we have been discussing carry the special name Bernoulli trials, because of their identification with the Swiss mathematician.

In this chapter, E_i will refer to the event "the elementary event E" which occurs on the ith trial. This is, in general, a compound event.*

For an arbitrary event $X = (E, \not E, E)$, we can give it directly, or we can give it as the intersection of event sets. It should be clear that $X = E_1 \cap \not E_2 \cap E_3$. This is the set of points where E occurs on the first trial, $\not E$ on the second, and E on the third trial.

We shall first investigate the probability of drawing a sample containing exactly r Es in an experiment where n Bernoulli trials are made. If we were interested in the probability of some specified ordered occurrence of the Es like $P[(E, \not E, E, \not E, E)]$, then if $P[E] = \frac{1}{4}$ and, if by assumption the trials are independent, Corollary 4.6.1 applies, and we have

$$\begin{aligned} P[(E, \not E, E, \not E, E)] &= P[E] \cdot P[\not E] \cdot P[E] \cdot P[\not E] \cdot P[E] \\ &= (\tfrac{1}{4})(\tfrac{3}{4})(\tfrac{1}{4})(\tfrac{3}{4})(\tfrac{1}{4}) \\ &= (\tfrac{1}{4})^3 \cdot (\tfrac{3}{4})^2 = .008775 \end{aligned}$$

It should be noted that, owing to the commutativity of factors, the probability would be the same for any other sequence of three Es and two $\not E$s.

Let us now approach the problem in a more general manner. We wish to find the probability of the compound event r Es and

* We could write it as

$$n\text{-tuple position} \quad \left(\underset{1}{\bigcup}, \underset{2}{\bigcup}, \underset{3}{\bigcup}, \ldots, \bigcup, \underset{i}{E}, \bigcup, \ldots, \underset{n-1}{\bigcup}, \underset{n}{\bigcup}\right)$$

Anything occurs on any trial but i, and E occurs there. In the case of a 3-tuple

$$E_2 = \{(\not E, E, \not E), (E, E, E), (E, E, \not E), (\not E, E, E)\}$$

This means that in the case of n trials we will consider the space of n-tuples as fundamental even though we will usually only deal with the $n + 1$ events $E_0, E_1, E_2, \ldots$. This approach means we are considering the *power* product $\{E, \not E\}^n$ as the domain set in our space. Thus the space has 2^n points.

$(n - r)$ $\not{E}$s without regard to order in n Bernoulli trials, if $P[E] = p$ for every trial.

We proceed with our problem. Any order of r Es and $(n - r)$ $\not{E}$s will have the same probability as any other. Hence we can find the probability for any specified order from whatever order happens to be the most convenient for us to use. The simplest order for our purposes is that in which all r of the Es precede all $n - r$ of the $\not{E}$s in the sequence. From Theorem 4.6.1 and its corollary,

$$P[(E, E, \ldots, E, \not{E}, \not{E}, \ldots, \not{E})] = P\left[\bigcap_{i=1}^{r} E_i \bigcap_{i=r+1}^{n} \not{E}_i\right]$$

$$= \left(\prod_{i=1}^{r} P[E_i]\right)\left(\prod_{i=r+1}^{n} P[\not{E}_i]\right) = p^r q^{n-r}$$

But that is the probability of a single arbitrary order. The event set for the compound event "without regard to order" ("any order will satisfy the condition") will contain as many points as there are ways of forming distinct arrangements (n-tuples) from r E elements and $(n - r)$ $\not{E}$ elements.

We know from Theorem 6.3.1 that a elements of one sort and b elements of another may be arranged in

$$\binom{a+b}{a} = \binom{a+b}{b} \text{ ways}$$

Hence r Es and $(n - r)$ $\not{E}$s may be arranged in

$$\binom{r + (n - r)}{r} = \binom{n}{r} \text{ ways}$$

In other words, the condition of r Es and $(n - r)$ $\not{E}$s is met with $\binom{n}{r}$ exclusive sample points, each with a *constant* probability of $p^r q^{n-r}$.

Since the points in our event set are exclusive, Theorem 4.3.1 applies, and we have

$$P[X \mid X = r\ E\text{s and } (n - r)\ \not{E}\text{s in any order whatever}]$$

$$= P[r\,E, (n - r)\,\not{E}] = \sum_{i=1}^{\binom{n}{r}} (p^r q^{n-r})$$

$$= \binom{n}{r} p^r q^{n-r} = \binom{n}{r} p^r (1 - p)^{n-r}$$

This is known as the *binomial probability* of exactly r occurrences of event E in n trials.

If the single-trial probability of an event E is $\frac{1}{4}$, then the probability that it will occur exactly five times in seven trials is

$$P[5E] = \binom{7}{5}\left(\frac{1}{4}\right)^5\left(1 - \frac{1}{4}\right)^{7-5}$$

$$= \left(\frac{7 \cdot 6}{2 \cdot 1}\right)\left(\frac{1}{4}\right)^5\left(\frac{3}{4}\right)^2$$

$$= 21\left(\frac{1}{1024}\right)\left(\frac{9}{16}\right)$$

$$= \frac{189}{16{,}384} = .0115$$

Two special cases are worth attention. The probability of exactly 0 occurrences in n trials is

$$\binom{n}{0}p^0q^{n-0} = 1 \cdot 1 \cdot q^n = q^n$$

The probability of exactly n occurrences in n trials is

$$\binom{n}{n}p^nq^{n-n} = 1 \cdot p^n \cdot 1 = p^n$$

Consider the probability of exactly x occurrences; then

$$P[x] = \binom{n}{x}p^xq^{n-x}$$

If we let x assume, in turn, all integral values from 0 through n, we shall have represented every possible outcome of the n trials; that is,

$$P[0] + P[1] + P[2] + \cdots + P[n]$$

$$= \binom{n}{0}p^0q^{n-0} + \binom{n}{1}pq^{n-1} + \binom{n}{2}p^2q^{n-2} + \cdots + \binom{n}{n}p^nq^{n-n}$$

The sum of this sequence of probabilities would give us the sum of the probabilities of every point in the sample space for n trials, and that sum should be equal to 1. Such a sum could be compactly represented as

$$\sum_{x=0}^{n} \binom{n}{x} p^x q^{n-x}$$

The probability of r or fewer occurrences would be

$$P[0 \leq x \leq r] = \sum_{x=0}^{r} \binom{n}{x} p^x q^{n-x}$$

The probability of r or more occurrences would be

$$P[r \leq x \leq n] = \sum_{x=r}^{n} \binom{n}{x} p^x q^{n-x}$$

9.2 THE BINOMIAL THEOREM

In elementary algebra there is an important theorem for raising the sum of two real terms, say x and y, to any specified nonnegative integral power n. In other words, this theorem, known as the *Binomial Theorem*, gives a general procedure for finding the value of $(x + y)^n$, with n a nonnegative integer.

For our purposes it is convenient to represent the real terms as q and p. We will review the derivation of this theorem.

$$(q + p)^1 = q + p$$

$$(q + p)^2 = q^2 + 2qp + p^2$$

$$(q + p)^3 = q^3 + 3q^2p + 3qp^2 + p^3$$

$$(q + p)^4 = q^4 + 4q^3p + 6q^2p^2 + 4qp^3 + p^4$$

and, in general,

$$(q + p)^n = q^n + \frac{n}{1}q^{n-1}p + \frac{n(n-1)}{2 \cdot 1}q^{n-2}p^2$$

$$+ \frac{n(n-1)(n-2)}{3 \cdot 2 \cdot 1}q^{n-3}p^3 + \ldots$$

$$+ \frac{n(n-1)(n-2)\ldots(n-r+1)}{r!}q^{n-r}p^r \ldots$$

$$+ \frac{n(n-1)\ldots 2}{(n-1)!}qp^{n-1} + p^n$$

Note that the general term, that is, the term involving p^r, can be rewritten

$$\frac{(n)_r}{r!}q^{n-r}p^r = \binom{n}{r}q^{n-r}p^r$$

Hence the expression $\binom{n}{r}$ is frequently called the *binomial coefficient*.

It may be shown by mathematical induction that this identity holds for any magnitude of n.

If we impose the condition that $q + p = 1$, we have an identity for the sum of terms in our binomial *probability* distribution, and the general term is identical with that which had already been derived by combinatorial analysis as the point probability of exactly r occurrences in n trials, that is, $\binom{n}{r}p^r q^{n-r}$.

The identity for the sum of all the terms is

$$(q + p)^n = \sum_{x=0}^{n} \binom{n}{x} p^x q^{n-x}$$

Remembering that $q + p = 1$, we have

$$1^n = \sum_{x=0}^{n} \binom{n}{x} p^x q^{n-x} = 1$$

In other words, the sum of the probabilities of all of our sample points is equal to 1, just as it is supposed to be. It is important to remember that this is not a uniform sample space, although the probabilities within each subset of point probabilities are uniform. Thus each term in the distribution may be thought of as a subset of size $\binom{n}{r}$ points, each with a probability of $p^r q^{n-r}$. The probability associated with each point will in general depend on r. For instance, given $n = 5$ trials and $p = \frac{1}{3}$, then each point in the subset of $r = 3$ occurrences has the probability

$$\left(\frac{1}{3}\right)^3 \left(\frac{2}{3}\right)^2 = .0164$$

and there are $\binom{5}{3} = 10$ such points. On the other hand, in the subset of points for $r = 4$ occurrences, the probability of each point is

$$\left(\frac{1}{3}\right)^4 \left(\frac{2}{3}\right)^1 = .0027$$

and there are $\binom{5}{4} = 5$ such points.

There is an interesting solution to the problem of the number of such points in the total sample space. The number of points will be equal, evidently, to

$$\binom{n}{0} + \binom{n}{1} + \cdots + \binom{n}{r} + \cdots + \binom{n}{n} = \sum_{x=0}^{n} \binom{n}{x}$$

Replace the restriction $q + p = 1$ with $q = p = 1$; then

$$\begin{aligned}(q + p)^n &= (1 + 1)^n = 2^n \\ &= \sum_{x=0}^{n} \binom{n}{x} p^x q^{n-x} \\ &= \sum_{x=0}^{n} \binom{n}{x} 1^x \cdot 1^{n-x}\end{aligned}$$

Since $1^x \cdot 1^{n-x} = 1$,

$$2^n = \sum_{x=0}^{n} \binom{n}{x}$$

In other words, the number of points in the sample space of a binomial probability distribution is 2^n. However, one must scrupulously avoid the assumption that the probability of each point is 2^{-n},* since the probabilities of the points vary as already indicated; that is, the sample space is not uniform because, although all of its points can be decomposed into subsets of a primitive space, if each element is separately identified (see Tables 9.6.1 and 9.6.2 on pp. 148 and 149), they will not be uniformly equal-sized subsets. It can be seen in Table 9.6.2, for instance, that the point "all male in three trials" decomposes only into itself (one point), whereas "all female in three trials" decomposes into nine points in that particular primitive space, with consequent probabilities of $\frac{1}{27}$ for "all male" and $\frac{9}{27}$ for "all female."

To find the probabilities of one or the other of various numbers of alternatives, we may make use of the fact that these are exclusive events, and

$$P[x_i \mid 1 \le i \le k] = \sum_{i=1}^{k} P[x_i] = \sum_{i=1}^{k} \binom{n}{x_i} p^{x_i} q^{n-x_i}$$

* An argument could be made that the sample space has $n + 1$ points, but this is not true for our derivation. We defined a sample space of 2^n points.

The subscription of the *x*s in the above expression indicates an arbitrary ordering of the *k* alternative outcomes. Thus we might be interested in the probability that in $n = 10$ trials, either three or eight occurrences would result. Let $E_1 = 3$ occurrences and $E_2 = 8$ occurrences; then

$$P[E_1 \cup E_2] = P[E_1] + P[E_2] = \binom{10}{3} p^3 q^7 + \binom{10}{8} p^8 q^2$$

Statistically, however, we would seldom be interested in anything other than the union of sequential sample points, and in particular the sequences at the extremes of the distribution, that is, the extreme ranges of values for the random variable *x*. Either

$$P[0 \leq x \leq r] = \sum_{x=0}^{r} \binom{n}{x} p^x q^{n-x}$$

or

$$P[r \leq x \leq n] = \sum_{x=r}^{n} \binom{n}{x} p^x q^{n-x}$$

9.3 THE USE OF TABLES OF BINOMIAL PROBABILITIES —THE HARVARD TABLES

Although point probabilities in the binomial probability distribution are relatively easy to compute, statistical application generally requires cumulative values. One of the most useful and conveniently available sources of such values is the Harvard *Tables of the Cumulative Binomial Probability Distribution.** This source will be used as our basic reference, and the general principles of its use apply with only minor modification to other such volumes. As in the case of the hypergeometric distribution, symmetry relationships reduce by an impressive amount the number of values that need to be printed. The actual printed values in the Harvard tables are

$$E(n, r, p) = P[r \leq x \leq n] = \sum_{x=r}^{n} \binom{n}{x} p^x q^{n-x}, \quad p \leq .50$$

* Cambridge, Mass.: Harvard University Press, 1955.

where $E(n, r, p)$ is a special notation comparable to $P[N, n, k, x]$ for the hypergeometric distribution.

Since $P[\not{E}] = 1 - P[E]$, it is evident that

$$P[0 \leq x \leq r] = 1 - \sum_{x=r+1}^{n} \binom{n}{x} p^x q^{n-x} = 1 - E(n, r + 1, p)$$

In other words, if we subtract from the probability for the total space the cumulative probability of all of the points in which there are more than r occurrences, we have left the cumulative probability of all the points in which there are r or fewer occurrences. In fact, the key to symmetry relationships lies in the implicit addition or subtraction of the appropriate sample points.

For instance, if $p > .50$, we can simply reverse our definition, letting q stand for the probability of an occurrence. If we had only to know the point probability, it would still be $\binom{n}{r}p^r q^{n-r}$, formally switching the arithmetic values of p for q, and of r for $n - r$, and conversely. Where cumulatives are concerned, however, such a switch is, in effect, an inversion of the order of the terms of the distribution. Since occurrences and nonoccurrences are mutually residual, their proportions are inversely associated. For example, it will be recalled that the probability of 0 occurrences is q^n and the probability of 0 nonoccurrences ($= n$ occurrences) is p^n. Therefore if we redefine the single trial probability of an occurrence as q instead of p, we must cumulate the probabilities of $n - r$ (substituted for r) occurrences as though 0 occurrences start on the right rather than the left tail extremity. Hence if $p > .50$,

$$P[0 \leq x \leq r] = \sum_{x=n-r}^{n} p^x q^{n-x} = E[n, n - r, 1 - p]$$

In short, in substituting $1 - p$ for p, we also had to substitute its exponent $n - r$ for r.

Finally, since

$$P[r \leq x \leq n] = 1 - P[0 \leq x \leq r - 1]$$

we may use for the case where $p > .50$

$$P[r \leq x \leq n] = 1 - E[n, n - (r - 1), 1 - p]$$
$$= 1 - E[n, n - r + 1, 1 - p]$$

These symmetries make it possible for us to use the Harvard tables for cumulating from either tail of the distribution and whether

Sample Page from *Tables of the Cumulative Binomial Probability Distribution**

n	r	p=0.09	p=0.10	p=0.11	p=0.12	p=1/8	p=0.13	p=0.14	p=0.15	p=0.16	p=1/6
16	0	1.00000	1.00000	1.00000	1.00000	1.00000	1.00000	1.00000	1.00000	1.00000	1.00000
	1	0.77886	0.81470	0.84503	0.87066	0.88193	0.89228	0.91047	0.92575	0.93856	0.94591
	2	0.42893	0.48527	0.53858	0.58847	0.61207	0.63473	0.67727	0.71610	0.75130	0.77283
	3	0.16937	0.21075	0.25451	0.29987	0.32292	0.34611	0.39255	0.43862	0.48380	0.51321
	4	0.04957	0.06841	0.09066	0.11621	0.13016	0.14484	0.17625	0.21011	0.24602	0.27090
	5	0.01106	0.01700	0.02485	0.03482	0.04066	0.04710	0.06182	0.07905	0.09882	0.11339
	6	0.00192	0.00330	0.00533	0.00818	0.00998	0.01205	0.01711	0.02354	0.03153	0.03779
	7	0.00026	0.00050	0.00090	0.00152	0.00194	0.00245	0.00376	0.00559	0.00803	0.01007
	8	0.00003	0.00006	0.00012	0.00023	0.00030	0.00040	0.00066	0.00106	0.00164	0.00215
	9	0.00000	0.00001	0.00001	0.00003	0.00004	0.00005	0.00009	0.00016	0.00027	0.00037
	10		0.00000	0.00000	0.00000	0.00000	0.00001	0.00001	0.00002	0.00003	0.00005
	11						0.00000	0.00000	0.00000	0.00000	0.00001
	12										0.00000
17	0	1.00000	1.00000	1.00000	1.00000	1.00000	1.00000	1.00000	1.00000	1.00000	1.00000
	1	0.79876	0.83323	0.86208	0.88618	0.89669	0.90628	0.92300	0.93689	0.94839	0.95493
	2	0.46042	0.51821	0.57229	0.62234	0.64580	0.66821	0.70992	0.74755	0.78126	0.80168
	3	0.19273	0.23820	0.28576	0.33450	0.35906	0.38363	0.43241	0.48024	0.52660	0.55648
	4	0.06035	0.08264	0.10869	0.13825	0.15425	0.17100	0.20654	0.24439	0.28406	0.31128
	5	0.01453	0.02214	0.03209	0.04459	0.05185	0.05981	0.07784	0.09871	0.12237	0.13964
	6	0.00274	0.00467	0.00747	0.01138	0.01381	0.01660	0.02337	0.03187	0.04230	0.05039
	7	0.00041	0.00078	0.00139	0.00232	0.00295	0.00369	0.00563	0.00828	0.01179	0.01469
	8	0.00005	0.00011	0.00021	0.00038	0.00051	0.00066	0.00110	0.00174	0.00266	0.00347
	9	0.00000	0.00001	0.00002	0.00005	0.00007	0.00010	0.00017	0.00030	0.00049	0.00066
	10		0.00000	0.00000	0.00001	0.00001	0.00001	0.00002	0.00004	0.00007	0.00010
	11				0.00000	0.00000	0.00000	0.00000	0.00000	0.00001	0.00001
	12									0.00000	0.00000
18	0	1.00000	1.00000	1.00000	1.00000	1.00000	1.00000	1.00000	1.00000	1.00000	1.00000
	1	0.81688	0.84991	0.87725	0.89984	0.90960	0.91846	0.93378	0.94635	0.95665	0.96244
	2	0.49088	0.54972	0.60417	0.65400	0.67716	0.69916	0.73975	0.77595	0.80800	0.82722
	3	0.21682	0.26620	0.31728	0.36904	0.39491	0.42062	0.47126	0.52034	0.56735	0.59735
	4	0.07226	0.09820	0.12816	0.16180	0.17986	0.19865	0.23816	0.27976	0.32287	0.35215
	5	0.01865	0.02819	0.04051	0.05583	0.06465	0.07426	0.09586	0.12056	0.14824	0.16825
	6	0.00380	0.00642	0.01018	0.01536	0.01857	0.02222	0.03099	0.04190	0.05511	0.06527
	7	0.00062	0.00117	0.00206	0.00341	0.00430	0.00537	0.00812	0.01182	0.01667	0.02064
	8	0.00008	0.00017	0.00034	0.00061	0.00081	0.00106	0.00173	0.00272	0.00412	0.00534
	9	0.00001	0.00002	0.00005	0.00009	0.00012	0.00017	0.00030	0.00051	0.00083	0.00113
	10	0.00000	0.00000	0.00000	0.00001	0.00002	0.00002	0.00004	0.00008	0.00014	0.00020
	11				0.00000	0.00000	0.00000	0.00000	0.00001	0.00002	0.00003
	12								0.00000	0.00000	0.00000
19	0	1.00000	1.00000	1.00000	1.00000	1.00000	1.00000	1.00000	1.00000	1.00000	1.00000
	1	0.83336	0.86491	0.89075	0.91186	0.92090	0.92906	0.94305	0.95440	0.96358	0.96870
	2	0.52022	0.57974	0.63421	0.68350	0.70622	0.72767	0.76691	0.80151	0.83179	0.84976
	3	0.24148	0.29456	0.34883	0.40324	0.43019	0.45683	0.50885	0.55868	0.60585	0.63566
	4	0.08527	0.11500	0.14897	0.18667	0.20674	0.22750	0.27079	0.31585	0.36199	0.39301
	5	0.02347	0.03519	0.05016	0.06854	0.07905	0.09043	0.11578	0.14444	0.17618	0.19890
	6	0.00514	0.00859	0.01352	0.02022	0.02433	0.02899	0.04007	0.05370	0.07001	0.08243
	7	0.00091	0.00170	0.00295	0.00484	0.00609	0.00756	0.01132	0.01633	0.02282	0.02808
	8	0.00013	0.00027	0.00053	0.00095	0.00125	0.00162	0.00262	0.00408	0.00613	0.00789
	9	0.00002	0.00004	0.00008	0.00015	0.00021	0.00028	0.00050	0.00084	0.00136	0.00183
	10	0.00000	0.00000	0.00001	0.00002	0.00003	0.00004	0.00008	0.00014	0.00025	0.00035
	11			0.00000	0.00000	0.00000	0.00000	0.00001	0.00002	0.00004	0.00006
	12							0.00000	0.00000	0.00000	0.00001
	13										0.00000
20	0	1.00000	1.00000	1.00000	1.00000	1.00000	1.00000	1.00000	1.00000	1.00000	1.00000
	1	0.84836	0.87842	0.90277	0.92244	0.93079	0.93829	0.95103	0.96124	0.96941	0.97392
	2	0.54840	0.60825	0.66243	0.71090	0.73305	0.75385	0.79157	0.82444	0.85287	0.86958
	3	0.26657	0.32307	0.38022	0.43687	0.46469	0.49204	0.54498	0.59510	0.64200	0.67134
	4	0.09933	0.13295	0.17095	0.21266	0.23467	0.25732	0.30412	0.35227	0.40100	0.43345
	5	0.02904	0.04317	0.06102	0.08272	0.09501	0.10825	0.13748	0.17015	0.20591	0.23125
	6	0.00679	0.01125	0.01755	0.02602	0.03117	0.03697	0.05067	0.06731	0.08700	0.10184
	7	0.00129	0.00239	0.00411	0.00669	0.00837	0.01035	0.01534	0.02194	0.03037	0.03714
	8	0.00020	0.00042	0.00079	0.00142	0.00185	0.00239	0.00384	0.00592	0.00880	0.01125
	9	0.00003	0.00006	0.00013	0.00025	0.00034	0.00046	0.00080	0.00133	0.00212	0.00284
	10	0.00000	0.00001	0.00002	0.00004	0.00005	0.00007	0.00014	0.00025	0.00043	0.00060
	11		0.00000	0.00000	0.00000	0.00001	0.00001	0.00002	0.00004	0.00007	0.00011
	12					0.00000	0.00000	0.00000	0.00000	0.00001	0.00002
	13									0.00000	0.00000

* Staff of the Computation Laboratory (Cambridge, Mass.: Harvard University Press, 1955), p. 59. Copyright, 1955, by the President and Fellows of Harvard College. Reproduced with the kind permission of the copyright owners.

or not $p > .50$. We shall have virtually no use for the point probabilities; however, these may be obtained by subtracting successive cumulative terms. This follows from the definition of cumulative. In the Harvard tables, $e[n, r, p]$ is used to designate *point* probabilities.

A summary of the essential information for using the Harvard tables is given herewith and is followed by a similar summary for use with Owen's *Handbook of Statistical Tables.*

Supplementary Instructions for Use with the Harvard Tables of the Cumulative Binomial Probability Distribution

Given a population of size N, k of whose elements are of one sort, and the remaining $N - k$ are another sort, the probability of drawing an element of the first sort in a single random trial is $p = k/N$. The probability of not drawing an element of the first sort is the same as the probability of drawing an element of the second sort, and is given by $q = 1 - p$. The probability that there will be *exactly* r occurrences of elements of the first sort in n random trials taken with replacement is given by the binomial term

$$P[r] = \binom{n}{r} q^{n-r} p^r = e(n, r, p)$$

where $e(n, r, p)$ is a condensed notation corresponding to that used in the Harvard tables.

The probability that there will be at least r occurrences (that is, r or more occurrences) is given by

$$P[r \leq x \leq n] = \sum_{x=r}^{n} \binom{n}{x} q^{n-x} p^x = E(n, r, p)$$

The usefulness of the Harvard tables may be greatly extended by using the following relationships:

(1) Exactly r occurrences:

$$P[r] = E(n, r, p) - E(n, r + 1, p) \qquad \text{if } p \leq .50$$

$$P[r] = E(n, n - r, 1 - p) - E(n, n - r + 1, 1 - p) \qquad \text{if } p > .50$$

(2) r or fewer occurrences:

$$P[0 \leq x \leq r] = 1 - E(n, r + 1, p) \qquad \text{if } p \leq .50$$

$$P[0 \leq x \leq r] = E(n, n - r, 1 - p) \qquad \text{if } p > .50$$

(3) r or more occurrences if $p > .50$:

$$P[r \leq x \leq n] = 1 - E(n, n - r + 1, 1 - p)$$

It will be recalled that the values for $P[r \leq x \leq n] = E(n, r, p)$, where $p \leq .50$ are given directly by the tables.

Binomial Distribution Symmetries for Owen's Handbook of Statistical Tables

On pp. 265–72 of Owen's *Handbook of Statistical Tables*, there is a table of values for the cumulative binomial probability distribution showing

$$P[0 \le j \le A] = B(n, A, p) \quad \text{for} \quad \sum_{j=0}^{n} \binom{n}{j} p^j (1-p)^{n-j}$$

for

$$2 \le n \le 25 \quad \text{and} \quad p = m/16; \quad m \text{ is an integer such that } 1 \le m \le 8$$

Hence the maximum value of p is $\frac{8}{16} = \frac{1}{2}$.

In contrast with the Harvard *Tables of the Cumulative Binomial Probability Distribution*, Owen's table shows then the probability that a random variate will be equal to or *less* than a prescribed value A rather than equal to or *greater* than a prescribed value r. Obviously the same symmetry formulas will not hold for both sets of tables. For Owen's table they are as follows.

(1) Exactly A occurrences—$b(n, A, p)$:

$$P[j = A] = B(n, A, p) - B(n, A-1, p) \qquad \text{if} \quad p \le \tfrac{8}{16}$$

$$P[j = A] = B(n, n-A, 1-p) - B(n, n-A-1, 1-p) \quad \text{if} \quad p > \tfrac{8}{16}$$

(2) A or fewer occurrences:

$$P[0 \le j \le A] = B(n, A, p) \qquad \text{if} \quad p \le \tfrac{8}{16}$$

Note that the above is the case for which the table values are given and hence requires only direct reading from the table.

$$P[0 \le j \le A] = 1 - B(n, n-A-1, 1-p)^* \qquad \text{if} \quad p > \tfrac{8}{16}$$

(3) A or more occurrences:

$$P[A \le j \le n] = 1 - B(n, A-1, p) \qquad \text{if} \quad p \le \tfrac{8}{16}$$

$$P[A \le j \le n] = B(n, n-A, 1-p) \qquad \text{if} \quad p > \tfrac{8}{16}$$

9.4 OTHER IMPORTANT TABLES

Another useful table is that of Sol Weintraub, *Tables of the Cumulative Binomial Probability Distribution for Small Values of p.*† The symmetries for the Harvard tables apply directly to it. Values of p in the Harvard tables, however, have only two-digit precision ranging from .01 through .50. The values of p in Weintraub's tables start with .00001, then skip to .0001 through .0009, and then run

* This does not agree with Owen's formula, p. 264, which the present writer claims to be in error.

† New York: Macmillan, 1963.

continuously from .001 through .100. Thus while they lack the range of values $.11 \leq p \leq .50$ of the Harvard tables, they give greater precision for values $<.100$. They also differ from the Harvard tables in that they omit the probabilities for $r = 0$. However, this cumulative probability is 1.00000 in every case.

Other important tables of binomial probabilities are as follows:

(1) National Bureau of Standards, *Tables of the Binomial Probability Distribution*, Applied Math. Series 6 (Washington, D.C.: U.S. Government Printing Office, 1950).

(2) U.S. Ordnance Corps, *Tables of the Cumulative Binomial Probabilities*, ORDP 20-1 (Washington, D.C.: Office of Technical Services, 1952).

(3) Romig, H. G., *Binomial Tables* (New York: John Wiley & Sons, Inc., 1953).

(4) Robertson, W. H., *Tables of the Binomial Distribution Function for Small Values of p* (Washington, D.C.: Office of Technical Services, U.S. Department of Commerce, 1960).

The ranges of values covered in the various tables differ somewhat from one to the other so that the user's needs and convenience will guide his choice.

9.5 FURTHER THEORETICAL CONSIDERATIONS

Use of the binomial model in statistical applications is similar to that for the hypergeometric distribution. It should be remembered, however, that use of the binomial model assumes that the sampling has been done *with independent trials*. If the size of the sample is very small relative to the size of the population from which it was drawn, this is not a crucial consideration. If we draw a sample of size 2 from a population of 1,000,000, both trials will to all intents and purposes be independent, owing to the very low probability of drawing a particular element twice, even if it is replaced. If, however, we draw a sample of size 2 from a population of size 2, the probability that a specified element will be included in the second draw is .50, which is, of course, high.

A specific comparison may be revealing. Given a "population" of five red balls and five white balls, what is the probability that a sample of size three will contain all red balls?

If the sample is drawn *with replacement*, the binomial model applies, and we get

$$P[3] = \left(\frac{1}{2}\right)^3 = \frac{1}{8} = .1250$$

If the sample is drawn *without replacement*, the hypergeometric model applies, and we get

$$P[3] = \frac{\binom{5}{3}\binom{5}{0}}{\binom{10}{3}} = \frac{1}{12} = .0833$$

9.6 FURTHER COMMENT ON THE CONCEPT OF POPULATION

Since great care has been taken in earlier chapters to stress that a population is a set and therefore every element in it has a unique identity, it may sound incongruous for us to speak of a population of five red balls and five white ones as we have just done, or of Caucasians and Negroes, as was done in the last chapter. The incongruity is only apparent. The classification of the elements either dichotomously or otherwise does not necessarily preclude their identifiability on the basis of other attributes. That separate identifiability is already implicit in the models because it was an explicit assumption in their development.

The following tables showing the points for samples drawn with replacement from a population of one man and two women illustrate the separate identifiability of the elements, even though the population is dichotomized into "men" and "women."

TABLE 9.6.1 / Composite Space of Ordered Sample Points for the Joint Occurrence of Elements Drawn with Replacement in Two Successive Trials from the Population of Three Elements, $P = \{M, W_1, W_2\}$

MM	W_1M	W_2M
MW_1	W_1W_1	W_2W_1
MW_2	W_1W_2	W_2W_2

TABLE 9.6.2 / Composite Space of Ordered Sample Points for the Joint Occurrence of Elements Drawn with Replacement in Three Successive Trials from the Population of Three Elements, $P = \{M, W_1, W_2\}$

MMM	MW_1M	MW_2M	W_1MM	W_1W_1M
W_1W_2M	W_2MM	W_2W_1M	W_2W_2M	MMW_1
MW_1W_1	MW_2W_1	W_1MW_1	$W_1W_1W_1$	$W_1W_2W_1$
W_2MW_1	$W_2W_1W_1$	$W_2W_2W_1$	MMW_2	MW_1W_2
MW_2W_2	W_1MW_2	$W_1W_1W_2$	$W_1W_2W_2$	W_2MW_2
$W_2W_1W_2$	$W_2W_2W_2$			

The above two tables are instructive in more than just one way. Observe that they represent the *primitive* spaces for binomial models.

If we wanted to know the probability that a sample of size 3 drawn with replacement from the three-element population M, W_1, W_2 would contain man twice and woman once, we could find it by counting points in Table 9.6.2:

$$P[2M, 1W] = \frac{\mathscr{E}}{S} = \frac{6}{27}$$

By the binomial formula,

$$P[2M, 1W] = \binom{3}{2}\left(\frac{1}{3}\right)^2\left(\frac{2}{3}\right)^1 = 3 \cdot \frac{1}{9} \cdot \frac{2}{3} = \frac{6}{27}$$

Given a population partitioned into exhaustive classes (two classes for the binomial case), the single-trial probability for a specified class equals the number of elements in the class divided by the number of elements in the population. In our illustration, the single-trial probability for a woman is $\frac{2}{3}$ and for a nonwoman (man) is $\frac{1}{3}$.

9.7 STATISTICAL INFERENCE WITH THE BINOMIAL PROBABILITY DISTRIBUTION

Statistical inference with a binomial model in the final analysis involves testing the hypothesis that the population from which the sample was drawn has the composition p. By saying "a composition p" we are taking cognizance of the fact that the proportion of elements in a population with a specified attribute is also the single-trial probability of drawing that element. A population of 60 males and 40 females obviously has a male composition of $p = .60$. This is also, of course, the single-trial probability of drawing a male if replacement occurs between trials. Essentially, two types of hypotheses may be tested. The less important case is that in which the population composition p is actually known and one is merely interested in determining whether the sample drawn was in fact random. The second and vastly more important case is that in which the randomness of the sample is assumed and the determination is to be made as to whether it was drawn from a population with the composition p. In the first case, the sample is known to have been drawn from such a population, and, in the second case, that is the fact to be determined. We shall confine our attention to this second case, where one of the following sets of hypotheses are used:

H_0: The true population proportion is p
H_1: The true population proportion is not p

H_0: The true population proportion is p or greater than p
H_1: The true population proportion is less than p

H_0: The true population proportion is p or less than p
H_1: The true population proportion is greater than p

The first is often called the two-tailed case, the second the left-tailed case, and the third the right-tailed case. A common source of confusion in practical application concerns the correct choice of the tail.

The random variable actually to be tested in the binomial sample is not the proportion but the *number* of occurrences of the event in the sample. A statistical test asks, Would the number r that is actually observed be a rare event under the hypothesis that the population from which it was drawn has the proportion p (equals the hypothesized single-trial probability)? The expected value of the random variable is the number of occurrences that would make the sample proportion equal to the population proportion. Since the sample size is n, the expected value is np—that is, the population proportion applied to the sample number. Knowing the expected value simplifies the logical choice of a direction (or the proper tail of the distribution) for the test.

The following rules may be applied:

(1) If $r = np$, there is nothing to test—immediate acceptance

of the null hypothesis is indicated. It means that the sample proportion is a perfect replica of the postulated population proportion. Otherwise we require a definition of rare event—that is, a probability, α—and the choice of tails.

(2) For a two-tailed test, H_0 is rejected if either $P[0 \leq x \leq r]$ or $P[r \leq x \leq n] \leq \alpha/2$. Rejection of the null hypothesis in this case implies only that the sample was drawn from a population for which the proportion was not p and hence different from that postulated.

(3) For a single-tailed test, a rational choice of tails must be made.

If $r < np$, it makes no sense to test $P[r \leq x \leq n]$, since one hardly supposes that an observed random variable less than the expected value creates a presumption of a true value greater than it. One would, under the circumstances, simply accept H_0. Given that $r < np$, the only directional alternative hypothesis it makes any sense to test is that the value of the proportion of Es in the population from which the sample was drawn is less than p. Hence one would reject H_0 if $P[0 \leq x \leq r] \leq \alpha$ and accept H_1, which states the true proportion is less than p.

By entirely similar reasoning, if H_1 were that the true population proportion is less than np and it is observed that $np < r$, one would immediately accept H_0. On the other hand, if H_1 is that the true population proportion is greater than p, then if $P[r \leq x \leq n] \leq \alpha$, one would accept H_1; otherwise one must conclude that H_0 may not be rejected.

9.8 APPLICATIONS OF THE BINOMIAL MODEL TO STATISTICAL PROBLEMS

The following applications of the binomial model involve artificial data and are intended to be suggestive. The experimental or observational control of extraneous factors is, of course, the responsibility of the scientific investigator and is a methodological rather than a statistical problem. For our purposes, we shall assume that the methodological problems have been solved and concentrate largely on the statistical aspects.

In the special applied context of drawing a sample of persons from a finite population, the use of the binomial model implies that when a person is drawn on two trials he be used on both as if he were different persons.

Since our concern is with statistical inference rather than estimation, our applications require tests of specific values of p. In other words, the investigator must know the specific value of p for which he is testing and must have a plausible rationale for testing that particular value.

1. A labor union has found by experience that it is futile to undertake a serious drive for a closed shop unless the membership at the start exceeds 30 percent of the labor force. A random sample of 600 workers taken with replacement yielded 207 union members. If a 1 percent probability of being wrong is an acceptable risk, is it worth their while to undertake the campaign?

Solution. Setting down our essential information, we have

$$n = 600 \quad \text{and} \quad p = .30$$

$$np = 600(.30) = 180 < 207 = r$$

$$\alpha = .01$$

H_0: The actual proportion of union members is 30 percent or less

H_1: The true proportion of union members exceeds 30 percent

Use of the Harvard tables shows

$$\begin{aligned} P[r \leq x \leq n] &= P[207 \leq x \leq 600] = E(n, r, p) \\ &= E(600, 207, .30) = .00974 < .01 = \alpha \end{aligned}$$

Therefore reject H_0 and conclude that a decision to make the drive is indicated.

The following problem is included for comparison with the hypergeometric problem of Section 8.7 of the previous chapter. Since sampling without replacement gives a better estimate of population parameters, the hypergeometric solution is much to be preferred for small samples.

2. A newspaper columnist wished to predict whether the United States Senate would bring a filibuster to an end by voting to close debate on a vital issue. He polled a random sample of 35 Senators taken with replacement and found cloture to be favored in 29 cases. Is he justified in predicting that the motion for cloture will be carried if he is willing to take a .01 risk of falsely rejecting the null hypothesis? Noting again that a two-thirds vote is required

to pass a motion to close debate, we may set $p = \frac{2}{3}$. We may state our hypotheses and present the essential information as follows:

$$H_0 : \tfrac{2}{3} \geq p$$

$$H_1 : \tfrac{2}{3} < p$$

$$n = 35$$

$$np = \tfrac{2}{3}(35) = 23.3 < 29$$

This indicates that further investigation is necessary. We therefore find

$$\begin{aligned} P[35, 29, \tfrac{2}{3}] &= E(n, r, p) = 1 - E[n, n - r + 1, 1 - p] \\ &= 1 - E[35, 35 - 29 + 1, \tfrac{1}{3}] = 1 - E[35, 7, \tfrac{1}{3}] \\ &= 1 - .97269 = .02731 > \alpha = .01 \end{aligned}$$

This indicates that H_0 may not be rejected. In fact, it would have required $r = 30$ with probability .00989 to reject H_0 when we use the binomial test with $\alpha = .01$.

3. A census determined that 21 percent of adult males in a depressed area were unemployed. A sample of 68 taken with replacement a year later showed 10 persons unemployed. If $\alpha = .05$, is there reason to suppose that the true unemployment rate has decreased? Although the sample here is small, the population size is not known, so we will use the binomial model. This illustrates that where the necessary information is lacking, our method is to make the best decision we can on the basis of available information.

Solution.

$$n = 68 \quad \text{and} \quad p = .21$$

$$\alpha = .05$$

$$np = 68(.21) = 14 > 10 = r$$

$$H_0 : p \geq .21$$

$$H_1 : p < .21$$

$$\begin{aligned} P[0 \leq x \leq 10] &= E(68, 10, .21) \\ &= 1 - E(n, r + 1, p) \\ &= 1 - E(68, 11, .21) \\ &= 1 - .87193 = .12307 > .05 = \alpha \end{aligned}$$

Therefore we may not reject H_0, and we conclude that there is no basis for the belief that the male unemployment rate has declined.

4. Sixteen respondents were instructed to appear for 20-minute interviews during a specified two-hour period. Assume that the respondents' arrival times will be random during the period. Every respondent has been assured that he will be interviewed immediately no matter when he arrives. How many interviewers will have to be available at the beginning of the interview period to insure that there is only a 1 percent chance for any respondent that he will in fact have to wait?

Since the maximum number of respondents that would have to wait (that is, the maximum length "queue") would decrease with each respondent that has been processed, the maximum probability that anyone will have to wait will prevail during the time that the first arrivals are still being interviewed. It is possible that arrivals would be so timed that every respondent is either being interviewed or waiting. If we can find the number of interviewers required during the period when a respondent's probability of having to wait is at a maximum, we will know the number of interviewers required to validate the guarantee at the prescribed risk level. Although we know that this probability is maximal until the first respondent has been processed, we do not know when the first applicant will appear. Any point in the interview time continuum is as likely to be encompassed by the first interview as any other. Similar reasoning applies to every applicant, each of whom is as likely as each and every other to be the first to arrive, or to occupy any order in the arrival times, including simultaneous arrivals.

Consider any point of time in the two-hour interval. Any respondent represents a 20-minute interview segment that may or may not encompass the point. Every 20-minute segment that encompasses the point is one of six linearly adjacent, mutually exclusive, continuous 20-minute time intervals that fall entirely within the time allotted for interviewing.*

This defines our single-trial sample space. For every sample point in the set of occurrences of the event "encompasses the time

* $6 \times 20 = 120$ minutes $= 2$ hours. Since respondents could arrive right at the end of the second hour, 2 hours and 20 minutes of interviewing time would have to be allotted. One and only one of the infinite number of sets of integral 20-minute segments would permit seven rather than six to fit in the 140 minute span, but since its probability is $p = 1/\infty \rightarrow 0$, it may be ignored.

point," there are five exclusive uniform points representing nonoccurrences. It must be remembered that we are speaking of opportunities for exclusive, continuous 20-minute intervals to occur. Such an interval could not occur in a segment of the interview period less than 20 minutes in length. Moreover, any overlapping interval would be accounted for in one of the other exclusive sets and must only be accounted for as part of such an exclusive set; otherwise there would be an "overcount."

In any case, we see that for every opportunity for an occurrence, there are five equal opportunities for a nonoccurrence; this indicates that occurrences occupy one-sixth of the sample space for a single trial and hence that $p = \frac{1}{6}$. In sum, no matter what point in the two-hour period one selects, there is a probability of $p = \frac{1}{6}$ for each and every respondent that his allotted 20 minutes will encompass it.

Our problem is now defined. What is the probability that r or more respondents will require interviewers at any point of time in the allotted two hours?

By stipulation, $\alpha = .01$. Since there are 16 respondents and each of these represents a "trial," $n = 16$. r is the permissible maximum of respondents for whom interviewers are to be supplied at any time; therefore $r =$ the number of interviewers required. Hence

$$P[r \leq x \leq n] = E(16, r, \tfrac{1}{6}) \leq \alpha = .01$$

Values for $n = 16$ and $p = \frac{1}{6}$ are tabulated on page 59 of the Harvard tables. We scan the probabilities and find that the maximum probability $\leq .01$ is .01007. We may ignore the last digit since only two-place precision is required. The corresponding value of r read from the tables is 7. This means that for any respondent the maximum risk that he will have to wait is .01 if $r = 7$ interviewers are available, since

$$P[7 \leq x \leq 16] = E(16, 7, \tfrac{1}{6}) = .01 \leq \alpha = .01$$

5. Tests of two points in time, or "before" and "after" exposure or treatment, may be analyzed with the binomial model. One method is to regard each subject that has undergone change in the anticipated direction after exposure to the treatment as an occurrence of E and those who have changed either in the opposite direction or not at all as $\not{E}$. One may then test the hypothesis that some specified proportion responded favorably to the treatment—25

percent, 50 percent, 60 percent, or some other proportion which then becomes the null hypothesis. Selecting an appropriate p becomes an estimation problem. While estimation is expressly excluded as an objective of the present book, a brief consideration of it in conjunction with the binomial model should be valuable. Estimation in this case involves finding minimum and maximum values of p (call them p_{lower} and p_{upper}) that define its plausible range of values in relation to the observed value of r. This range of values is called the confidence interval. To find the lower boundary one enters the tables to find a $p_{\text{lower}} = P[r \leq x \leq n] \doteq \alpha/2$. That is, n, r, and α are known, and a corresponding value of p is found with the use of the tables. Such a value of p_{lower} is interpreted as the lowest value of p at which the observed value r would not fall into the range of rare events under the right-tailed null hypothesis.

$$p_{\text{lower}} = p$$

such that

$$P[r \text{ or more occurrences}] = \frac{\alpha}{2}$$

To find the upper boundary, the tables are consulted to find

$$p_{\text{upper}} = P[0 \leq x \leq r] \doteq \frac{\alpha}{2}$$

This is interpreted to mean the highest value of p for which the observed value of r would not fall into the range of rare events under the left-tailed null hypothesis.

$$p_{\text{upper}} = p$$

such that

$$P[r \text{ or fewer occurrences}] = \frac{\alpha}{2}$$

These two values, p_{lower} and p_{upper}, are, respectively, the lower and upper boundaries of the confidence interval. Its length equals $p_{\text{upper}} - p_{\text{lower}}$. The interval is identified as a percentage obtained as $1 - \alpha$. Thus if $\alpha = .05$, we speak of a 95 percent confidence interval, which means, in effect, that there is a 95 percent probability that the true p is encompassed by the interval. It is important to recognize that it is the interval and not p that is the random variable; p is fixed at whatever value it actually is.

Finding a value for p as the dependent variable is not nearly as convenient as finding values for r or α from the tables; however, it is entirely feasible and well worth the effort. One may even find an appropriate minimum sample size n if p, r, and α are given.

6. As with the hypergeometric model, the binomial model may be used as a median test. A binomial test is essentially a percentile test, and the median is just the fiftieth percentile.

The median score for college seniors on an attitude schedule was determined. Of the sociology majors who were tested, 20 were at or above the median and 10 were below. Does the attitude tend to prevail more strongly among sociology majors than among the general group of seniors if $\alpha = .01$?

Solution. The fact that the median is the reference point implies $p = .50$.

$$H_0\colon\ p \le .50$$

$$H_1\colon\ .50 < p$$

$$P[20 \le x \le 30] = E(30, 20, .50) = .04937 > .01 = \alpha$$

Therefore accept H_0 that the sociology majors are not different from the other seniors. Note that if α had been set at .05, we would have rejected H_0 in favor of H_1.

9.9 THE NUMBER OF TRIALS REQUIRED FOR A SPECIFIED PROBABILITY OF AT LEAST ONE OCCURRENCE

If we remove from a sample space all of the points that represent zero occurrences, we must necessarily have left all of the points representing one or more occurrences, which means the same as "at least one occurrence." Call the event "at least one occurrence," E, and "no occurrences," $\not{E}$. Applying a formula previously derived, we have

$$P[E] = 1 - P[\not{E}] \quad \text{implies} \quad P[0 < x] = 1 - P[x = 0]$$

In short, the probability of at least one occurrence equals 1 minus the probability of no occurrences.

In the binomial distribution, the probability of no occurrences is $P[0 = x] = q^n$. Hence

$$P[0 < x] = 1 - q^n.$$

From this we may easily derive the number of trials, n, required to achieve a specified probability of at least one success. From the previous formula, we may state

$$\begin{aligned} q^n &= 1 - P[0 < x] \\ \ln q^n &= \ln (1 - P[0 < x]) \\ n \ln q &= \ln (1 - P[0 < x]) \\ n &= \frac{\ln (1 - P[0 < x])}{\ln q} \\ &= \frac{\ln (1 - P[0 < x])}{\ln (1 - p)} \end{aligned}$$

Example

It has been determined that the probability that the head of a household will be home during certain hours is 60 percent. If an interviewer wishes to contact the head of a particular household, for how many possible trips must he budget his time if he wishes to be 99 percent certain of making the contact?

$$\begin{aligned} n &= \frac{\ln (1 - .99)}{\ln (1 - .60)} = \frac{\ln (.01)}{\ln (.40)} = \frac{-4.65017}{-0.91629} \\ &= 5.0258 \doteq 5 \end{aligned}$$

Hence he must be prepared to make five trips, if necessary.

9.10 SPECIAL BINOMIAL PROBLEM

If r balls are distributed among N cells, what is the probability that exactly k balls will land in some single specified cell?

1. COMBINATORIAL APPROACH. k balls may be selected from among r to occupy the specified cell in $\binom{r}{k}$ ways. For each of these ways, the

remaining $r - k$ balls may be distributed among the remaining $N - 1$ cells in $(N - 1)^{r-k}$ ways. The size of the sample space is N^r. Hence

$$P[k] = \binom{r}{k}(N - 1)^{r-k}\frac{1}{N^r}$$

2. BINOMIAL MODEL APPROACH. If we approach this problem with the binomial model, the single-trial probability that a ball will occupy the specified cell is

$$p = \frac{1}{N} \quad \text{and} \quad q = \frac{N - 1}{N}$$

The probability of exactly k occurrences in r trials is thus

$$P[k] = \binom{r}{k}\left(\frac{1}{N}\right)^k\left(\frac{N - 1}{N}\right)^{r-k}$$

Since both of these approaches are valid, they should yield identical answers. Show that

$$\binom{r}{k}(N - 1)^{r-k}\frac{1}{N^r} = \binom{r}{k}\left(\frac{1}{N}\right)^k\left(\frac{N - 1}{N}\right)^{r-k}$$

PROBLEMS

These problems on binomial distribution and its applications may be worked in any order you prefer. Scan all the problems before you start work.

1. Theoretical considerations:

a. Why has the theory of the binomial distribution been developed using 2^n points instead of $n + 1$? Note that for five tosses of a coin we observe one of the digits 0, 1, 2, 3, 4, 5 as a result. There are $5 + 1 = 6$ results. Why are there also 2^n possible results?

b. If $n + 1$ points were used and $n = 10$, to what would the event $\{7\}$ or the point 7 refer?

c. If $p \neq q$ or, equivalently, $p \neq \frac{1}{2}$, explain why the binomial distribution is not primitive even when we consider all 2^n points.

2. In these typical problems, state an H_0 and an H_1. Determine whether a "one-tailed" or "two-tailed" test is implied, and state why one or the other should be used. Test the hypotheses.

a. It is believed that the religious composition of a city is changing from being 40 percent Catholic. A random sample of 100 has 30 Catholics. Examine these data using the procedure outlined above.

b. Another random sample shows 20 percent of the 40 male Protestants are unskilled whereas 6 percent of the general labor force is unskilled. Use H_0: "Protestants tend to be over-represented in the unskilled labor force compared to the general population," to analyze the data given. Does H_0 mean Protestants are under-represented in the skilled occupations? No! Why?

c. Voting can be visualized as a binomial situation. In an election each of the 1000 electors votes for one of two candidates. If p is considered at .51, .52, and .55, respectively, for party x, what are the respective probabilities that party y will win when for some reason a binomial model applies?

d. Expanding on the voting model, assume 45 percent of the voters are totally committed to each party, then only 10 percent remain to vote "randomly." Assume chance factors act on these voters so that each person has a given p value for the random decision to vote for x or against y. Use the p values .51, .55, and .60 to determine the three probabilities of y winning.

e. If the voting population is 10,000, how is the probability of y winning affected compared to having only 1000 electors (in part c). Why?

3. A model for inmarriage can be expressed in terms of a binomial model. Assume each groom has an available bride population. Also assume all brides of every ethnic group are "equally available" to all grooms and that the population is large enough so that a model with replacement can be used, rather than the hypergeometric model presented in Chapter 8.*

a. Each groom has an available bride population with n persons, k of those being of his ethnic (religious, social

* Beaman and Versloot presented a paper on these methods to the Rural Sociological Society in Miami, 1966. Geographical, religious-ethnic group interactions, and other factors may be taken into account very easily.

status, or another variable could be used) group. Use the binomial model with $k/n = .45\,k$ to calculate the probability of 60 percent inmarriage or more when the ratio $k/n = .45$ means the bride population is 45 percent British.

(1) Ten marriages are observed. *Hint:* What is the probability of six or more *E*s, given $p = .45$?

(2) One hundred marriages are observed.

(3) One thousand marriages are observed.

b. Assume in the above that the samples resulted in 6, 60, and 600 inmarriages.

(1) State reasonable hypotheses H_0, implying the number of inmarriages observed could have occurred by chance. Indicate acceptance or rejection of the H_0.

(2) The ratios 6/10, 60/100, and 600/1000 are equal. If H_0 is the ratio $k/n = .45$, why is H_0 accepted for 6/10, rejected for 600/1000, while its acceptance is very dependent on the significance level for 60/100?

(3) What does accepting H_0 imply in the above cases?

4. A psychology student announces that he can select people who are or will be upwardly mobile. He does this by examining photographs of their head and shoulders. According to his theory, one person in 10 will meet his criteria. To test his ability, one person in a sample should meet his criteria.

a. How big must a sample be to ensure this at the 5 percent level?

b. In a nontrivial vein, use the following proportions to determine the sample size needed to be 97 percent sure that at least one person in the implied category will be present in a random sample.

(1) Unskilled workers are 6 percent of the labor force.

(2) Two percent of the people aged 35 to 40 will die in a given year.

(3) A city has a suicide rate of three per 1000 per year.

CHAPTER 10

OCCUPANCY NUMBERS AND THE SPACE FOR UNORDERED SAMPLES TAKEN WITH REPLACEMENT

IN CHAPTER 5 we considered the space for independent samples, as exemplified by ordered samples taken with replacement. In this chapter we shall consider the space for *unordered* samples taken with replacement. As a preliminary approach, let us investigate the following prototypical problem.

10.1 OCCUPANCY NUMBERS

If a sample of size $r = 12$ is drawn *with replacement* from the five-element population *a*, *b*, *c*, *d*, and *e*, what is the probability it will contain four *a*s, three *d*s, and five *e*s in *any order*?

We shall approach our solution to this particular problem with the primitive sample space; that is, the space for *ordered* samples taken with replacement. It is assumed in this model that *unordered* sample points are compound points that are composed of the various arrangements (ordered points) that qualify as occurrences of them and hence that the *primitive* space will be the space of all distinguishable ordered points. The size of the space for all possible *ordered* samples taken with replacement is, it will be recalled,

$S = n^r$, which, in this case, means $S = 5^{12}$. To find the requisite probability, then, it remains only to determine the size of the subset of that sample space that consists of points meeting the condition: contains four *a*s, three *d*s, and five *e*s in any order.

We can redefine our problem in terms of the ball-and-cell model. By Theorem 5.6.1, the 12 balls may be partitioned into three distinct subpopulations of sizes 4, 2, and 5 to occupy cells *a*, *d*, and *e*, respectively, in

$$\frac{12!}{4!3!5!} = \mathscr{E} \quad \text{ways}$$

Hence

$$P[4a, 3d, 5e] = \frac{12!}{4!3!5!} \cdot 5^{-12}$$

We may represent the ball-and-cell model for the compound space of unordered points by assigning indistinguishable balls, as follows:

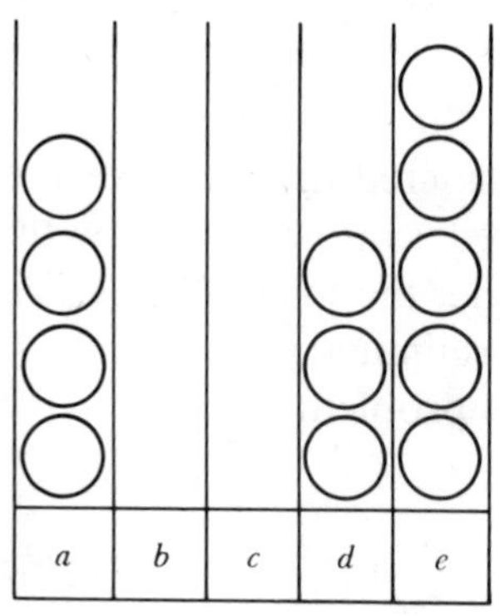

Because there is in this case no necessity to distinguish the balls, we can convey the same information by replacing the balls with integers representing their numbers, as follows:

4	0	0	3	5
a	*b*	*c*	*d*	*e*

Numbers assigned in this fashion are called *occupancy* numbers. Note that where no balls occur an occupancy number of zero is assigned. We can see from our initial problem that the number of points in the primitive sample space where this ball-and-cell model is used is equal to the factorial of the sum of the occupancy numbers (equals number of trials) divided by the product of their factorials; that is,

$$\frac{(4 + 0 + 0 + 3 + 5)!}{4!0!0!3!5!} = \frac{12!}{4!3!5!}$$

If we represent the occupancy numbers as r_i, we may depict a generalized model of a sample point for unordered samples taken with replacement as*

r_1	r_2	r_3	• • •	$r_{\nu-1}$	r_ν
A_1	A_2	A_3	• • •	$A_{\nu-1}$	A_ν

By the application of Theorem 5.6.1, the distinguishable balls (ordered trials) may be partitioned into ordered subpopulations of sizes $r_1, r_2, \ldots, r_v$ to occupy cells $A_1, A_2, \ldots, A_v$ in

$$\mathscr{E} = \frac{\left(\sum_{i=1}^{v} r_i\right)!}{\prod_{i=1}^{v} r_i!} \quad \text{ways}$$

This formula applies only to the primitive sample space, which, it will be recalled, is defined as a uniform space. This further implies that a ball is as likely to fall into one cell as another. Where this equiprobability of the selection of elements does not hold but where, nevertheless, the probability for each element remains constant from trial to trial, we may use the multinomial model whose derivation is presented in the following section.

10.2 MULTINOMIAL TERMS

For conveniently compact notation, the following definitions are introduced.

* Note that the subscript here is used to identify not place in a trial sequence but rather the cell occupied.

DEFINITION 10.2.1. $[r_i E_i]_k$ is an *unordered* array of r_1 occurrences of event E_1, r_2 occurrences of event $E_2, \ldots, r_k$ occurrences of event E_k. For example,

$$[3E_1, 2E_2, 2E_3] = [E_1, E_1, E_1, E_2, E_2, E_3, E_3] = [r_i E_i]_3$$

such that $r_1 = 3$, $r_2 = 2$, and $r_3 = 2$.

DEFINITION 10.2.2. $(r_i E_i)_k$ is any specific *arbitrary order* of r_1 occurrences of event E_1, r_2 occurrences of $E_2, \ldots, r_k$ occurrences of event E_k. For example, one might stipulate "let $(r_i E_i)_3$ equal $(E_2, E_1, E_3, E_3, E_1, E_2)$," or one might merely say "let $(r_i E_i)_3$ represent some specific arbitrary order of three E_1s, two E_2s, and two E_3s."

We reiterate that E_i does not refer here to an occurrence on the ith trial but has another meaning in the context of the multinomial model. As with many other fields, a symbol has different meanings in different contexts.

THEOREM 10.2.1

$$P[[r_i E_i]_k] = \frac{\left(\sum_{i=1}^{k} r_i\right)!}{\prod_{i=1}^{k} r_i!} \prod_{i=1}^{k} p_i^{r_i}$$

where r_i is the number of occurrences of event E_i in N trials, $p_i = P[E_i]$ the *constant* single trial probability of E_i,

$$N = \sum_{i=1}^{k} r_i, \qquad \sum_{i=1}^{k} p_i = 1$$

and the E_i are independent events.

PROOF. From Theorem 4.6.1, we know that the probability of a sequence of independent events in some stipulated order is equal to the product of their respective probabilities; that is,

$$P[(E_1, E_2, \ldots, E_k)] = \prod_{i=1}^{k} P[E_i]$$

By the property of commutativity with respect to real numbers, any arbitrary order of occurrence of these events will have the same probability as any other arbitrary order. For convenience we shall choose the sequence corresponding to the order of magnitude of the *i*s. Hence

$$P[(r_i E_i)_k] = \left(\prod_{i=1}^{r_1} p_1\right)\left(\prod_{i=1}^{r_2} p_2\right)\cdots\left(\prod_{i=1}^{r_k} p_k\right)$$

$$= (p_1^{r_1})(p_2^{r_2})\cdots(p_k^{r_k}) = \prod_{i=1}^{k} p_i^{r_i}$$

But this is the probability of only one arbitrary order of occurrence of the events. *Any* arbitrary order will satisfy the condition $[r_i E_i]_k$. The number of such orders corresponds to the possible number of linear arrangements of $r_1 E_1$ elements, $r_2 E_2$ elements, $\ldots, r_k E_k$ elements. This is given by Theorem 6.3.2 as

$$\frac{\left(\sum_{i=1}^{k} r_i\right)!}{\prod_{i=1}^{k} r_i!} = \frac{N!}{r_1! r_2! \ldots r_k!}$$

Since the probability given each arbitrary order of the elements has the same value, we may, by applying Theorem 4.3.1, obtain the probability of their union as the product of that value and the number of such arbitrary orders. We obtain

$$P[[r_i E_i]_k] = \frac{N!}{r_1! r_2! \ldots r_k!}(p_1^{r_1})(p_2^{r_2})\ldots(p_k^{r_k})$$

and the theorem is proved.

To illustrate the concrete meaning of this multinomial term, suppose there is a population that is 20 percent Negro, 10 percent Oriental, and 70 percent Caucasian. If a random sample of size 15 is drawn with replacement and without respect to order, what is the probability it will contain exactly five Negroes, four Orientals and six Caucasians? Note that

$$p_1 + p_2 + p_3 = .2 + .1 + .7 = 1.0$$

From Theorem 10.2.1, with $r_1 E_1 = 5$ Negroes, $r_2 E_2 = 4$ Orientals, and $r_3E_3 = 6$ Caucasians we have

$$P[[r_iE_i]_3] = \frac{15!}{5!4!6!} \cdot (.2)^5(.1)^4(.7)^6$$
$$= 114{,}660\,(.00032)(.0001)(.117649)$$
$$= .00043$$

The computation of exact probabilities from multinomial terms does not have much practical application, (see Section 11.5, footnote) but the model itself is conceptually very important.

10.3 THE EVENT SETS FOR UNORDERED SAMPLES TAKEN WITH REPLACEMENT

A sample of size N is to be drawn *with* replacement and without regard to order from a population whose elements are evenly partitioned into k mutually exclusive and jointly exhaustive categories $E_1, E_2, E_3, \ldots, E_k$. The corresponding numbers of the elements appearing in the sample are designated $r_1, r_2, r_3, \ldots, r_k$. These r_i are occupancy numbers, because they may be used to represent the number of indistinguishable balls in each cell of a ball-and-cell model. Schematically we have

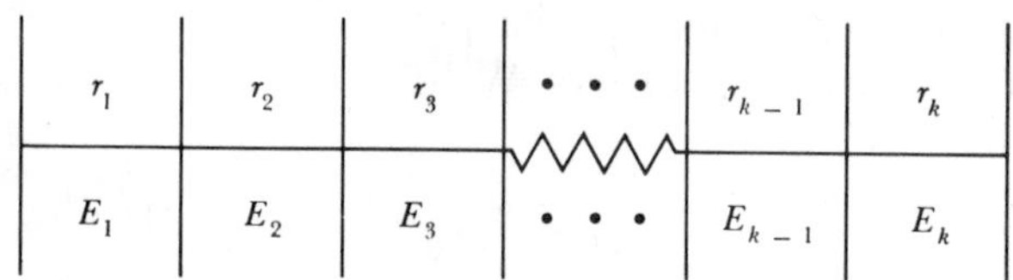

$r_i = 0$ is not excluded. Obviously,

$$N = \sum_{i=1}^{k} r_i$$

While N is a constant, the r_i are to be considered random variables whose values may vary from sample to sample. The samples are to be distinguishable by differences in the numbers of the various specified elements they contain, that is, by the cohorts of ordered occupancy numbers that characterize them. For instance, points *aaabbc* and *cababa* would both be represented as

3	2	1	0	0
a	*b*	*c*	*d*	*e*

and hence be indistinguishable. However, *bbbccd* would be a different point although it is represented with the same array of occupancy numbers, because the numbers are assigned to a different order of cells.

THEOREM 10.3.1. Given a population whose elements occur in equal proportions in k exclusive and exhaustive categories, E_i, $i = 1, 2, \ldots, k$, the number of distinguishable event sets that may be defined for an unordered sample of size N drawn *with* replacement is

$$\binom{k + N - 1}{N}$$

PROOF.* We may think of the group of k linearly arranged cells as consisting of two end walls and $k - 1$ separating walls ($k + 1$ walls), all represented as vertical lines. We may further think of the balls as occupying the cells in a horizontal line instead of in a stacked manner, allowing each cell to become as wide or as narrow as is necessary to accommodate the number of balls assigned to it, illustrated by

| | | O O O | O | | O O | | O O O O |

This example represents the ordered occupancy cohort 00310204. In general, we may now think of the balls and lines as a linear arrangement of two distinguishable types of elements: $k + 1$ wall elements and N ball elements. The two end walls must remain fixed, but if we calculate all possible linear arrangements of the remaining $k - 1$ walls and the N balls, we will have accounted for all possible ordered cohorts of occupancy numbers r_i. From Theorem 6.3.1, we know that the number of such arrangements of $(k - 1)$ elements of one sort and N of another is

$$\binom{(k - 1) + N}{k - 1} = \binom{k + N - 1}{N}$$

and the theorem is proved.

* This proof closely follows Feller's.

One should not jump to the conclusion that all the event sets defined on the sample space have the *theoretical* probability

$$\binom{k+N-1}{N}^{-1}$$

The events are, in fact, not uniformly probable in theory, because the greater the occurrence of repetitions of elements in the sample point the fewer the distinguishable arrangements of them, and hence the fewer the points in an event set that meet the condition.

For instance, the probability that a sample of size 6 drawn from a six-element population will contain four *a*s and two *b*s is

$$\frac{6!}{4!2!} \cdot 6^{-6} = \frac{15}{6^6}$$

The probability that it will contain one of each of the elements in the population is

$$\frac{6!}{6^6} = \frac{720}{6^6}$$

This second probability is 48 times greater than the first—an impressive difference.

In Table 10.3.1, we can see that only one point in the whole 125-point space meets the condition "contains three *a*s." Three points meet the condition "contains two *a*s and one *b*" and six points meet the condition "contains one *a*, one *b*, and one *c*." Each separate subset of ordered points in the table represents only a single event defined as "unordered samples containing specified numbers of specified elements." By inspection we see that these subsets of ordered points vary in size from 1 to 6 in this case, and there are 35 such subsets. Hence we see that 35 events with varying probabilities are defined on the sample space. Five of the events have probability $\frac{1}{125}$, 20 have probability $\frac{3}{125}$ and 10 have probability $\frac{6}{125}$. Thus

$$5\left(\frac{1}{125}\right) + 20\left(\frac{3}{125}\right) + 10\left(\frac{6}{125}\right) = 1$$

as we might expect.

TABLE 10.3.1 / A Partitioning of the Sample Points in Table 4.1.1 into Subsets of Points Containing the Same Elements in Different Orders

aaa	*bbb*	*ccc*	*ddd*	*eee*
aab	*bba*	*cca*	*dda*	*eea*
aba	*bab*	*cac*	*dad*	*eae*
baa	*abb*	*acc*	*add*	*aee*
aac	*bbc*	*ccb*	*ddb*	*eeb*
aca	*bcb*	*cbc*	*dbd*	*ebe*
caa	*cbb*	*bcc*	*bdd*	*bee*
aad	*bbd*	*ccd*	*ddc*	*eec*
ada	*bdb*	*cdc*	*dcd*	*ece*
daa	*dbb*	*dcc*	*cdd*	*cee*
aae	*bbe*	*cce*	*dde*	*eed*
aea	*beb*	*cec*	*ded*	*ede*
eaa	*ebb*	*ecc*	*edd*	*dee*
abc	*abd*	*abe*	*acd*	*ace*
acb	*adb*	*aeb*	*adc*	*aec*
bac	*bad*	*bae*	*cad*	*cae*
bca	*bda*	*bea*	*cda*	*cea*
cab	*dab*	*eab*	*dac*	*eac*
cba	*dba*	*eba*	*dca*	*eca*
ade	*bcd*	*bce*	*bde*	*cde*
aed	*bdc*	*bec*	*bed*	*ced*
dae	*cbd*	*cbe*	*dbe*	*dce*
dea	*cdb*	*ceb*	*deb*	*dec*
ead	*dbc*	*ebc*	*ebd*	*ecd*
eda	*dcb*	*ecb*	*edb*	*edc*

If we calculate the number of such compound events by the formula of Theorem 10.3.1, we get, from $k = 5$ and $N = 3$,

$$\binom{5+3-1}{3} = \binom{7}{3} = \frac{(7)_3}{3!} = 35$$

which agrees with our count.

Since the r_i are the numbers of the corresponding E_i elements in the sample, the probability of any of the specified events defined on the space is

$$P[[r_i E_i]_k] = \frac{N!}{r_1! r_2! \ldots r_k!} \cdot \left(\frac{1}{k}\right)^N$$

where

$$N = \sum_{i=1}^{k} r_i$$

For example,

$$P[2a, 1d] = \frac{3!}{2!1!}\left(\frac{1}{5}\right)^3 = \frac{3}{125}$$

as above. This formula is, of course, a special case of the multinomial term in which the p_i ($= 1/k$ for every i) can be gathered under a single exponent because they are all equal. That is,

$$\left(\frac{1}{k}\right)^{r_1}\left(\frac{1}{k}\right)^{r_2} \cdots \left(\frac{1}{k}\right)^{r_k} = \left(\frac{1}{k}\right)^N$$

The sampling situation discussed in this section should not be confused with the case in which only some of the r_i are specified. For example, the probability that an unordered sample of size 7 taken with replacement from a k-element population would contain exactly three *a*s and two *b*s would be

$$P[3a, 2b] = \frac{7!}{3!2!} \cdot (k - 5)^2 \cdot k^{-7}$$

Or if with reference to Table 10.3.1 we asked the probability that an event set would contain exactly two *a*s without specifying the remaining sample element, we can see by inspection that

$$P[2a] = \frac{12}{125}$$

whereas if we specify the remaining element as, say, b we get

$$P[2a, 1b] = \frac{3}{125}$$

We should also avoid confusing the cases in which the elements are specified from those in which only the occupancy numbers are specified, for example, the probability that the sample will contain one element of one sort, two of another, and three of another without specifying which elements they are to be. This case has already been discussed in Section 10.1.

One final caution: one must not reach conclusions about *empirical* probabilities from a priori models. The fact that the sampling specifications we have used do not lead to a uniform probability of

$$\binom{k+N-1}{N}^{-1}$$

does not justify the conclusion that empirical sample spaces could not have theoretically uniform probabilities of that form, indeed, empirical sample spaces fitting such a model actually exist, and they are referred to as Bose–Einstein statistics.*

10.4 THE COMPOSITION OF THE MULTINOMIAL SAMPLE SPACE

The binomial distribution is the special case of the multinomial distribution in which k (the number of exclusive categories) = 2. Obviously, in this case,

$$\sum_{i=1}^{k} p_i = \sum_{i=1}^{2} p_i = p_1 + p_2 = 1$$

hence $p_2 = 1 - p_1 = q$.

We recall that the binomial sample space contains $N + 1$ subsets of equiprobable points corresponding to each term in the distribution, and that the size of each such subset equals the binomial coefficient of the corresponding term. We further saw that the total sum of the elements in the subsets so defined was equal to the sum of the coefficients of all the terms, and that that sum is 2^N.

Highly analogous statements may be made about the composition of the multinomial sample space. For instance, we know that

* See Feller, *An Introduction to Probability Theory and Its Application*, *op. cit.*, pp. 38–40.

the number of equiprobable points for each term, each with probability

$$\prod_{i=1}^{k} p_i^{r_i}$$

is given by the corresponding multinomial coefficient of the term; that is,

$$\frac{\left(\sum_{i=1}^{k} r_i\right)!}{\prod_{i=1}^{k} r_i!} = \frac{N!}{r_1! r_2! \ldots r_k!}$$

The total of all of the points in these subsets would again in a highly analogous manner be equal to the sum of the multinomial coefficients for the whole distribution. It is easy to see that, for the binomial case, the number of terms in the distribution is $N + 1$, since the sum is

$$\sum_{x=0}^{N} \binom{N}{x} = \sum_{x=1}^{N+1} \binom{N}{x-1}$$

The number of terms in the multinomial distribution is not as obvious, but it may readily be determined. There will be as many terms in the distribution as there are distinct arrays of integral values that can be assigned to the r_i under the restriction that

$$\sum_{i=1}^{k} r_i = N, \quad r_i = 0 \quad \text{not excluded}$$

By direct application of Theorem 10.3.1, we know that all such possible cohorts of r_i may be formed in $\binom{k+N-1}{N}$ ways, hence that is the number of terms in the multinomial distribution. Each of these terms corresponds to a compound event, each of which has a probability of

$$\frac{N!}{\prod_{i=1}^{k} r_i!} \prod_{i=1}^{k} p_i^{r_i}$$

with each such event being at least partially decomposable into

$$\frac{N!}{\prod_{i=1}^{k} r_i!}$$

subevents each with probability

$$\prod_{i=1}^{k} p_i^{r_i}$$

As a test case, we know that the binomial has $N + 1$ terms. For the binomial, $k = 2$ and

$$\binom{k+N-1}{N} = \binom{2+N-1}{N} = \binom{N+1}{N} = \frac{(N+1)_N}{N!} = \frac{(N+1)!}{N!}$$

$$= N + 1$$

just as it should. Note that

$$(N + 1)_N = (N + 1)(N)(N - 1)\dots 2 = (N + 1)_{N+1} = (N + 1)!$$

because the last factor needed to complete the factorial is 1, which has no effect on the product.

At the risk of creating a notational monster, the total number of points in the subsets of equiprobable points may be represented compactly. If we order the cohorts of r_i in either an arbitrary or systematic way, the total number of points in the term subsets of equiprobable points is

$$\sum_{j=1}^{\binom{k+N-1}{N}} \frac{\left(\sum_{i=1}^{k} r_{ij}\right)!}{\prod_{i=1}^{k} r_{ij}!} = N! \sum_{j=1}^{\binom{k+N-1}{N}} \left(\prod_{i=1}^{k} r_{ij}!\right)^{-1}$$

where j identifies the jth cohort.

Again, if we test this model with the binomial case, we get

$$\sum_{j=1}^{N+1} \frac{N!}{\prod_{i=1}^{2} r_{ij}!} = \sum_{j=0}^{N} \frac{N!}{r_j!(N - r_j)!} = \sum_{j=0}^{N} \binom{N}{r_j}$$

The systematic order of r_j is that in which $r_0 = 0, r_1 = 1, \ldots, r_N = N$, or, in general, $r_j = j$. Hence we get

$$\sum_{j=0}^{N} \binom{N}{j} = 2^N$$

just as we anticipated.

We have already seen in Section 9.2 that the sum of the probabilities of the events in a binomial distribution meets the required condition of totaling 1. This is also true of the multinomial distribution. We have just seen that there is one compound event with probability

$$\frac{\left(\sum_{i=1}^{k} r_i\right)!}{\prod_{i=1}^{k} r_i!} \prod_{i=1}^{k} p_i^{r_i}$$

for each of the $\binom{k+N-1}{N}$ distinct unordered k-sized arrays of positive integral values the r_i can assume under the condition that

$$\sum_{i=1}^{k} r_i = N$$

Since these exhaust all possible outcomes of a set of exclusive events, the sum of their probabilities must equal 1 by Theorem 4.3.2, provided that a primitive space exists. By varying proportions of cells representing each event rather than assigning only one cell to an event, a primitive sample space can theoretically be constructed for any exhaustive set of events whose probabilities are rational numbers. This is essentially what we did for the binomial case in constructing Tables 9.6.1 and 9.6.2. Conversely, any exhaustive set of probabilities that are rational numbers implies the existence of a primitive sample space. Our conclusion is justified, then, for at least finite sample spaces as defined herein because the probabilities of their subsets are always rational numbers.

10.5 UNORDERED SAMPLES OF UNSPECIFIED ELEMENTS

We have already considered the specific problem of finding the probability that an unordered sample of size 12 would contain four *as*, three *d*s and five *e*s. We also noted that the 4, 3, and 5 may be thought of as occupancy numbers. Suppose we now asked the probability that a random sample of size 12 drawn from a common population contained four elements of one unspecified sort, three of a second sort, and five of still another sort. In this case, the condition would be met not only by $[5a, 3d, 4e]$ but also, for instance, by $[5b, 3c, 4a]$ or any other combination of three elements such that there were three of one, four of another, and five of still a third in any order whatever. In short, we have changed the problem to one concerned with the occurrence of the specified occupancy numbers without reference to the particular cells they happen to occupy. We would then be seeking $P[3, 4, 5]$ in this particular case.

A more general statement of the problem is: If an unordered sample of size n is randomly drawn from a population of v elements, what is the probability that it will contain r_1 unspecified elements of one sort, r_2 of another sort, r_3 of another, ..., and finally r_v of a final sort? Note that

$$\sum_{i=1}^{v} r_i = n$$

and that $r_i = 0$ is not excluded.

Again, we will operate with the primitive sample space in which $S = n^r$.

We have already seen in Section 10.1 that if the elements are specified, the ball-and-cell model represents the situation by an assignment of occupancy numbers to the appropriate cells and that the number of sample points qualifying as an occurrence is

$$\frac{\left(\sum_{i=1}^{v} r_i\right)!}{\prod_{i=1}^{v} r_i!}$$

This number is the same for any specified arrangement of the specified occupancy numbers. If we can find all possible distinguishable linear arrangements of those occupancy numbers among the v cells, we have a factor for determining the total number of sample points containing the specified numbers of unspecified elements. If every occupancy number were different, the number of such arrangements would be $v!$, but we do not need to be limited to this case.

The number of distinguishable arrangements of occupancy numbers among the cells, and hence the magnitude of our factor, will depend upon the proportions of repeated occupancy numbers. This may be shown more readily with a specific problem.

If an unordered sample of size $n = 24$ is drawn with replacement from the $v = 10$ element population $a, b, c, d, e, f, g, h, i$, and j, what is the probability that it will contain four elements of each of five sorts and two each of two other sorts? In other words, exactly seven of the 10 elements will be represented in the sample in the proportions 4:4:4:4:4:2:2.

One appropriate arbitrary order of occupancy numbers might be the following:

4	2	0	4	4	2	0	0	4	4
a	*b*	*c*	*d*	*e*	*f*	*g*	*h*	*i*	*j*

The number of primitive sample points containing four *a*s, two *b*s, no *c*s, four *d*s, and so on, would be

$$\frac{(4+2+0+4+4+2+0+0+4+4)!}{4!2!0!4!4!2!0!0!4!4!} = \frac{24!}{(4!)^5(2!)^2(0!)^3}$$

But any distinguishable order of the same occupancy numbers would also qualify as an occurrence. There are as many such orders as there are distinguishable arrangements of five 4s, two 2s, and three 0s; that is, five elements of one sort, two of another, and three of still a third. We know from Theorem 6.3.2 that this may be accomplished in $[(5 + 2 + 3)!]/5!2!3!$ different ways. Hence the answer to our problem is

$$P[4, 4, 4, 4, 4, 2, 2, 0, 0, 0] = \frac{24!}{(4!)^5(2!)^2(0!)^3} \cdot \frac{10!}{5!2!3!} \cdot 10^{-24}$$

It is not necessary to complete the arithmetic, but a thorough understanding of the solution and the reasoning by which it is derived is mandatory. By this method we shall obtain values for probabilities associated with χ^2. It does not seem profitable to develop a general notation for the second factor, but it will be noted that its numerator is the sum of the exponents of the factorials in the first factor and the denominator is the product of the factorials of those exponents.

PROBLEMS

1. Show the ball-and-cell models and give occupancy number diagrams for the following conditions:

a. When a sample of size 10 is drawn from housing in five conditions of good to very bad. The numbers in each category are 1, 3, 2, 2, 2, going from good to very bad.

b. When the following table gives a breakdown of use of the parks.

AGE GROUP	PARK USERS		PARK NONUSERS	
	MALES	FEMALES	MALES	FEMALES
Young	5	2	10	4
Old	3	4	5	2

c. When a study of 30 people interviewed indicates that 10 were in favor and 15 were against the views the interviewer expressed.

2. A large population has the following ethnic distribution:

	BRITISH	GERMAN	FRENCH	OTHER
% Population	50	30	10	10

Assume that a sample of size 10 is drawn and answer the following questions. (In this example, an n-tuple gives the numbers in each ethnic group in the order given by the table.)

a. What is the probability of (5, 3, 1, 1)?
b. What is the probability of (3, 5, 1, 1)?
c. Why do the answers of parts a and b differ?
d. If each group were 25 percent of the population, would the answers to parts a and b differ?
e. What are the probabilities of (4, 5, 0, 1) and (4, 5, 1, 0)? Why are the probabilities equal?
f. Use the binomial to determine the probability of at least one German.
g. How large a group must be drawn to be 99 percent certain of having at least one German?

3. The extension of the above leads to an interesting application of Boole's inequality.

a. How large a group must be drawn to be certain of at least one German and one "other"? *Hint:*

$$
\begin{aligned}
P[\text{1 German and 1 "other"}] = 1 &- P[\text{no German}] \\
&- P[\text{no "other"}] \\
&+ P[\text{no German and} \\
&\quad \text{no "other"}].
\end{aligned}
$$

b. How large a group must be drawn to be 99 percent certain of one German, one Frenchman, and one "other"? For a hint, see Chapter 11, Problem 4, and review Boole's inequality (Chapter 4). Use $P[x \text{ and } y \text{ and } z] \geq 1 - P[\text{not } x] - P[\text{not } y] - P[\text{not } z]$.
c. When each of four groups is 25 percent of a large population, how large a group must be drawn to be 99 percent certain one person from each of the four groups is drawn? Use the method illustrated above.

4. A population is made up of transients, movers, and stayers in the ratio 1/1/2. A sample of size 5 is drawn.

a. What is the probability that two to four movers will be drawn using a multinomial model?

b. Use the binomial distribution $p = 1/4$, $q = 3/4$ to determine the probability calculated above. Why does the answer to part a agree with the answer to this question?
c. What is the probability of no transients, but one or more stayers and one or more movers? Determine the set of simple events that constitute this event. Careful examination of the simple events will indicate that you can check your result using binomial probabilities.

5. A purchasing agent sees no a priori reason that a particular buyer should prefer one color of a certain cotton fabric to another. A test was performed with the following results:

	RED	YELLOW	BLUE	GREEN
Persons Purchasing Fabric	10	14	12	20

a. How probable is any point like the one in the above table?
b. How probable is the outcome that all numbers in the table are 14s?
c. Formulate an H_0 and H_1 in terms of the ideas in Section 10.5.
d. Suggest how a statistical test of H_0 might be performed. What is H_1 in this case?

CHAPTER 11

THE CHI-SQUARE STATISTIC

THE STATISTIC known as χ^2 (chi-square) may be defined in different ways. We shall develop this topic as we have the previous ones in a context of countable sample spaces that can be visualized in terms of concrete sampling procedures.

Chi-square has a general definition and actually has many distributional forms. Certain of these forms are under given conditions close to the χ^2 distribution tabulated in many texts. In this book it is not necessary to understand the definition of the tabulated χ^2 or to be able to prove certain approximations. A more pressing problem is to assess the statistical measures in terms of their stochastic meaning vis-à-vis the conditions of the substantive investigations. We shall envisage χ^2 largely as a measure of "goodness of fit" with a stochastic rationale that can be found in the multinomial distribution. Only in very simple cases could the practical difficulties of computing probabilities from the multinomial distribution itself be surmounted, owing to the volume of arithmetic involved, but it is still the appropriate conceptual model to use for sampling assumptions and the interpretation of results. The assumptions are virtually identical with those of the binomial which, as we have seen, is a special case of the multinomial. The alternative outcomes for any single trial must be exclusive and exhaustive, and the probability of every outcome must remain constant from trial to trial. It is not at all necessary that the probabilities of the outcomes of different trials be equal to each other, however. It will be helpful here to discuss trial-to-trial constancy within the framework of statistical independence, discussed in Section 4.6.

11.1 THE INDEPENDENCE OF TRIALS

In a discussion of events that may be classified by multiple attributes, it is desirable to introduce a notation capable of reflecting these relationships. Subscripts representing a nominal level of measurement should serve this purpose. For instance, the events that a respondent will be either a Catholic, Jew, Protestant, or "other" might be represented, respectively, as E_1, E_2, E_3, or E_4, and the symbol E_i would be the general representation of an event in which i would be a random variable in the category of religion that could assume the values 1, 2, 3, or 4. For more categories of classification we would add more subscripts. Thus j might stand for economic status, k, nationality, and so forth, and the general representation of an event classified by w categories of which v is the wth is $E_{ijk...v}$. We may additionally identify the order of the trial by the subscript L (for trial identifier) and denote the event and the trial identifier $E_{ijk...v,L}$.

Thus that might represent the fifth trial ($L = 5$) of the event that the element drawn is a white, Protestant, college-educated radio announcer. In this case, any numerical values associated with the other subscripts would identify subclasses of race, education, religion, and occupation.

We may depict the trial-to-trial independence of such an event as

$$P[E_{ijk...v,L} \mid E_{ijk...v,M}] = P[E_{ijk...v}] \quad \text{for all} \quad M \neq L$$

We may represent the required condition of exclusiveness as

$$E_{ijk...v} \cap E_{(ijk...v)'} = \phi$$

where the prime sign means "not." Used in conjunction with the parentheses, it implies that the two events belong to different categories if at least one of the subscripted values differs in any subcategory. If the prime were associated with *each* subscript, it would imply that the events differed in *every* category, which is far more restrictive than the condition we wish to represent, being only one of the $2^w - 1$ ways in which the two events could differ if there are w subscripts.*

11.2 χ^2 AS A MEASURE OF "GOODNESS OF FIT"

In application of the χ^2 measure, almost everything of importance can be demonstrated with its simplest cases and then extended to more complex situations with negligible additional knowledge. For that reason, one- and two-subscript variables corresponding to one or two dimensions of classification will suffice for most of our discussion.

Like the statistical models we have thus far presented, use of the χ^2 measure requires only a nominal level of measurement; that is, it may be used if the elements can be counted and unequivocally classified into exclusive categories. Unlike the previous models, however, it is much less restricted by this level of measurement, since the ease with which subcategories can be increased in any dimension permits a continuous measurement function to be subdivided into as many segments as needed for a feasible degree of precision. This feature also enables the model to handle quantitative and qualitative variables simultaneously. The value of such a feature for sociological research hardly needs to be stressed—particularly when the mildness of the required assumptions is considered. The potentialities of this model should become appreciated as our discussion evolves.

Suppose we wish to test the hypothesis that the composition of a population is 20 percent single, 50 percent married, 10 percent widowed, and 20 percent divorced. A sample of size 60 is taken with replacement, and it yields 6 single, 26 married, 10 widowed, and 18 divorced. In asking how good a "fit" the sample is, we are asking how close the observed frequencies are to the expected frequencies.

* For an example of a different event as we mean here, one could have $E_{ij'klm'\ldots v}$, where the differences occur only in the sense that $j' \neq j$ and $m' \neq m$. The conceptual apparatus for concluding that there are $2^w - 1$ possible differences of this sort should now be at the disposal of the reader. If he wishes to demonstrate it for himself, his task will be facilitated greatly by using the ball-and-cell model.

The population proportions are evidently the probabilities under the null hypothesis. Partitioning the sample into these proportions will give us the "expected" sample frequencies. The sum of the elements in the partitions will, of course, give us the sample size again. That is,

$$\sum_{i=1}^{k} Np_i = .2(60) + .5(60) + .1(60) + .2(60)$$

$$= 12 + 30 + 6 + 12 = 60$$

We may thus compare the observed with the expected values as follows:

	S	M	W	D	TOTALS
Observed (r_i)	6	26	10	18	60
Expected (Np_i)	12	30	6	12	60

We can assess the fit by some measure that takes account of the differences between the observed and expected values. A widely used measure is χ^2 defined as

$$\chi^2 = \sum_{i=1}^{k} \frac{(r_i - Np_i)^2}{Np_i}$$

where r_i is the observed frequency, Np_i is the expected frequency, and k is the number of categories. In the above illustration, we get

$$\chi^2 = \frac{(6-12)^2}{12} + \frac{(26-30)^2}{30} + \frac{(10-6)^2}{6} + \frac{(18-12)^2}{12}$$

$$= \frac{6^2}{12} + \frac{4^2}{30} + \frac{4^2}{6} + \frac{6^2}{12} = 9.2$$

It is obvious that for any specified number of terms the larger the value of χ^2 the poorer the fit, and that a perfect fit would yield $\chi^2 = 0$. A perfect fit would occur if every observed value exactly equaled its expected value; in this case, we would have a string of terms with numerators of 0 divided by the expected frequency. To help us decide the point at which we define the fit to be good or bad, we use the probability that a fit just as bad or worse would occur; that is, we define a region of rejection consisting of all values of χ^2 as large or larger than some specified value, which means on the right tail of the distribution. Tables giving approximate values of χ^2 corresponding to commonly used confidence levels (αs) are commonplace. In using such tables, however, one must take account of k, the number of categories, since more categories would mean more terms and could yield a large value of χ^2 even if the fit were very good. To allow for this fact, the χ^2 tables provide separate listings of critical values according to the number of *degrees of freedom*, commonly abbreviated "df." This term refers to the number of categories that can vary in size before the remaining ones are arithmetically determinate or fixed. For instance, in the above sample of 60, after one has set the number of single at 12, the number of married at 30, and the number of widowed at 3, the only value the remaining category of "divorced" can assume is $60 - (12 + 30 + 6) = 12$. Thus the number of degrees of freedom is 3, the number of terms inside the parentheses,

Suppose we wish now to test our null hypothesis,

$$H_0: p_1 = .20, \qquad p_2 = .50, \quad p_3 = .10, \quad \text{and} \quad p_4 = .20$$

If we are willing to take a 5 percent risk of rejecting H_0 even if it should be true, we would set $\alpha = .05$. Turning to the table of Appendix A,* we find in the row for df = 3 the value of χ^2 associated with $\alpha = .05$ to be 7.815. This means that if H_0 is true, a sample with a value of $\chi^2 = 7.815$ or larger would occur only five times in every 100 such investigations, on the average. In other words, the region of rejection consists of all values of $\chi^2 \geq 7.815$. Since our observed value is $\chi^2 = 9.2 > 7.815 = \chi^2_{\alpha=.05}$, it is a "rare event" and we therefore reject H_0.

Our substantive conclusion is that we do not have an acceptable "fit." It is unlikely that our sample would have been drawn from a population with the composition specified in H_0.

After we have derived a computationally convenient identity, we shall take a closer look at the meaning of "the probabilities associated with χ^2."

11.3 A THEOREM ON THE χ^2 IDENTITY

Computation of the value of the observed χ^2 may be shortened considerably by use of the identity derived in the following theorem. The economy of effort that it permits should compensate for any

* In the appendix table the notation for df is n.

diversionary effect it might have at this point.* Given:

N = the size of a sample drawn with replacement and without regard to order

k = the size of a set of mutually exclusive and jointly exhaustive categories E_i into which the elements of a population may be classified

$p_i = P[E_i]$, the single-trial probability of event E_i

r_i = the number of occurrences of E_i in the sample

Note that

$$\sum_{i=1}^{k} r_i = N, \qquad \sum_{i=1}^{k} p_i = 1$$

and Np_i is the expected frequency of E_i for the sample.

THEOREM 11.3.1

$$\chi^2_{(\text{exact})} = \left(\sum_{i=1}^{k} \frac{r_i^2}{Np_i}\right) - N$$

PROOF. By definition,

$$\begin{aligned}
\chi^2_{(\text{exact})} &= \sum_{i=1}^{k} \frac{(r_i - Np_i)^2}{Np_i} \\
&= \sum_{i=1}^{k} \frac{r_i^2 - 2r_iNp_i + (Np_i)^2}{Np_i} \\
&= \sum_{i=1}^{k} \frac{r_i^2}{Np_i} - 2\sum_{i=1}^{k} r_i + N\sum_{i=1}^{k} p_i \\
&= \sum_{i=1}^{k} \frac{r_i^2}{Np_i} - 2N + N(1) \\
&= \left(\sum_{i=1}^{k} \frac{r_i^2}{Np_i}\right) - N
\end{aligned}$$

and the theorem is proved.

* In computer applications the use of this identity may not be advantageous because of problems of floating-point precision in the case of a large number of categories. In this case, the preferable basic form may be

$$\sum_{i=1}^{k} \left[\frac{(r_i - Np_i)^2}{Np_i}\right]$$

11.4 THE PROBABILITIES ASSOCIATED WITH THE χ^2 MEASURE

Chi-square is a measure with which a probability is associated and, as such, is a *random variable.* We shall illustrate the nature of this association by constructing a table of values based on a simple experiment—the random distribution of six indistinguishable balls among three cells. On any given trial the probability for each cell is $p = \frac{1}{3}$, and hence its expectancy is $Np = 6 \cdot (\frac{1}{3}) = 2$. Uniform probabilities occasionally occur in, but would not typify, χ^2 applications; this assumption leads to results that will require special comment. The restriction in any case simplifies the computations and the construction of the table, and we shall dispense with it after it has served this purpose.

For our experiment, the occupancy numbers r_i will be allowed to assume integral values from 0 through 6 under the restriction that for any set of them

$$\sum_{i=1}^{3} r_i = 6$$

Owing to the fact that the expected values are uniform ($Np_i = 2$, for every i), any array of three occupancy numbers will yield the same value of χ^2 regardless of the order in which they occupy the cells. They will also, for the same reason, yield the same associated probabilities. In other words, except where the values of r_i also happen to be uniform, the value of χ^2 is a compound event; this would not be the case in the typical application.

Let us for illustrative purposes compute the χ^2 and its associated probability for the following configuration of balls.

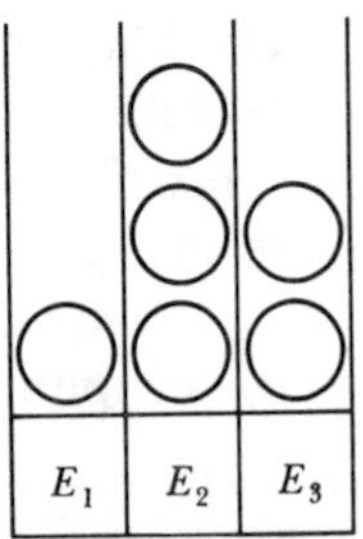

This gives us the ordered occupancy numbers $r_1 = 1$, $r_2 = 3$, $r_3 = 2$.

$$\chi^2 = \left(\sum_{i=1}^{k} \frac{r_i^2}{Np_i}\right) - N = \left(\sum_{i=1}^{3} \frac{r_i^2}{2}\right) - 6$$
$$= \tfrac{1}{2}(1^2 + 3^2 + 2^2) - 6 = 7 - 6 = 1$$

Owing to commutativity of addition, the same occupancy numbers in any order would yield the same value of χ^2. Three different occupancy numbers can be arranged in $3! = 6$ different ways, so there are at least six points in the space of unordered samples with this same value of χ^2.*

The associated probability may be obtained by the method discussed in Section 10.5. Subpopulations of balls of sizes 1, 3, and 2 may be selected to occupy the cells in a specified order in $6!/(1!3!2!)$ ways. But, as we have just observed, any order of these occupancy numbers will be associated with $\chi^2 = 1$. Three distinct occupancy numbers can be ordered in 3! ways. The size of the primitive sample space is 3^6. Since we do not know a priori whether other possible arrays of occupancy numbers will also yield $\chi^2 = 1$, we will cautiously express our results as

$$P[\chi^2 = 1] \geq 3!\frac{6!}{1!3!2!}3^{-6}$$

although it happens in this case that we could in fact omit the inequality sign.

One should now be able to understand the construction of Table 11.4.1. All of the calculations except the values of χ^2 are included in the table itself.

Although the scope of this table is too restricted for most practical uses, an illustrative application should be instructive. As suggested at the beginning of the chapter, the commonly published values of χ^2 are accurate for the definition for which they are given. They are, in fact, a very good approximation for the χ^2 we are using, if expected cell frequencies are mostly 8 to 10 or greater. If even 25 percent of the expected cell frequencies are under 4 to 6, and no expected frequencies are zero, the published tables still give an

* The implicit sample space is nonuniform because some arrays of occupancy numbers contain repetitions of elements, for example, 3, 3, 0.

TABLE 11.4.1 / Probabilities Associated with Chi-Square for the Random Distribution of Six Balls Among Three Cells

OCCUPANCY NUMBERS	EXACT	POINT PROBABILITY	CUMULATIVE PROBABILITY
r_1, r_2, r_3	χ^2	$P[r_1, r_2, r_3]$	$P[\chi^2 \geq \chi^2_{(\text{exact})}]$
2, 2, 2	0	$\frac{6!}{2!2!2!} \cdot \frac{3!}{3!} \cdot 3^{-6} = .1234$	1.0000
3, 2, 1	1	$\frac{6!}{3!2!1!} \cdot 3! \cdot 3^{-6} = .4938$	.8766
3, 3, 0	3	$\frac{6!}{3!3!0!} \cdot \frac{3!}{2!} \cdot 3^{-6} = .0823$	.3828
4, 1, 1	3	$\frac{6!}{4!1!1!} \cdot \frac{3!}{2!} \cdot 3^{-6} = .1235$	
4, 2, 0	4	$\frac{6!}{4!2!0!} \cdot 3! \cdot 3^{-6} = .1235$	.1770
5, 1, 0	7	$\frac{6!}{5!1!0!} \cdot 3! \cdot 3^{-6} = .0494$	.0535
6, 0, 0	12	$\frac{6!}{6!0!0!} \cdot \frac{3!}{2!} \cdot 3^{-6} = .0041$	.0041

approximation that is quite good. Where these conditions are not met, it is sometimes feasible to make a table of exact values to fit a particular investigation.

In an experiment in small group dynamics it was desired to ascertain for a three-member experimental group whether the factor of personal dominance might be exerting a consistent effect on their collective responses and hence constitute an intrusive biasing factor on the observations. Six situations were observed in which the personal dominance of one or another member of the group clearly influenced its reactions. On these six occasions, A was dominant once, B not at all, and C five times. If $\alpha = .05$, should the hypothesis that the factor of personal dominance is uniformly distributed among the three subjects be rejected? Since Table 11.4.1 provides the atypical service of supplying the values of χ^2 from the occupancy numbers, we do not need to recalculate it here. For occupancy numbers 5, 1, 0, we see that $\chi^2 = 7$ and that it has a cumulative probability of .05 (rounded). This means that under the null hypothesis the observed pattern of dominance would be a rare event, and we conclude that uniformity of the subjects with respect to dominance may not be assumed.

11.5 χ^2 AND THE MULTINOMIAL MODEL

The exact probabilities for Table 11.4.1 could have been found from the multinomial distribution also. For instance, to find the probability for occupancy numbers 3, 2, 1, we would have

$$P[3E_1, 2E_2, 1E_3] = \frac{6!}{3!2!1!}\left(\frac{1}{3}\right)^3\left(\frac{1}{3}\right)^2\left(\frac{1}{3}\right)^1 = \frac{6 \cdot 5 \cdot 4}{2} \cdot \frac{1}{3^6}$$

But *all* orders of the r_i have to be considered; for example,

$$P[1E_1, 3E_2, 2E_3] = \frac{6!}{1!3!2!}\left(\frac{1}{3}\right)^1\left(\frac{1}{3}\right)^3\left(\frac{1}{3}\right)^2$$

In this case, since the p_is are all equal, the χ^2s for each group order would be equal to each other and their respective probabilities would be equal to each other. Therefore we can assign the r_is to the E_is in all possible orders ($= 3!$) and get

$$P[r_1, r_2, r_3] = P[1, 2, 3] = 3! \cdot \frac{6 \cdot 5 \cdot 4}{2} \cdot \frac{1}{3^6} = .4938$$

which agrees with the tabulated result where

$$[r_1, r_2, r_3] = [3, 2, 1]$$

If the p_is were not equal, then, in general, the χ^2 values for each arrangement of occupancy numbers would not be equal and neither would the probabilities corresponding to the occupancy numbers, because different assignments of the r_i as exponents would attach them to different p_is as bases, affecting both the $(r_i - Np_i)^2$ and the $p_i^{r_i}$.

This can readily be seen by comparing the following two cases:

I. $(.2)^1(.5)^2(.3)^3 = .00135$
II. $(.2)^3(.5)^1(.3)^2 = .00036$

Thus I $\neq$ II even though the p_is are identical sets and the r_is are identical sets in the two cases. Remembering that

$$\chi^2_{(\text{exact})} = \sum_{i=1}^{k} \frac{r_i^2}{Np_i} - N$$

we get

$$\chi^2_{\text{I}} = \frac{1^2}{6(.2)} + \frac{2^2}{6(.5)} + \frac{3^2}{6(.3)} - 6 = 1.16667$$

$$\chi^2_{\text{II}} = \frac{3^2}{6(.2)} + \frac{1^2}{6(.5)} + \frac{2^2}{6(.3)} - 6 = 4.0555$$

Hence $\chi^2_{\text{I}} \neq \chi^2_{\text{II}}$.

The multinomial distribution would rescue us, then, from the restriction of uniform probabilities, but its direct use, much beyond the binomial case, would require an extraordinary amount of computation.* It is therefore fortunate that the published values of

---

* The large number of calculations that would be required for the number of arrangements of the r_i that even a relatively small value of k would entail, further compounded by the requirement of cumulative frequencies, possibly hastened the discovery of the χ^2 function from which the popular published tables are calculated. Consider the problem of finding the distribution for a sample of size N drawn with replacement from a population containing k categories of elements. We want $P[r_i]$, when

$$\sum_{i=1}^{k} r_i = N \quad \text{and} \quad \sum_{i=1}^{k} p_i = 1$$

The multinomial model is

$$P[[r_i E_i]_k] = \frac{\left(\sum_{i=1}^{k} r_i\right)!}{\prod_{i=1}^{k} r_i!} \cdot \prod_{i=1}^{k} p_i^{r_i}$$

To find $P[(r_i E_i)_k]$ would require $k!$ calculations of

$$\prod_{i=1}^{k} p_i^{r_i}$$

to allow for all possible assignments of the r_i to the p_i, although the multinomial coefficient would remain constant. $k!$ calculations of χ^2 would also be required.

In addition, finding the cumulatives would require repeating the above for all k-dimensioned groups of nonnegative integers r_i such that

$$\sum_{i=1}^{k} r_i = N$$

where N is the sample size. The number of such groups would be $\binom{k+N-1}{N} = \binom{k+N-1}{k-1}$ by Theorem 10.3.1. This represents all distinct k-element arrays of occupancy numbers whose sum equals N. Hence the number of calculations for the cumulative values for $P[(r_i E_i)_k]$ is $k!\binom{k+N-1}{N}$ for the probabilities and an identical number for the values of the corresponding χ^2s.

Thus for the very modest values $k = 4$ and $N = 12$, we get

$$4!\binom{4+12-1}{12} = 4!\binom{15}{12} = 4!\binom{15}{3} = \frac{24 \cdot 15 \cdot 14 \cdot 13}{3!}$$

$$= 4 \cdot 15 \cdot 14 \cdot 13 = 10{,}920 \text{ calculations each}$$

for the probabilities and the χ^2s, not to mention the labor of laying out the arrangements for calculation.

probabilities associated with χ^2 serve as excellent approximations for other distributions associated with χ^2. The multinomial model, on the other hand, is very useful for interpretive conceptualization of a number of research applications.

To this end, a further discussion of our ball-and-cell experiment may be in order. We know from Chapter 5 that the random distribution of six indistinguishable balls among three distinguishable cells is exactly equivalent to drawing an unordered sample of size 6 with replacement (obviously) from a population of three elements. From this we may correctly infer that valid use of the χ^2 distribution presupposes that the samples have been taken *with* replacement or at least from such a large population that the probability of drawing the same element twice would be negligible anyway, so that the trials are to all intents and purposes independent. To this extent, the model and Table 11.4.1, which was constructed from it, are useful aids to understanding. As was previously suggested, however, we must be cautious of overinference from the unique situation arising from the uniform trial probabilities. These led to uniform expectancies, which in turn led to values of χ^2 associated with atypically large segments of the sample space. That is, all orders of the occupancy numbers were associated with a given value of χ^2, and consequently a given value of χ^2 was associated with the probability of one or another of those orders. This implies, however, that the *cells* are unordered.

For illustration, consider the example at the beginning of this chapter concerning the probability that a sample of size 60 would contain 6 single, 26 married, 10 widowed, and 18 divorced under the hypothesis of the expected frequencies. This is a typical χ^2 application. If our test were analogous to our illustrative table, however, we would have been finding the probability of 6 of one sort, 26 of another, 10 of another, and 18 of a final sort, so that, for instance, 18 single, 6 married, 26 widowed, and 10 divorced would have been as much of an occurrence as that actually observed. Our associated probability would have been much higher. In this case, however, while such a probability could logically be sought, it could not be associated with a single value of χ^2 but only with one or the other of 4! of them.

We repeat for emphasis that typical applications of χ^2 undertake to test for the fit of ordered cells (implying ordered occupancy numbers), although important exceptions exist.

11.6 AN APPLICATION OF THE χ^2 MEASURE

In Section 11.2, we used the χ^2 statistic to test the hypothesis that an observed sample had been drawn from a population of a specified composition. Presumably there was some theoretical basis for supposing that the population had such a composition, and this suggests an extremely important type of application of the χ^2 statistic—that is, the determination of whether observed results are consonant with those predicted by some theory.

Notice that, in contrast to the examples of application of other tests we have considered, acceptance of the null hypothesis in this case, rather than the rejection of it, lends credibility to the theory of primary interest. Hoel provides an example of this application in testing the theory of Mendelian inheritance.*

Application of Mendelian theory suggests that four types of specimens should occur in the ratio 9:3:3:1. A sample of $N = 240$ plants yielded 120, 40, 55, 25 in the four categories. At $\alpha = .01$, is the theory inconsistent with the observed results?

$$9 + 3 + 3 + 1 = 16$$

$$H_0\colon p_1 = \frac{9}{16}, p_2 = p_3 = \frac{3}{16}, p_4 = \frac{1}{16}$$

H_1: The p_i of the population are not as indicated

$$Np_1 = \frac{9}{16} \cdot 240 = 135$$

$$Np_2 = \frac{3}{16} \cdot 240 = 45$$

$$Np_3 = \frac{3}{16} \cdot 240 = 45$$

$$Np_4 = \frac{1}{16} \cdot 240 = 15$$

The total is $N = 240$.

* Adapted from Paul G. Hoel, *Introduction to Mathematical Statistics*, 2nd ed. (New York: John Wiley & Sons, Inc., 1947 and 1954), p. 163.

$$\chi^2 = \sum_{i=1}^{k} \frac{r_i^2}{Np_i} - N$$

$$= \frac{120^2}{135} + \frac{40^2}{45} + \frac{55^2}{45} + \frac{25^2}{15} - 240$$

$$= 106.7 + 35.5 + 67.2 + 41.7 - 240 = 11.1$$

With df $= 3$, $P[11.34 \leq \chi^2] = .01$.

Since $\chi_\alpha^2 = 11.34 \geq \chi^2 = 11.1$, we conclude that the observations do not discredit the theory.

In the applications of the χ^2 test most widely used in sociology at present, it is the rejection of H_0 that is anticipated; this indicates that the deviations of the observed from the expected frequencies are due not to "chance" but to an actual condition of dependence among factors being investigated. We proceed to a discussion of the model most popular among sociologists.

11.7 THE χ^2 CONTINGENCY TABLE

The χ^2 contingency table is unquestionably the most familiar application of the statistic. Many of its users are even unaware that the term "χ^2 test" has a broader denotation. The contingency table is, in any case, an extremely versatile and valuable instrument which paradoxically finds frequent inappropriate employment because of its simplicity and yet is often erroneously overlooked in favor of complex parametric models requiring highly questionable assumptions about the data.

The 2×2 χ^2 contingency table is similar in form to the Fisher exact table of the same dimensions, but the sampling assumptions and the methods of determining the probabilities are quite different in the two cases. Unlike the case of the Fisher test, use of the χ^2 contingency table assumes that the samples have been taken with independent trials, and it uses the χ^2 measure as a rational way of defining region of rejection in multidimensional space. This latter feature makes the extension of its size and dimensions a relatively simple matter—in marked contrast to the Fisher test.

The similarity with the Fisher table can be seen in the following 2×2 χ^2 table.

ROW CHARACTERISTIC	COLUMN CHARACTERISTIC B_1	B_2	MARGINAL TOTAL
A_1	$x(= r_{11})$	$k - x(= r_{12})$	$k(= \mu_1)$
A_2	$n - x(= r_{21})$	$N - n - k + x(= r_{22})$	$N - k(= \mu_2)$
Marginal total	$n(= \nu_1)$	$N - n(= \nu_2)$	N

The null hypothesis to be tested is that the row and column characteristics are independent. If the range of values of variable A is $\{A_1, A_2\}$ and of variable B is $\{B_1, B_2\}$, where

$$A_1 = \text{Upper income} \qquad B_1 = \text{Protestant}$$
$$A_2 = \text{Lower income} \qquad B_2 = \text{Non-Protestant}$$

then we might have

H_0: A and B are statistically independent
H_1: A and B are statistically dependent (that is, there is a tendency for income categories to vary with religious categories)

We may express the hypotheses in the notation of conditional probability as follows: Let x represent any of the N element selections in the total sample; then

$$H_0: P[x \in A_i \mid x \in B_j] = P[x \in A_i] \quad \text{for all } B_j \text{ and } A_i$$

$$H_1: P[x \in A_i \mid x \in B_j] \neq P[x \in A_i] \quad \text{for some } B_j \text{ and } A_i$$

One way of stating H_0 is that whatever causes an element to be assigned to its column category is independent of whatever causes it to be assigned to its row category. Testing the null hypothesis requires that appropriate expected frequencies be assigned to each cell.

Suppose that the individuals in a human population can be classified by certain broad categories, C_i, as exemplified by C_1 = ethnic identity, C_2 = sex, C_3 = religious background, C_4 = occupation. Suppose further that these categories can take on different values, such as:

CATEGORIES	POSSIBLE VALUES
C_1	10 (10 ethnic groups)
C_2	2 (male, female)
C_3	8 (8 denominations)
C_4	10 (10 occupation categories)

If we think of the C_i as sets and their values as their respective elements, we could generate a set of ordered 4-tuples representing every possible cross-classification as the set product,

$$C_1 \times C_2 \times C_3 \times C_4 = \prod_{i=1}^{4} C_i$$

of size

$$\prod_{i=1}^{4} n_i = 10 \times 2 \times 8 \times 10 = 1600 \quad \text{“cells”}$$

Each cell could be regarded as a four-element “vector” in an N space (where $N = 4$ dimensions, in this case), as, for example, if X_i represents any value (subcategory) of C_i, then one cell might be

$$(X_1, X_2, X_3, X_4) = (\text{Scotch, female, Presbyterian, factory worker})$$

Each such cell would have an occupancy number of r individuals,

$$0 \leq r \leq (\text{total number of individuals in the population})$$

With 1600 cells, something of the order of 10,000 or more individuals would have to be involved in order for meaningful statistical results to be obtained. In practice, then, it is generally not feasible to attempt to handle more than a few categories. Even a space to handle (C_1, C_2) would contain $10 \times 2 = 20$ cells.

To be able to work with arrays of cells of the type just discussed it is necessary to have a terminology to denote certain totals. For the present, we will discuss the two-dimensional case with newly defined C_i, but our definitions will be general enough for the N-dimensional case.

The following table illustrates a two-dimensional categorization with “marginal totals.”

TABLE 11.7.1

RELIGION (C_1)	ECONOMIC CLASS (C_2)			RELIGION
	LOWER	MIDDLE	UPPER	TOTALS
Catholic	30	33	12	75
Protestant	18	41	20	79
Jew	8	24	7	39
Other	5	11	6	22
Economic class totals	61	109	45	215

The number in each cell represents, of course, the number of observed cases out of the 215 total that belong to the cross-classification represented by that particular cell. For example, if values are assigned such that

$$(X_1, X_2) = (\text{Protestant, upper})$$

then the occupancy number is 20. It will be convenient to introduce a notation whereby n preceding an ordered tuple of categories will mean the number of elements in the cells defined by the tuple. Thus

$$n(\text{Protestant, upper}) = 20$$

An instruction to "sum out over," say, the religious categories could be abbreviated as

$$\text{Marginal totals for each economic class} = \text{total on } C_2 = \sum_{C_1} n(C_1, C_2)$$

This would therefore be an instruction to total the columns in Table 11.7.1. If we let r_{ij} be the occupancy number, where i means the ith category in C_1 and j means the jth category in C_2, then, for instance, $r_{11} = 30$, $r_{3,2} = 24$, and so forth. Hence

$$\text{Total on } C_2 = \sum_{C_1} n(C_1, C_2) = \sum_i r_{ij} \quad \text{for every } j$$

Thus it tells us to obtain the values for each element in a total vector as

$$\sum_i r_{ij} = \begin{cases} r_{11} + r_{21} + r_{31} + r_{41} = 30 + 18 + 8 + 5 = 61 = v_1, \\ r_{12} + r_{22} + r_{32} + r_{42} = 109 = v_2, \\ r_{13} + r_{23} + r_{33} + r_{43} = 45 = v_3 \end{cases}$$

Hence our total vector is $(v_1, v_2, v_3) = (61, 109, 45)$. Similarly,

$$\text{Total on } C_1 = \sum_{C_2} n(C_1, C_2)$$

would be obtained as $\sum_J r_{ij} =$

$$r_{11} + r_{12} + r_{13} = 75 = \mu_1,$$
$$r_{21} + r_{22} + r_{23} = 79 = \mu_2$$

and so forth.

In the three-dimensional case, the cells could be represented as cube-shaped subdivisions of a larger cube. In this case, if we let k be the kth subcategory of C_3, then

$$\text{Total on } C_1 = \sum_{C_2 C_3} n(C_1, C_2, C_3) = \sum_{jk} r_{ijk} \quad \text{for every } i$$

Moreover,

$$\text{Total on } C_1 \text{ and } C_2 = \sum_{C_3} n(C_1, C_2, C_3) = \sum_{k} r_{ijk} \quad \text{for every } (i, j)$$

The same notational systems extrapolate to higher dimensions, but geometric representation of the cells becomes impossible.

The hypothesis we will often wish to test is that certain characteristics occur independently of each other. This means we wish to see if a "product space model" is an acceptable model in terms of our observations. If the sample elements (cases) are assigned by some stochastic process to the cells, then each cell has some probability associated with it that can be thought of as either the single-trial probability that a randomly selected element will be assigned to it or as its "expected" proportion of elements if all of them are assigned. That probability will be some kind of resultant of the probabilities of the subcategories that define the cell. The characteristics C_i can be considered to have distributions $P[C_i = X_i]$, where X_i represents any specified value (subcategory) of C_i. Thus if the C_i are independent, then

$$P[C_1 = X_1, C_2 = X_2, \ldots, C_k = X_k] = \prod_{i=1}^{k} P[C_i = X_i]$$

That is, if the various categories are independent, then the probability for any cell will equal the product of the probabilities of the subcategories that define it.

However, if we don't know the probabilities, the problem becomes: how do we estimate them? In Section 8.3 we presented the maximum-likelihood method and saw that in a random sample the most likely estimate of the population proportions was the proportions observed in the total sample. The observed proportions can be calculated from the marginal totals.

Thus using the marginal distributions we can calculate the probability of a cell as

$$P[C_1 = X_1, C_2 = X_2, \ldots, C_k = X_k]$$

$$= P[X_1, X_2, \ldots, X_k] = \prod_{i=1}^{k} P[C_i = X_i]$$

If we let

τ_{x_i} = the number of element assignments to subcategory X_i

and if N draws are made, the expected number, n_e, of observations in this cell would be

$$n_e(X_1, X_2, \ldots, X_k) = N \cdot P[X_1] \cdot P[X_2] \cdot \ldots \cdot P[X_k]$$
$$= N \cdot \frac{\tau_{x_1}}{N} \cdot \frac{\tau_{x_2}}{N} \cdot \ldots \cdot \frac{\tau_{x_k}}{N}$$
$$= \frac{1}{N^{k-1}} \prod_{i=1}^{k} \tau_{x_i}$$

In the two-dimensional case, this gives

$$n_e(X_1, X_2) = \frac{(\tau_{x_1})(\tau_{x_2})}{N}$$

The fact that this formula is symmetrical reflects the notion of independence.

If we let the values that can be assumed by τ_{x_1} be $\mu_1, \mu_2, \ldots, \mu_n$, and those that can be assumed by τ_{x_2} be $\nu_1, \nu_2, \ldots, \nu_m$, we can represent a generalized two-dimensional contingency table as in Table 11.7.2. If

$$(\tau_{x_1}, \tau_{x_2}) = (\mu_i, \nu_j)$$

then the expected value, η_{ij}, for the cell in the ith row and the jth column is

$$\eta_{ij} = \frac{\mu_i \nu_j}{N}$$

Owing to the rectangular pattern of the cells, the expression for χ^2 in the general notation appears considerably more complicated than it actually is: the computation procedure, once the expected values have been established, is identical with that for the linear pattern; however, we will present it for reference.

$$\chi^2 = \frac{\sum_{i=1}^{n} \sum_{j=1}^{m} (\eta_{ij} - r_{ij})^2}{\eta_{ij}} = \left(\sum_{i=1}^{n} \sum_{j=1}^{m} \frac{r_{ij}^2}{\eta_{ij}} \right) - N$$

TABLE 11.7.2 / Generalized Two-Dimensional Contingency Table

DEPENDENT CHARACTERISTIC	INDEPENDENT CHARACTERISTIC I_1	$I_2 \cdots$	$I_j \cdots$	I_m	MARGINAL TOTAL
D_1	r_{11}	r_{12}	r_{1j}	r_{1m}	$\sum_{j=1}^{m} r_{1j} = \mu_1$
D_2	r_{21}	r_{22}	r_{2j}	r_{2m}	$\sum_{j=1}^{m} r_{2j} = \mu_2$
$\vdots$	$\vdots$	$\vdots$	$\vdots$	$\vdots$	$\vdots$
D_i	r_{i1}	r_{i2}	r_{ij}	r_{im}	$\sum_{j=1}^{m} r_{ij} = \mu_i$
$\vdots$	$\vdots$	$\vdots$	$\vdots$	$\vdots$	$\vdots$
D_n	r_{n1}	r_{n2}	r_{nj}	r_{nm}	$\sum_{j=1}^{m} r_{nj} = \mu_n$
Marginal total	$\sum_{i=1}^{n} r_{i1} = \nu_1$	$\sum_{i=1}^{n} r_{i2} \cdots = \nu_2$	$\sum_{i=1}^{n} r_{ij} \cdots = \nu_j$	$\sum_{i=1}^{n} r_{im} = \nu_m$	$\sum_{i=1}^{n} \sum_{j=1}^{m} r_{ij} = N$

This means we follow cell by cell the same procedures as for a linear arrangement of the cells—that is,

> χ^2 = the sum, diminished by N, of the ratios of the squares of each of the observed frequencies to their corresponding expected frequencies.

However, we must determine the number of degrees of freedom, df. As we have already seen, the number of cells in a table of k-dimensions will be the continued product

$$\prod_{i=1}^{k} n_i$$

where n_i is the number of subcategories in C_i. The number of cells is the "potential number of degrees of freedom." In getting the actual number it is necessary to diminish the potential number to account for the fact that the observations have been used in establishing the distributions of the characteristics. This is accomplished by using the formula

$$\text{df} = \prod_{i=1}^{k} (n_i - 1)$$

In the two-dimensional case for m subcategories of C_1 and n subcategories of C_2, there are $m \times n$ potential degrees of freedom. However, we only had to calculate $m - 1$ and $n - 1$ in each case and the remaining one was known. Thus we lost $(m - 1) + (n - 1)$ degrees of freedom. However, since the fact that there is a fixed number of cases results in a loss of one more degree of freedom, then

$$\begin{aligned} \text{df} &= m \times n - (m - 1) - (n - 1) - 1 \\ &= m \times n - m - n + 1 \\ &= (m - 1)(n - 1) \end{aligned}$$

We could also consider how many cells must be known, given the marginal totals, before all the others are known. This would give the same result.

As we have already indicated, χ^2, defined in terms of deviations of observed from expected cell frequencies, is sufficiently well approximated by the commonly available tables of probabilities associated with χ^2, provided one observes simple rules about minimum allowable expected frequencies for cells. One of the outstanding features of χ^2 as a statistical measure is its extraordinary flexibility. Regardless of whether one increases the number of categories in any or all dimensions or whether one increases the number of dimensions, the general computational procedures and the formulation of the statistical hypotheses remain essentially the same. χ^2 affords us the great convenience of having a one-dimensional parameter for determining whether an observation in an N-dimensional space is consistent with a given hypothesis. The general null hypothesis is that the C_i are independent. That is, given that X_i is a variable that can assume the value of any subcategory of C_i, then for any random observation x occurring in any of the N independent trials, we have

$$H_0\colon\ P[x \in X_i \mid x \in X_j] = P[x \in X_i] \quad \text{for all } X_j \text{ and } X_i$$

$$H_1\colon\ P[x \in X_i \mid x \in X_j] \neq P[x \in X_i] \quad \text{for some } X_j \text{ and } X_i$$

In more "substantive" language, H_0 implies that whatever determines the occurrence of each and every specified attribute of an observed datum operates independently of whatever determines the occurrence of each and every other specified attribute. It should be noted that the populations involved are populations of *attributes*; hence the "elements" are the attributes of such things as people rather than the things themselves. The greater the average deviations of the observed frequencies in the cells from the expected frequencies, the greater the basis for doubt as to the hypothesis that the C_i are independent, and the higher the numerical value of χ^2. Thus for any fixed number of degrees of freedom, a region of rejection with probability α may be defined. A value of χ^2 falling within the region of rejection implies that the distribution of the observations would be a rare event under the null hypothesis.

We may now turn to some examples. In any investigation the only statistical conclusion that may legitimately be drawn is that either the C_i are independent or they are not. This is mighty thin soup for the investigator for whom the field of statistics is instrumental rather than consummatory. We shall take some liberties that presuppose far more watertight experimental control and methodological justification than could feasibly be made explicit without creating confusing distraction from the matters that are of more central concern to this work. With this understood, we consciously sacrifice "statistical purity" for "motivation," in order to suggest possibilities for application.

11.8 APPLICATIONS OF THE χ^2 CONTINGENCY MODEL

One example of a straightforward application could be an investigator who wished to have a basis for assessing in connection with the "gored ox theory" (attitudes on public issues depend upon whose ox is being gored) whether the attitudes of U.S. residents toward the Vietnam war and their vulnerability to the consequences of that war are associated. Suppose he reasons that, if these two variables were found by investigation to be statistically independent, he would at least have a basis for discrediting the theory, and that if they were statistically dependent, the theory would merit further study. Is the evidence inconsistent with the "gored ox" hypothesis, if $\alpha = .02$?

	INVOLVEMENT CATEGORY		
POLICY FAVORED	ELIGIBLE OR CLOSE RELATIVE ELIGIBLE FOR MILITARY DRAFT	NOT ELIGIBLE AND NO CLOSE RELATIVE ELIGIBLE	MARGINAL TOTALS
Escalate	6	13	19
Negotiate	28	11	39
Withdraw	16	8	24
No response	8	10	18
Marginal totals	58	42	100

H_0: Policy preference is independent of personal involvement, that is $P[x \in \text{row } i \mid x \in \text{col } j] = P[x \in \text{row } i]$

H_1: Policy preference and personal involvement are dependent

It should be noted that the *substantive theory* in question is "directional" in the sense that one would expect that those who have the most to lose on account of involvement will be inclined to oppose the war, and those with the least to lose will show differentially greater enthusiasm for it.

Subjecting the above data to the χ^2 test will give only a limited amount of information for assessing the theory. It will enable one to determine whether the relevant variables are *statistically* independent or dependent. It cannot, however, discriminate between which, if either, of the variables is the independent variable and which the dependent variable if they should indeed prove to be statistically dependent. Furthermore, it cannot distinguish the nature of the function that would describe the general relationship of the variables. One would not even know from the test alone whether a finding of statistical dependence implied the diametric opposite of the theory, that is, those who stand to bear the brunt of the war favor it more than those who do not.

However, the interest in scientific investigations is seldom limited to statistical independence, and there has to be some theoretical reason for conducting an investigation in the first place. For instance, it would be rather naïve to be led by a finding of dependence to continue to investigate the theory if the actual pattern of the data implied the diametric opposite of the theory. The point is that no data should be mechanically analyzed by a statistical model before it has been given the necessary "eyeball" tests to see whether it makes sense to run the test in the first place. While such procedures might be methodological rather than statistical, our applied orientation justifies the inclusion of at least one example of the preliminary eyeballing procedures. Before applying the statistical test then, it might well be advisable to set up a table of percentages.

	PERCENTAGES FAVORING INDICATED POLICY					
	ELIGIBLE		NOT ELIGIBLE		MARGINAL TOTAL	
Escalate	10.3		31.0		19.0	
Negotiate	48.3	75.9	26.2	45.2	39.0	63.0
Withdraw	27.6		19.0		24.0	
No response	13.8		23.8		18.0	
Marginal total	100.0		100.0		100.0	

By comparing the cell percentages to the population percentages in the Marginal Total column, we may immediately assess the implications of the data taken at face value. The percentage of the Eligibles is the lesser in the Escalate category and the greater in the Withdraw category. Moreover, the cumulative Negotiate–Withdraw class is largest for the Eligible characteristic. All in all, the distribution of the data is consistent with the theory, and it therefore makes sense to test for dependence.

Our first step is to compute the expected frequencies, η_{ij}, for each cell.

$$\eta_{ij} = \frac{\mu_i \nu_j}{N}$$

EXPECTED FREQUENCIES

POLICY FAVORED	INVOLVEMENT CATEGORY ELIGIBLE	NOT ELIGIBLE
Escalate	$\frac{(58)(19)}{100} = 11.02$	$\frac{(42)(19)}{100} = 7.98$
Negotiate	$\frac{(58)(39)}{100} = 22.62$	$\frac{(42)(39)}{100} = 16.38$
Withdraw	$\frac{(58)(24)}{100} = 13.92$	$\frac{(42)(24)}{100} = 10.08$
No response	$\frac{(58)(18)}{100} = 10.44$	$\frac{(42)(18)}{100} = 7.56$
Total	58.00	42.00

$$\chi^2 = \sum_{i=1}^{4} \sum_{j=1}^{2} \frac{r_{ij}^2}{\eta_{ij}} - 100$$

$$= \left(\frac{6^2}{11.02} + \frac{13^2}{7.98} + \frac{28^2}{22.62} + \frac{11^2}{16.38} + \frac{16^2}{13.92} + \frac{8^2}{10.08} + \frac{8^2}{10.44} + \frac{10^2}{7.56} \right) - 100$$

$$= (3.27 + 21.18 + 34.66 + 7.39 + 18.39 + 6.35 + 6.13 + 13.23) - 100$$

$$= 10.6$$

Since there are four rows and two columns, we find the number of degrees of freedom to be

$$\text{df} = (4 - 1)(2 - 1) = (3) \cdot (1) = 3$$

From the table of values associated with χ^2 (Appendix A), we see that, for df $= 3$ and $\alpha = .02$, the region of rejection is defined by $9.84 \leq \chi^2$. Since $9.84 \leq 10.6 = \chi^2$, we reject H_0 and accept the conclusion that the categories are statistically dependent. Since the statistical evidence is not inconsistent with the theory (as would have been the case if H_0 were accepted), tentative acceptance of the theory pending further investigation is justified. In practice, scientific theories tend to be accepted when sufficiently variegated attempts to discredit them fail to do so. There is no absolute "critical test," statistical or otherwise, of an empirical theory.

A second example of an application of the χ^2 contingency model could involve a market research organization that wished to assure itself that the race of its interviewers did not bias the answers of the respondents. Suppose a sample of respondents was randomly assigned to the participating interviewers, who were instructed to ask an appropriate question calling for a "yes" or "no" answer, with the tabulated results as follows:

RACE OF INTERVIEWERS	ANSWERS TO QUESTIONS YES	NO	NO RESPONSE	MARGINAL TOTALS
Negro	21	4	10	35
Caucasian	63	15	14	92
Oriental	14	7	5	26
Marginal totals	98	26	29	153

Here the substantive direction of the dependence is that "race" is the independent category and "response" the category whose dependence is in question. There is no need to investigate the racial patterning of the responses, since the substantive hypothesis does not require it.

The reader should set $\alpha = .05$, state the null and alternative hypotheses, find χ^2, and render the correct decision.

Our problem can be categorized as "respondent bias toward the interviewer" to distinguish it from "interviewer bias" problems, in which the interviewer's manner of presenting the question biases the results. By making specific individuals the independent category, as suggested by the following form, interviewer bias can be assessed.

INTERVIEWER	ANSWER TO QUESTION YES	NO	NO RESPONSE	MARGINAL TOTALS
Tom Jones				
John Brown				
Joe Fink				
Smedley Whiffle				
Marginal totals				

H_0: $P[\text{Answer}_j \mid \text{Interviewer}_i] = P[\text{Answer}_j]$
H_1: The categories "interviewer" and "response" are dependent

If H_1 were accepted, the conclusion that the differential responses are affected by individual differences among the interviewers would not require a wildly intuitive leap.

We have previously mentioned the ability of the χ^2 model to handle continuous measurements to a required degree of precision in any or all of its dimensions. This is because the subcategories may easily be increased in any dimension. Thus for instance, if a study investigates culture-linked differences in precision of judgment with respect to the length of physical objects, and the range of differences covers 4 inches, one could, on the basis of the degree of discrimination needed, have four categories with 1-inch ranges, eight with $\frac{1}{2}$-inch ranges, or 16 with $\frac{1}{4}$-inch ranges, and so forth. We have already mentioned that this flexibility makes it possible to relate quantitative and qualitative variables in the same model—as implied by this example. Thus an experimental sample of Eskimo, Indian, and Caucasian children in an Alaskan school might be tested for different abilities to judge lengths of objects. There is also, however, another important type of application, in which only continuous or, in some cases, ordinal levels of measurement might be assessed.

For instance, if one has computed a correlation coefficient for two continuous measurements and finds it necessary to accept the null hypothesis of no correlation, he cannot properly infer that there is no dependence between the variables. He can only conclude that *if* any dependence exists it is described by some function other than the one implicit in the model he used. For instance, if the actual function relating the variables were a perfect semicircle, the *linear* correlation coefficient would be 0. When we consider that there are infinitely more functions than the one embodied in any particular parametric model, rejecting the null hypothesis does not tell us very much. The same data may be tested with a χ^2 contingency table, however, and a decision made as to whether there is *any* significant dependence among the variables, without specificity as to function. There are those who regard this lack of specificity as a weakness of the test, but it is sometimes possible to make an informed guess as to the function by inspecting the pattern of concentration of elements on the grid formed by the cells. In the example to follow one might surmise the relationship of the variables to be parabolic.

Example

An investigator computed the linear coefficient of correlation between wages and age for a group of semiskilled workers and found no significant correlation. He then classified each laborer by his age hextile and wage quartile, with the results tabulated below. Do these data sustain his original hunch that there is some determinate relationship between wages and age if he is willing to run a .001 risk of being wrong?

INCOME QUARTILE	AGE HEXTILE FROM YOUNGEST TO OLDEST I	II	III	IV	V	VI	TOTAL
4	1	1	9	2	1	1	15
3	2	7	0	5	1	0	15
2	6	1	1	1	5	1	15
1	1	1	0	2	3	8	15
Total	10	10	10	10	10	10	60

H_0: Age and wage level tend to vary independently of each other

H_1: Age and wage level are related (statistically dependent)

$$K = 24 = \text{number of cells}$$

$$p_i = \frac{1}{24}, \quad \text{for every } i$$

$$Np_i = \frac{60}{24} = 2.5, \quad \text{for every } i$$

$$\chi^2 = \sum_{i=1}^{K} \frac{r_i^2}{Np_i} - N = \sum_{i=1}^{24} \frac{r_i^2}{2.5} - 60$$

$$= \frac{1}{2.5} \sum_{i=1}^{24} r_i^2 - 60 = \frac{312}{2.5} - 60$$

$$= 124.8 - 60 = 64.8$$

$$P[37.697 \leq \chi^2] < .001$$

where

$$\text{df} = (5)(3) = 15$$

Hence

$$\chi^2_\alpha = 37.697 \leq 64.8 = \chi^2$$

Therefore conclude a dependency relationship between age and wage level. Substantive considerations enable us to surmise that "wages tend to depend on age."

It may be noted that an expected frequency of only 2.5 per cell does not meet the required standard for validity, but the formal procedure and rationale would be valid for a sample of sufficient size. Where cell frequencies are too low, decreasing the numbers of subcategories and hence increasing the density of cell occupancy will often rectify the situation.

11.9 χ^2 CONTINGENCY MODELS OF HIGHER DIMENSIONS

The rectangular contingency tables that have occupied our attention thus far are widely used, but higher dimension models incorporating three or more categories of characteristics are seldom employed. Such a model enables one to investigate dependence among multiple categories. In view of the extensive lip service that is paid to "multiple factors" in the social sciences, the infrequency with which this model is used suggests a general unawareness of its existence. While a visual geometric representation of the table beyond three dimensions is not feasible, practical extension of it to any number of dimensions that are likely to be wanted is accomplished with little difficulty. The only practical complication of consequence is that multivariate tabulations of the data are necessary because there are more intersections per cell, but computer programs to perform this task are becoming available. (See Appendix C.)

The three-dimensional table may be represented as a rectangular parallelepiped with cells as pictured in Figure 11.9.1. The categories are then arranged along three axes instead of just two. As in the previous section, the number of observed cases in any cell could be represented as r_{ijk}, where each subscript may assume the values of all subcategories of its corresponding class. Thus r_{213} would represent the number of observed elements in cell

$$(X_1, X_2, X_3) = (a_2, b_1, c_3)$$

If there are s_1 subcategories of a, s_2 of b and s_3 of c, then there would be $s_1 \times s_2 \times s_3$ cells, and the cell with the largest subscripts would be $(a_{s_1}, b_{s_2}, c_{s_3})$.

FIGURE 11.9.1 / Three-Dimensional χ^2 Contingency Table

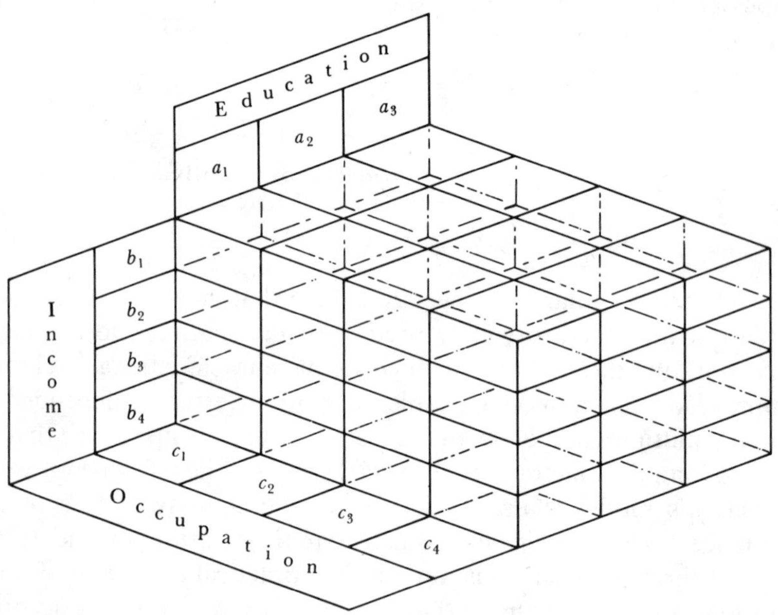

In higher dimensional cases, more methods of analysis become available. The sample equivalent of the two-dimensional case is the case where the assumption under H_0 is that all of the major categories C_i are independent. There are, of course, as many dimensions as there are such categories. For simpler exposition we shall concentrate our discussion largely on the three-dimensional case, but the extrapolation to higher dimensions is perfectly straightforward. The hypothesis for any number of dimensions, k, is as follows:

> The *expected* number of observations in a cell (that is, $\eta_{ijk\ldots v}$, where v may assume any of the values of C_k)* is determined by the probability that all characteristics will occur, given that each characteristic has its marginal distribution and the characteristics are independent. If $k = 3$ and there are N observations, as in Figure 11.9.1, then

$$\eta_{a_2 b_3 c_1} = N \times P[a_2] \times P[b_3] \times P[c_1]$$

$$= N \times \frac{\tau_{a_2}}{N} \times \frac{\tau_{b_3}}{N} \times \frac{\tau_{c_1}}{N} = \frac{\tau_{a_2} \times \tau_{b_3} \times \tau_{c_1}}{N^2}$$

This means the univariate tabulations for each variable and the trivariate tabulation for N must be obtained.

Suppose $n = 3$ dimensions, and each of the C_i contains two subcategories:

The range of variable X_1 in $C_1 = \{+, -\}$
The range of variable X_2 in $C_2 = \{0, 1\}$
The range of variable X_3 in $C_3 = \{\text{yes, no}\}$

The contingency table could then be visualized as a cube or other rectangular parallelepiped segmented into $2 \times 2 \times 2$, or eight cells. If we severed it—on a plane parallel to the plane defined by two of the axes—into two slices, each slice being one cell in width (as though we were halving a block), we might represent an observed distribution with tabulations of the cell occupancies, r_{ijk}, as in Table 11.9.2. Examples of how the marginal totals in this table were obtained would be

$$\tau_+ = 50 + 30 + 25 + 16 = 121$$

$$\tau_0 = 50 + 40 + 25 + 21 = 136$$

$$\tau_{\text{no}} = 25 + 21 + 16 + 9 = 71$$

* Note that the subscripts of η are cell (and hence value) identifiers, whereas the subscript of c is a category (or variable) identifier. Therefore do not confuse the k of c_k with the k in $\eta_{ijk\ldots v}$. The k subscript of η stands for any of the values c_3 can assume. If there are k categories, then the v subscript of η stands for any of the values c_k can assume.

TABLE 11.9.2 / A Three-Dimensional Distribution

X_3 = Yes

		X_1 +	X_1 −
X_2	0	50	40
	1	30	20

X_3 = No

		X_1 +	X_1 −
X_2	0	25	21
	1	16	9

Marginal Totals

	τ_+	τ_-	N
X_1	121	90	211

	τ_0	τ_1	N
X_2	136	75	211

	τ_{Yes}	τ_{No}	N
X_3	140	71	211

To find the expected frequency for a certain cell—say, $(X_1, X_2, X_3) = (+, 0, \text{no})$—we would have

$$\eta_{+,0,\text{no}} = n_e(+, 0, \text{no}) = \frac{\tau_+ \cdot \tau_0 \cdot \tau_{\text{no}}}{N^2}$$

$$= \frac{121 \times 136 \times 71}{(211)^2} = 26$$

The *observed* frequency for the same cell is, of course,

$$r_{+,\,0,\,\text{no}} = 25$$

The predicted values under H_0 could be calculated in this way for each of the eight cells, and χ^2 with 1 df could be calculated in a straightforward manner as though they were the cells of a univariate distribution.

We notice that just as in the two-dimensional case, the sum of the marginal totals in any dimension is equal to N—a fact which serves as a useful computational cross check.

The degrees of freedom were obtained by the formula presented in Section 11.7. That is,

$$\text{df} = \prod_{i=1}^{3} (n_i - 1) = (2 - 1)(2 - 1)(2 - 1) = 1$$

If we had set up our hypotheses formally, we would have had

H_0: The categories C_i are independent
H_1: Some of the categories C_i are dependent

In other words, this model tests the general hypothesis of overall independence.

If we wish to have a different hypothesis—that two variables be held as control—we can set up a model such as the following three-dimensional illustration.

TABLE 11.9.3 / A Three-Dimensional Distribution with the Categories of Two Dimensions Held Constant

C_1 \ $C_{2,3}$	$X_2 = 0$		$X_2 = 1$		Marginal Totals
	$X_3 =$ Yes	$X_3 =$ No	$X_3 =$ Yes	$X_3 =$ No	
$X_1 = +$	50	25	30	16	121
$X_1 = -$	40	21	20	9	90
Marginal Totals	90	46	50	25	211

Here we have actually combined C_2 and C_3 into a single category $C_{2,3}$ but with four values:

$$\{\{0, \text{yes}\}, \{0, \text{no}\}, \{1, \text{yes}\}, \{1, \text{no}\}\}$$

In effect, then, we have here only a two-dimensional table with the dimensions C_1 and $C_{2,3}$. It is therefore treated just like any other two-dimensional table. Thus the expected value for

$$(X_1, (X_2, X_3)) = (+, (0, \text{yes}))$$

is

$$\eta_{+,(0,\text{yes})} = \frac{\tau_+ \cdot \tau_{(0,\text{yes})}}{N} = \frac{121 \times 90}{211} = 51$$

$$\text{df} = (2 - 1)(4 - 1) = 3$$

χ^2 is calculated in the usual way, and the hypotheses are

H_0: C_1 and $C_{2,3}$ are independent
H_1: C_1 and $C_{2,3}$ are dependent

It is not necessary for C_2 and C_3 to be independent of each other. They may be thought of as dividing the cases into groups in which homogenous behavior might be expected.* In four dimensions our two previous methods could be combined—that is, two variables could be combined and the null hypothesis become a three-way independence, or three could be combined, or two groups of two categories be established to test for two-way independence, and so forth. For only four dimensions, $1 + \binom{4}{3} + \binom{4}{2} + 3 = 14$ distinct tests could be made. The number of possibilities obviously proliferates greatly with each additional dimension. However, sound scientific procedure would ordinarily require a theoretical rationale for the particular structure of category combinations; this would drastically reduce the number feasible to test.

Suppose C_1, C_2, C_3, and C_4 have, respectively, n_1, n_2, n_3, and n_4 subcategories. If C_2 and C_3 are combined to give $n_2 \times n_3$ categories, then

$$\text{df} = (n_1 - 1)[(n_2 \times n_3) - 1](n_4 - 1)$$

If C_2, C_3, and C_4 are combined, then

$$\text{df} = (n_1 - 1)[(n_2 \times n_3 \times n_4) - 1]$$

And, of course, if they are combined as two pairs—say, C_1 with C_2 and C_3 with C_4—then

$$\text{df} = [(n_1 \times n_2) - 1][(n_3 \times n_4) - 1]$$

The general principle extends to other combinations and higher dimensions.

PROBLEMS

1. **a.** Use the following distributions to state an H_0. Test it using χ^2.

	BRITISH	FRENCH	GERMAN	POLISH	METIS	OTHER
Theoretical probabilities	.43	.12	.10	.05	.05	.25
Observed frequency	53	10	14	6	2	26

* If C_2 were age then $C_{2,3}$ would be age-specific values of C_3.

b. In drawing six persons at random, it is expected about 50 percent will claim to be Republicans. Sixty independent samples give the following:

Number of Republicans	0	1	2	3	4	5	6
Number of samples with given number of Republicans	1	8	13	18	13	5	2

Do these results indicate a binomial distribution with $p = .5$?

c. It is considered desirable to determine that the hypergeometric model is really valid in a given situation. The test is used repeatedly on independent samples. The table is always of the following form:

	AFTER EFFECT	NO AFTER EFFECT	
Received treatment			5
No treatment			5
Total			10

The number treated with no after effect was distributed as follows:

Number with no after effect	0	1	2	3	4	5	6	7	8	9	10
Number of samples with given result	0	0	2	12	25	30	21	12	3	2	1

(1) Test to see if this meets the hypergeometric distribution.

(2) Test to see if the binomial distribution with $p = q = \frac{1}{2}$ is better.

(3) Why do the distributions obtained in parts a and b differ? How do they differ?

2. Use the χ^2 test for Problems 8.2, 8.3, and 8.5 of Chapter 8. Compare the results of the Fisher exact test and the χ^2 test. Note that Siegel (see Bibliography) discusses comparison of tests in some detail and gives reference to material at a more advanced level.

3. For each one of the following bivariate tables, state an H_0 and test it; then answer the other questions about the table or results. The tables are taken from a real study, but the data are not. The tables are constructed to illustrate statistical points. The category titles are given to allow the reader to think of the tables in an applied context. The 120 persons referred to may be thought of as persons in prison for a criminal offense.

a. Why might the significance of the result shown in the table below be challenged? Of what importance is it that alcoholism and number of convictions both increase with age?

PREVIOUS RECORD	PREVIOUS USE OF ALCOHOL		
	NONE	MODERATE	ALCOHOLIC
Yes	20	20	20
No	20	30	10

b. The age group in the table below is based on age at last conviction. Is this pattern unexpected in terms of the comment made in part a? Does the χ^2 really show us anything important?

USE OF ALCOHOL	AGE GROUP		
	UNDER 21	21–30	31 AND UP
None	10	12	18
Moderate	8	17	25
Alcoholic	3	12	15

c. Is it possible that the apparent lack of relation is explained by a third variable? (See table below.) Explain how this might happen.

CRIMES INVOLVED IN	PREVIOUS CONVICTIONS	
	NO	YES
Violent	30	30
Nonviolent	30	30

d. In the table below, young and old refer to age at conviction. Can you explain this table in terms of longer criminal careers and longer sentences for violent crimes? Explain how you can derive the table in part c from the table below.

CRIMES INVOLVED IN	PREVIOUS CONVICTIONS			
	NO		YES	
	YOUNG	OLD	YOUNG	OLD
Violent	20	10	10	20
Nonviolent	10	20	20	10

e. The tables in part c and d illustrate how a table that has an insignificant χ^2 can be formed by summing the data that are significant with respect to a third variable. The following tables illustrate how an apparently significant table can be the sum of insignificant components. Examine these tables, test each, and comment on your findings.

CRIME RESULTING IN THIS CONVICTION	UNDER 25	25 OR OVER
Minor theft	40	20
Other	20	40

CRIME RESULTING IN THIS CONVICTION	PREVIOUS CONVICTIONS					
	NONE		1		2 OR MORE	
	UNDER 25	25 OR OVER	UNDER 25	25 OR OVER	UNDER 25	25 OR OVER
Minor theft	30	5	9	9	1	6
Other	6	1	9	9	5	30

Which variable is really important, or is one variable important? Can you explain the last table in terms of a developing criminal career?

4. For this trivariate example, perform the three-dimensional and the three two-dimensional χ^2 test. If all four tests are to be performed with no a priori information, Boole's inequality indicates the χ^2 must be chosen so that $P(\chi^2 \geq x) = \frac{1}{4}x$. If each χ^2 test is performed at the 1 percent level, since four tests are to be performed, conclusions can be drawn only at the 4 percent level. If the 1 percent level is desired, each hypothesis must be tested at the .025 level. Draw conclusions for each individual hypothesis, assuming the others are not being tested. Then draw overall conclusions.

REFLEXES	PROFESSIONAL		CLERICAL	
	MALE	FEMALE	MALE	FEMALE
Good	20	12	15	14
Average or poor	14	7	6	4

5. Examine the park and school data given below and explain why there are such differences in the ratio of the number of parks to the number of schools in certain municipalities.*

* These are real data on 13 municipal areas. Area 13 had a population of approximately 230,000 in 1961. Other areas had populations of 10,000 and up. These areas have 25,000 acres of residential land. There were about 500,000 people in the area in 1961. The table is from a recreation study in which Beaman worked with Professor J. B. Leicester of the University of Saskatchewan. Other problems in this book draw indirectly on this and other recreation studies with Professor Leicester.

NUMBER	MUNICIPALITY						
	1	2	3	4	5	6	7
Parks	34	3	14	34	18	1	62
Schools	16	8	12	21	11	2	27

NUMBER	MUNICIPALITY						
	8	9	10	11	12	13	TOTAL
Parks	39	24	29	12	29	159	458
Schools	21	21	13	5	13	110	280

a. Is χ^2 significant at either the .01 or .05 level?
b. Write briefly on why these differences can occur and if it is valid to say that there is a significant difference in the park-school ratio even if χ^2 is not significant.
c. Apply another test—for example, a median test—using the park-school ratios in each municipality, and determine whether something significant can be obtained by using a different test.

CHAPTER 12

THE POISSON DISTRIBUTION

THE POISSON PROBABILITY distribution is widely used in the physical sciences, engineering, economics, and theoretical mathematical statistics. The almost total neglect of this distribution by sociologists is rather ironic, since its discoverer, Poisson, was a sociologist who developed it to investigate phenomena such as Paris crime rates.

When we considered the binomial model, we were dealing with a two-parameter distribution, the parameters being n, the size of the sample, and p, the single-trial probability. Once these two values were fixed, a specific probability distribution was defined for all random variables x, such that x is an integer and $0 \leq x \leq n$. The Poisson distribution is a one-parameter distribution, with the parameter being conventionally represented as λ. The distribution is

$$\left\{\left(x, \frac{\lambda^x e^{-\lambda}}{x!}\right) | \lambda \text{ is a positive real number; } x \text{ is an integer } 0 \leq x\right\}$$

The constant e in the probability expression is a special transcendental real number whose exact value cannot be stated because it possesses an endless nonrepeating decimal component. However, its value may be stated to any required degree of precision—for example, its value to five decimal places is 2.71828. We shall say more about this number later; for now it is enough to know that it may be used like any other real number.

The probability of exactly k occurrences of some specified event where Poisson sampling conditions are met may be expressed as

$$P[(k, \lambda)] = \frac{\lambda^k e^{-\lambda}}{k!}$$

Practical application of the distribution requires that λ be given some valid meaningful interpretation. One such interpretation that is especially suited to the social and behavioral sciences is as follows: Given an event E such that $P[E]$ has the constant trial-to-trial value p, and given that c is a positive real constant and n is the number of trials, let $np = c$. Now if $n \to \infty$, we define $\lambda = c$. This says that, as n becomes indeterminately large, the constant value c may be regarded as the λ in the Poisson distribution. It is evident that as $n \to \infty$, $p \to 0$; that is, the larger the value of n, the closer p approaches the limiting value zero. This in effect implies an interpretation of the Poisson distribution as a limiting case of the binomial distribution as the number of Bernoulli trials becomes very large and the single-trial probability becomes very small.

Except, perhaps, for certain instances in which time might be involved, not many sampling experiments in the social sciences will meet these sampling conditions. However, there are still numerous circumstances in which the Poisson distribution may be usefully employed for very close approximations to binomial probabilities where n is reasonably large, p quite small, and λ is of moderate magnitude. The Poisson distribution is also useful for determining expected frequencies that are to be used in conjunction with the χ^2 model in experiments involving the distribution of elements among large numbers of cells. In addition, it provides an important theoretical basis for matching experiments. It can be used under certain circumstances when only the density of occurrences (that is, the average number of cases per some unit such as a minute or a square mile) is known but n and p are not—provided circumstances justify the assumption that n is very large.

The only interpretation of the Poisson distribution we shall try to justify formally is that it gives a very close approximation to the binomial distribution for large n and small p. Nevertheless, we will present illustrations of other interpretive uses in which a reasonable intuitive justification can be suggested.

Because "limits" are involved, we must introduce certain propositions from the calculus. However, if the reader will accept two or three of these propositions on faith, the following theoretical discussion should not be difficult to understand. The next section therefore considers some important background material, largely from the calculus.

12.1 THE CONSTANT e AND THE FUNCTIONS e^x, e^{-x}, AND $\ln x$

The constant e is an irrational real number; that is, it has no fractional form. Like any other irrational number—for instance, π (= 3.1416...)—it is an endless nonrepeating decimal expression. It emerges as a consequence of mathematical considerations, has some extremely interesting properties, and is of great practical value in both science and mathematics. It has all of the properties common to members of the class of real numbers, and algebraic expressions of these apply equally to it. For instance, just as we may write 2^2 or 2^x, we may write e^2 or e^x. The expression e^x tends to assume irrational values also, but conspicuous exceptions would be $e^0 = 1$ and $e^{\ln a} = a$, for the case of rational values of a. Determination of the values of e^x may be accomplished by the application of a useful device from the calculus known as Taylor's formula, which provides a means for determining to any required degree of precision the values of many important functions, for instance, $\sin X$. This technique generates an infinite series. The Taylor series for e^x is

IDENTITY 12.1.1

$$e^x = \sum_{k=0}^{\infty} \frac{x^k}{k!} = \frac{x^0}{0!} + \frac{x^1}{1!} + \frac{x^2}{2!} + \cdots + \frac{x^n}{n!} + \cdots$$

It is important to recognize that the converse is also true; that is, when a series of this sort emerges from mathematical operations, it equals e^x. We may illustrate the use of the series to find the value of e itself.

$$e = e^1 = \sum_{k=0}^{\infty} \frac{1^k}{k!} = \frac{1^0}{0!} + \frac{1^1}{1!} + \frac{1^2}{2!} + \frac{1^3}{3!} + \frac{1^4}{4!} + \frac{1^5}{5!} + \frac{1^6}{6!} + \frac{1^7}{7!} + \frac{1^8}{8!} + \cdots$$

$$= 1 + 1 + \frac{1}{2} + \frac{1}{6} + \frac{1}{24} + \frac{1}{120} + \frac{1}{720} + \frac{1}{5040} + \frac{1}{40{,}320} + \cdots$$

If we tabulate the values of these terms to five decimal places, along with their cumulative sums, we get

VALUE OF TERM	CUMULATIVE VALUE
1.00000	1.00000
1.00000	2.00000
.50000	2.50000
.16667	2.66667
.04166	2.70833
.00833	2.71666
.00138	2.71804
.00019	2.71823
.00002	2.71825

The last cumulation can be seen to have converged very close to 2.71828. It is apparent, because of the rapid growth of the factorial denominators, that the further along the term occurs in the sequence the less its tendency to affect the digits in the preceding cumulations.

By formal substitution of $-x$ for x in the Taylor series for e^x, we can obtain the series for e^{-x}:

$$e^{-x} = \frac{(-x)^0}{0!} + \frac{(-x)^1}{1!} + \frac{(-x)^2}{2!} + \frac{(-x)^3}{3!} + \cdots + \frac{(-x)^n}{n!} + \cdots$$

$$= 1 - \frac{x}{1!} + \frac{x^2}{2!} - \frac{x^3}{3!} + \cdots$$

Thus we see that e^{-x} has terms identical to those of e^x, but the terms are alternately added and subtracted. This is compactly stated in the following.

IDENTITY 12.1.2

$$e^{-x} = \sum_{k=0}^{\infty} \frac{(-1)^k x^k}{k!}$$

IDENTITY 12.1.2 COROLLARY

$$e^{-1} = 1 - 1 + \frac{1}{2!} - \frac{1}{3!} + \frac{1}{4!} - \cdots + \frac{(-1)^n}{n!} + \cdots$$

in particular.

It will be recalled from elementary algebra that, by definition of a logarithm,

$$\log_a a^x = x$$

This simply says that *by definition* the variable exponent x whose base is the constant a is called the logarithm of the number a^x. That is, if $N = a^x$, then $\log_a N = x$.

The converse statement is equally important: if $\log_a N = x$, then $N = a^x$. For example, $\log_2 8 = \log_2 2^3 = 3$. Conversely, given that $\log_2 N = 3$, we know immediately that $N = 2^3 = 8$.

Since e is a perfectly good real number, it can serve as the base of a set of logarithms; that is, $\log_e e^x = x$. Logarithms based on e are called *natural logarithms* and are customarily denoted simply by ln. Thus $\ln N = \log_e N$. Note that if $\ln N = x$, then $N = e^x$.

We require one other identity from the calculus:

$$-\ln(1 - p) = p + \frac{p^2}{2} + \frac{p^3}{3} + \cdots + \frac{p^n}{n} + \cdots$$

At first glance, the right-hand side may seem to resemble the Taylor series for e^x, but the denominators are not factorials, the first term is not $f(0)$, and the series is obtained by a somewhat different method. It may be represented compactly as follows:

IDENTITY 12.1.3

$$\ln(1 - p) = -\sum_{k=1}^{\infty} \frac{p^k}{k}$$

We now have the information from calculus necessary to show that the Poisson distribution may serve as a useful model for large n and small p.

12.2 THE POISSON PROBABILITY OF ZERO OCCURRENCES

We shall derive the Poisson distribution by developing an iterative formula; that is, we shall establish a procedure whereby the kth term can be obtained with little effort, provided the $(k - 1)$st term is already known. Since finding the kth term depends upon knowing the $(k - 1)$st term, success depends upon being able to find a value for a prior term. It follows that if the first term in the sequence is known, all of the others can be derived from it by successive iteration. The logical first term in a Poisson distribution is the one that gives the probability of exactly zero occurrences. We proceed to find such a term.

As previously stated, applications of the Poisson distribution often involve finding the probability of events that have a very low relative frequency of occurrence and hence a very large complement set of nonoccurrences. Physical examples often cited are the probabilities that lightning will strike in some area or that a man will be kicked by a horse. There are many sociological examples, such as crime rates, suicide rates, and so forth. Thus at a typical rate of 10 per 100,000, the probability of a person's committing suicide is .0001.

It will be useful for our subsequent discussion to introduce an abbreviated notation for the general binomial term

$$b[k; n, p] = \binom{n}{k} p^k (1 - p)^{n-k}$$

We shall similarly represent the Poisson term as $p[x; \lambda]$.

Under the assumption of independent Bernoulli trials, let p be a very small single trial probability; that is, assume that the small probability p is constant from trial to trial.

Let $\lambda = np$, where n is of a magnitude that yields moderate values of λ. Since p is very small, this implies a very large n. Since

$$b[x; n, p] = \binom{n}{x} p^x (1 - p)^{n-x}$$

then the probability of zero occurrences in n trials is

$$b[0; n, p] = \binom{n}{0} p^0(1-p)^{n-0} = (1-p)^n$$

Hence

$$\ln b[0; n, p] = \ln(1-p)^n = n \cdot \ln(1-p) = -n \sum_{k=1}^{\infty} \frac{p^k}{k}$$

by Identity 12.1.3. Since $\lambda = np$, then $p = \lambda/n$, and, by substitution

$$\ln b[0; n, p] = -n \sum_{k=1}^{\infty} \left(\frac{\lambda}{n}\right)^k \frac{1}{k} = \sum_{k=1}^{\infty} -\frac{\lambda^k}{kn^{k-1}}$$

$$= -\lambda - \frac{\lambda^2}{2n} - \frac{\lambda^3}{3n^2} - \cdots - \frac{\lambda^r}{rn^{r-1}} - \cdots$$

Since, by stipulation, λ is of moderate magnitude and n is very large,* the terms after the first have a negligible effect on the total sum, and

$$\ln b[0; n, p] \doteq -\lambda$$

Thus

$$b[0; n, p] \doteq e^{-\lambda}$$

Since we may think of the Poisson term as a binomial term in which $np = \lambda$, we may logically use the following identity:

IDENTITY 12.2.1

$$p[0; \lambda] = b[0; n, p] \doteq e^{-\lambda}$$

This says that for some given $\lambda = np$, the probability of no occurrences in a very large number of trials (that is, as $n \to \infty$) with a very small p (that is, $p \to 0$), is $e^{-\lambda}$. This provides us with a starting point for obtaining the probabilities in which $k > 0$, from an iterative formula.

---

* Moreover, this series certainly converges for any value of $n \geq \lambda^2 > 1$, being dominated by the geometric series

$$-\sum_{k=1}^{\infty} \frac{1}{\lambda^{k-2}}$$

12.3 THE POISSON PROBABILITY OF k OCCURRENCES

The ratio of two adjacent binomial terms yields the following identity:

IDENTITY 12.3.1

$$\frac{b[k; n, p]}{b[k-1; n, p]} = \frac{np - p(k-1)}{k(1-p)}$$

PROOF. The left-hand ratio can be rewritten

$$\frac{\binom{n}{k}p^k(1-p)^{n-k}}{\binom{n}{k-1}p^{k-1}(1-p)^{n-k+1}} = \frac{n!}{k!(n-k)!} \cdot \frac{(k-1)!(n-k+1)!}{n!} \cdot \frac{p}{(1-p)}$$

$$= \frac{p(n-k+1)}{k(1-p)} = \frac{np - p(k-1)}{k(1-p)}$$

and the identity is established.

Since $\lambda = np$, we may rewrite Identity 12.3.1 as

$$\frac{p[k; \lambda]}{p[k-1; \lambda]} = \frac{\lambda - p(k-1)}{k(1-p)}$$

However, the use of λ implies that p is very small; hence we can say that as $p \to 0$, $p(k-1) \to 0$, and $(1-p) \to 1$. Hence

$$\frac{p[k; \lambda]}{p[k-1; \lambda]} \doteq \frac{\lambda}{k}$$

and

$$p[k; \lambda] \doteq p[k-1; \lambda] \cdot \frac{\lambda}{k}$$

This is our iterative formula. Since we know from Identity 12.2.1 that $p[0;\lambda] = e^{-\lambda}$, we can write, for $k = 1, 2, 3, \ldots, r$

$$p[1;\lambda] \doteq \frac{\lambda}{1}e^{-\lambda} = \lambda e^{-\lambda}$$

$$p[2;\lambda] \doteq \left(\frac{\lambda}{1}e^{-\lambda}\right)\frac{\lambda}{2} = \frac{\lambda^2 e^{-\lambda}}{2\cdot 1}$$

$$p[3;\lambda] \doteq \left(\frac{\lambda^2 e^{-\lambda}}{2\cdot 1}\right)\frac{\lambda}{3} = \frac{\lambda^3 e^{-\lambda}}{3\cdot 2\cdot 1}$$

and, in general

$$p[k;\lambda] = \frac{\lambda^k e^{-\lambda}}{k!}$$

This is the general Poisson term. The probability of k or fewer occurrences would be

$$p[x \leq k;\lambda] \doteq \sum_{x=0}^{k} \frac{\lambda^x e^{-\lambda}}{x!} = e^{-\lambda} \sum_{x=0}^{k} \frac{\lambda^x}{x!}$$

As $n \to \infty$, there is no upper limit on k, so the complete Poisson distribution is

$$p[x \leq \infty;\lambda] = e^{-\lambda} \sum_{x=0}^{\infty} \frac{\lambda^x}{x!}$$

But we recognize by Identity 12.1.1 that

$$\sum_{x=0}^{\infty} \frac{\lambda^x}{x!} = e^{\lambda}$$

Hence

$$p[x \leq \infty;\lambda] = e^{-\lambda}e^{\lambda} = e^0 = 1$$

which is exactly what the sum of the complete set of probabilities of exclusive events should total.

For reasons that should now be obvious, the probability of k or more occurrences is

$$p[k \leq x;\lambda] = 1 - \sum_{x=0}^{k-1} \frac{e^{-\lambda}\lambda^x}{x!} = 1 - p[x < k;\lambda]$$

Tables of values for the Poisson distribution can be obtained given k and λ. One of the most useful of these, authored by General Electric Company, is *Tables of Terms of Poisson Distribution.**

Sample Page from *Tables of the Individual and Cumulative Terms of Poisson Distribution*†

TABLE OF THE POISSON DISTRIBUTION
INDIVIDUAL AND CUMMULATIVE TERMS

	U = 0.5600000			U = 0.5700000		
X	P(X)	C(X)	D(X)	P(X)	C(X)	D(X)
0	.57120907	.57120907	1.00000000	.56552544	.56552544	1.00000000
1	.31987708	.89108614	.42879093	.32234950	.88787494	.43447456
2	.08956558	.98065172	.10891386	.09186961	.97974455	.11212505
3	.01671891	.99737063	.01934827	.01745523	.99719977	.02025545
4	.00234065	.99971128	.00262937	.00248737	.99968714	.00280022
5	.00026215	.99997343	.00028872	.00028356	.99997070	.00031285
6	.00002447	.99999790	.00002657	.00002694	.99999765	.00002929
7	.00000196	.99999986	.00000210	.00000219	.99999984	.00000235
8	.00000014	.99999999	.00000014	.00000016	.99999999	.00000016
	U = 0.5800000			U = 0.5900000		
0	.55989837	.55989837	1.00000000	.55432729	.55432729	1.00000000
1	.32474105	.88463942	.44010163	.32705310	.88138038	.44567271
2	.09417490	.97881432	.11536058	.09648066	.97786105	.11861961
3	.01820715	.99702147	.02118567	.01897453	.99683557	.02213895
4	.00264004	.99966151	.00297853	.00279874	.99963432	.00316442
5	.00030624	.99996775	.00033849	.00033025	.99996457	.00036568
6	.00002960	.99999736	.00003224	.00003247	.99999705	.00003542
7	.00000245	.99999981	.00000264	.00000274	.99999978	.00000295
8	.00000018	.99999999	.00000019	.00000020	.99999999	.00000021
	U = 0.6000000			U = 0.6100000		
0	.54881164	.54881164	1.00000000	.54335087	.54335087	1.00000000
1	.32928698	.87809862	.45118836	.33144403	.87479489	.45664913
2	.09878609	.97688472	.12190138	.10109043	.97588532	.12520510
3	.01975722	.99664193	.02311528	.02055505	.99644038	.02411467
4	.00296358	.99960551	.00335806	.00313465	.99957503	.00355962
5	.00035563	.99996115	.00039448	.00038243	.99995745	.00042497
6	.00003556	.99999671	.00003885	.00003888	.99999633	.00004254
7	.00000305	.99999975	.00000329	.00000339	.99999972	.00000366
8	.00000023	.99999999	.00000024	.00000026	.99999998	.00000028
9				.00000002	.99999999	.00000002
	U = 0.6200000			U = 0.6300000		
0	.53794444	.53794444	1.00000000	.53259180	.53259180	1.00000000
1	.33352555	.87146999	.46205556	.33553283	.86812463	.46740820
2	.10339292	.97486291	.12853001	.10569284	.97381748	.13187536
3	.02136787	.99623078	.02513709	.02219550	.99601298	.02618252
4	.00331202	.99954280	.00376922	.00349579	.99950877	.00398702
5	.00041069	.99995349	.00045720	.00044047	.99994924	.00049123
6	.00004244	.99999592	.00004651	.00004625	.99999548	.00005076
7	.00000376	.99999969	.00000407	.00000416	.99999965	.00000451
8	.00000029	.99999998	.00000031	.00000033	.99999998	.00000035
9	.00000002	.99999999	.00000002	.00000002	.99999999	.00000002

* New York: D. Van Nostrand Co., Inc., 1962.

† General Electric Company, Defense Systems Department (New York: D. Van Nostrand Company, Inc., 1962, p. 75). Copyright by the General Electric Company. Reproduced with kind permission of the copyright owners.

In these tables the information is given under the headings $P(x)$, $C(x)$, $D(x)$, where $U = \lambda$, and

$$P(x) = p[k;\lambda]$$
$$C(x) = p[x \leq k;\lambda]$$
$$D(x) = p[k \leq x;\lambda]$$

Tables such as these make it possible to solve many useful and interesting problems. Where existing tables of Poisson values do not contain the required parameters, the probabilities can be found from the basic formulas in conjunction with other extensive tables of values of e^x and e^{-x}.*

Example

A sociologist living in a town of 5268 people suspected that the four suicides that had occurred among the local residents in a single year was an unusually large number for the population size. By comparing the age-sex-race standardized rate of the U.S. with the structure of the local resident population, he obtained an adjusted rate for the country at large of 11.8 per 100,000, or .000118. Using $\alpha = .01$, he was then able to test H_0: $p \leq .000118$ against $H_1: .000118 < p$ as follows:

$$\lambda = np = 5268\,(.000118) \doteq .62$$
$$p[k \leq x;\lambda] = p[4 \leq x;.62]$$

From the General Electric tables, where $\lambda = .62$, he found

$$D(4) = .00377 < .01 = \alpha$$

He therefore rejected H_0 and concluded that the local rate was unusually high. It should be added parenthetically that a determination had to be made that the suicides were independent events—for instance, that the victims were not closely related by blood or marriage and that none had been jointly involved in suicide pacts. The assumption is also made that these factors have a negligible effect on the national rate.

* *Tables of the Exponential Function e^x*, National Bureau of Standards, Applied Mathematics Series No. 14, U.S. Government Printing Office, 1951.

12.4 λ AS A MEASURE OF DENSITY

The potentiality of the Poisson model for application is greatly extended if it is recognized that λ is a measure of density—that is, a measure of the average number of occurrences per unit of measurement. For instance, if $n = 500$ balls are distributed among 100 cells, the density is $\bar{x} = \frac{500}{100} = 5$ balls/cell.* It is also to be noted that the single-trial probability that a ball will fall into any specified cell is $p = \frac{1}{100}$.

$$np = 500 \cdot \tfrac{1}{100} = 5$$

illustrates the well-known relationship that $\bar{x} = np$.

It has already been shown that where p is sufficiently small and λ is of moderate magnitude, $\lambda \doteq np$. Hence where these conditions are met, $\bar{x} \doteq \lambda$.

This fact makes it possible to use $\bar{x}$ for λ even where n and p are not known, as long as n is sufficiently large. Examples would be the average number of occurrence points per unit area in a plane, or per unit volume of a solid, where the total number of points is infinitely large. A common physical example is the problem of finding the probability that a unit length of steel strapping coming through a rolling mill will contain k or more flaws, if the average number of flaws per unit is known to be $\bar{x}$ under normal operation. The point probability would be

$$p(k\,;\bar{x}) = \frac{\bar{x}^k e^{-\bar{x}}}{k!}$$

and the solution would be $D(k)$, given $\lambda = \bar{x}$. The null hypothesis that operation was normal would be rejected if $D(k) \leq \alpha$, for a specified $\lambda = \bar{x}$, an experimental constant.

Analogous considerations enable one to operate with a λ equal to the average number of occurrences per unit of time, since the obviously continuous nature of the time continuum implies $n = \infty$, where n represents the total number of instants in time in which an event could occur.

* $\bar{x} \doteq \lambda$, where $\bar{x}$ stands for the arithmetic mean. In parametric statistics, and in terms of primitive sample spaces, it may be defined as the ratio of the sum of the points in the space to the number of points in that space, assuming that "sum" is defined on an interval scale. See Siegel, *op. cit.*, pp. 26–28, for discussion of interval scale.

The units, of course, must be uniform in order to meet the requirement under the null hypothesis that the single-trial probabilities remain constant. For the same reason, we must assume that instantaneous events in a segment of the time continuum could not occur at exactly the same instant.

The following example may suggest applications to the social sciences, provided we assume (as we have throughout this book) that the *methodological* aspects of the investigation are under control.

Example

The average weekly rate of reported delinquencies in a particular area was three per 1000 inhabitants. Later, after months of effort by social workers sent into the area, 22 delinquencies were reported in a four-week period. If the average population of the area was 2980, does this contradict the subjective assessment of the workers that their efforts were having a salutary effect?

Solution. The original weekly rate was .003, but since this is to be applied to a four-week period, we have

$$H_0: p = 4(.003) = .012 \quad \text{and} \quad H_1: p < .012.$$

$$\lambda = np = 2980\,(.012) \doteq 36$$

We need

$$p[x \leq 22; 36] = C(22) = .00846 < .01 = \alpha$$

Therefore conclude that the statistical evidence does not contradict the subjective assessment.

12.5 A POISSON QUEUING PROBLEM

Suppose a certain facility is available where surplus food is distributed during three hours on the day the food arrives. There are 923 qualified recipients, and distribution requires an average of 5 minutes of a clerk's time for each recipient. How many clerks would have to be on duty until the first recipient arrived to be 95 percent certain that no recipient would have to wait to be served? Assume that random forces determine the arrival time of recipients over the three-hour period (otherwise we could redefine our problem to cover only the period of peak load).

Solution. Think of the recipients as being 923 random trials, each having a probability of 5 minutes/180 minutes, or .0277 minutes, of requiring a clerk's attention at any time during the three hours. The number of recipients present at any given time is the number of occurrences, k; hence we need k clerks to handle k recipients. Until at least one customer arrives, the possibility exists for every point of time in the distribution period that any number of recipients $x, 0 \leq x \leq 923$, could arrive at the same time. Since the time of arrival of the first recipient is not known, one point in time is as likely to occur as any other. Moreover, that point is the one for which the maximum number of clerks is needed. After that, n diminishes as rapidly as recipients are processed. Since our problem requires us to be concerned only with the maximum potential demand for volunteers, the solution is

$$\lambda = np = 923(.0277) \doteq 26$$

By the conditions imposed,

$$p(k \leq x; \lambda) = p(k \leq x; 26) = .05$$

From the General Electric tables we find under $\lambda = 26$ that $D(k) \doteq .05$, if $k = 35$. That is, $D(35) = .05284$. To be conservative, 36 clerks could be assigned—in which case, if they remained on duty the whole period, the maximum probability of a recipient having to wait at any point in time would be $D(36) = .03632$. Stated differently, the probability one would have to wait any time is $p \leq .03632$.

It might also be noted that, with $\alpha = .05$, the maximum number of recipients that can be expected to have to wait at one time is $.05(923) \doteq 46$. Hence 46 is the expected maximum length of the queues that might form. In other words, the selection of α is a decision as to the maximum number of people that will have to wait. Conversely, a decision as to how many persons it is feasible to make wait at any single time would determine α.

12.6 THE NUMBER OF TRIALS REQUIRED FOR A SPECIFIED CERTAINTY OF AT LEAST ONE SUCCESS

A formula for a specified certainty of at least one success for the Poisson model may be derived in much the same manner as for the binomial model. The probability of at least one success is 1 minus the probability of 0 successes. Conversely, the probability of 0 successes is 1 minus the probability of at least one success; that is, $1 - p[0 < x; \lambda]$. We saw in Section 12.2 that the Poisson probability of 0 successes is $e^{-\lambda}$. Hence

$$e^{-\lambda} = 1 - p[0 < x; \lambda]$$

Taking the logarithm of both sides of the equation, we get

$$\ln e^{-\lambda} = \ln (1 - p[0 < x; \lambda])$$

Hence

$$-\lambda = \ln (1 - p[0 < x; \lambda])$$

Multiplying both sides of the equation by -1 and recognizing that $\lambda = np$, we obtain

$$np = -\ln (1 - p[0 < x; \lambda])$$

and finally

$$n = \frac{-\ln (1 - p[0 < x; \lambda])}{p}$$

The logarithm of a number between 0 and 1 will always be negative, and therefore the numerator must be negative if n is to be positive.

We would expect from the assumptions implicit in the Poisson distribution that n will be quite large if a high degree of confidence is to be expected, since the single-trial probability, p, is by stipulation very small. This is ensured in our model for determining n by the fact that the closer a number less than 1 gets to 0, the higher is the *absolute* value of its logarithm. For example,

$$\ln (.9999) = -.00010$$

whereas

$$\ln (.0001) = -9.21034$$

Obviously,

$$|-.000010| < |-9.21034|$$

We may illustrate the use of our formula with the following example: An archeologist knew from collective experience that intact specimens occur on the average of two per 10,000 cubic feet of earth removed from a particular type of site. How many cubic feet of earth would he have to budget for removal in order to be 95 percent certain of obtaining an intact specimen? We have as given

$$p = .0002 \quad \text{and} \quad P[0 < X; \lambda] = .95$$

Therefore

$$n = \frac{-\ln(1 - .95)}{.0002} = \frac{-\ln(.05)}{.0002}$$

$$= \frac{-(-2.99573)}{.0002} = 14{,}979 \text{ cu. ft} \doteq 15{,}000 \text{ cu. ft}$$

As a check on our answer, it is evident that

$$\lambda = np = (14{,}979).0002 = 2.99573 \doteq 3.0$$

From the General Electric tables, where $\lambda = 3.0$,

$$D(1) = .95495 \doteq .95$$

12.7 COMBINING THE POISSON AND χ^2 MODELS

A combined use of the Poisson and χ^2 distributions provides a powerful model that would seem to have great potential application for the social and behavioral scientist. The ultra-rigid, self-styled "humanist" who denies that human motives and tastes can ever be assessed statistically would be forced to adopt absurd premises to discredit the statistical determination of whether, for instance, the German High Command sought particular targets or indiscriminate civilian targets in its bomb raids on London in World War II. By imposing a grid on the map so as to partition London into 576 areas of one-fourth square kilometers each, it was possible to record the number of strikes for every such square.

A statistical demonstration of the randomness of the hits clearly establishes that the targets were the general population, unless one attributes it to the technical ineptitude of the Germans—a premise unsubstantiated by historical evidence. The details of this study, presented with characteristic excellence by Feller,* will not be reproduced here. However, his stochastic model is formally identical to the one developed and illustrated below with a somewhat different example.

Suppose that v balls are to be distributed randomly among N cells. The density—the average number of balls per cell—is thus v/N. The single-trial probability that a ball will occupy a specified cell is $1/N$. If N is sufficiently large, then $1/N$ will be very small, and the probability of exactly k occurrences for a specified cell in a large number of trials will be sufficiently close to $p(k; \lambda = v/N)$. This being so, the proportion of the N cells that can be expected to contain k balls will be $N \cdot p(k; v/N)$. Since, by stipulation, all v of the balls are distributed, it has to be true that

$$\sum_{x=0}^{v} p\left(x; \frac{v}{N}\right) = 1$$

because this is the sum of the probabilities of every possible alternative, and the events $x = 0, x = 1, \ldots, x = v$ are exclusive. It is evident, then, that

$$N \sum_{x=0}^{v} p\left(x; \frac{v}{N}\right) = N \cdot 1 = N$$

Furthermore,

IDENTITY 12.7.1

$$N \sum_{x=0}^{v} p\left(x; \frac{v}{N}\right) = N \cdot p\left(0; \frac{v}{N}\right) + N \cdot p\left(1; \frac{v}{N}\right) + \cdots + N \cdot p\left(v; \frac{v}{N}\right) = N$$

The terms in this sum represent the numbers of cells that might be expected to contain x balls, where $x = 0, 1, 2, \ldots, v$.

* Feller, *op. cit.*, pp. 150–152.

Since the single-trial probability $1/N$ is, by stipulation, very small, one correctly expects that the terms on the tails of the distribution might decline precipitously at some point. For instance, $p(v; v/N)$ is the probability that all of the balls will fall into a single cell. With small $1/N$, this becomes a negligible quantity. At some point, therefore, it might be convenient to truncate the string of terms by consolidating the cases of m or more occurrences per cell, as follows:

$$\left[N\sum_{x=0}^{m-1} p\left(x;\frac{v}{N}\right)\right] + N\cdot p\left(m \le x;\frac{v}{N}\right) = \left[N\sum_{x=0}^{m-1} p\left(x;\frac{v}{N}\right)\right] + N\cdot D(m)$$

A consolidated term on the left tail would be

$$N\cdot p\left(x \le m;\frac{v}{N}\right) = N\cdot C(m)$$

The terms in Identity 12.7.1, then, represent expected numbers of cells containing x balls *under the null hypothesis that the distribution of the balls was random* rather than systematically patterned. Systematic patterning, then, is H_1.

We accept or reject H_0 on the basis of whether the fit of the *observed* number of cells (frequencies) to the expected numbers of cells for each x is acceptable by the χ^2 criterion. For convenience we shall represent the expected frequencies of cells containing k balls as N_k, where $N_k = N\cdot p(k; v/N)$.

The following example should clarify the method. In an effort to determine whether the assessment of nonobjective art has any reliable basis, a panel of 187 art critics were asked to indicate their first preference in a collection of 100 new nonobjective paintings ranging from previously unviewed works by eminent artists to the finger paintings of baboons. The methodological precaution of randomizing the order of viewing was taken. Here the single-trial probability that any particular painting will be selected under the null hypothesis is

$$p = .01 \quad \text{and} \quad \lambda = \frac{187}{100} = 1.87 \doteq 1.9$$

Since λ is also equal to $vp = 187(.01)$, 1.9 is the expected number of *choices for each painting*, but this should not be confused with N_k, which is *the expected number of paintings* for any given number of choices, k. The *observed* number of paintings chosen k times for the various values of k is shown in the second column of Table 12.7.1. The values of $p(k; \lambda = 1.9) = P_k$ in the third column were obtained from the General Electric tables. The entries in column four are obtained from $N_k = NP_k = 100\, P_k$. Column five contains the squares of the observed frequencies of paintings receiving k choices, divided by the corresponding expected frequencies, as an intermediate step in the calculation of χ^2 by the method of Theorem 11.3.1.

TABLE 12.7.1 / First Preferences of Art Critics from 100 Nonobjective Paintings

I	II	III	IV	V
NO. OF TIMES CHOSEN $(= k)$	NO OF PAINTINGS CHOSEN k TIMES $(= F_k)$	PROBABILITY THAT A PAINTING WILL BE CHOSEN k TIMES UNDER H_0 $[= p(k; 1.9) = P_k]$	EXPECTED FREQUENCY OF PICTURES RECEIVING k CHOICES $[N \cdot P_k = 100 \cdot P_k\ (= N_k)]$	$\dfrac{F_k^2}{N_k}$
0	18	.14957	15.0	21.60
1	35	.28418	28.4	43.13
2	20	.26997	27.0	14.81
3	15	.17098	17.1	13.16
4	5	.08122	8.1	3.09
5	4	.03086	3.1	5.16
$x \vert 6 \leq x$	3	.01322	1.3	6.9
	100	1.00000	100.0	101.72

H_0: The judgment of the experts is random
H_1: The judgment of the experts is patterned

$$\chi^2 = 107.85 - 100 = 7.85$$

Since 0 through $6 \leq x$ represents seven categories, df $= 7 - 1 = 6$. If $\alpha = .01$, then

$$\chi_\alpha^2 = \chi_{.01}^2 = 16.81 > 7.85 = \chi^2$$

Therefore H_0 may not be rejected, and art criticism remains suspect in this instance. This means that there was no patterned tendency to reject certain paintings and to prefer others.

The table should be largely self-explanatory. A $p = .01$ may be pushing the definition of "very small." This could have been improved by providing more paintings, but the gain might be erased by practical considerations such as the number of paintings it is reasonable to ask a respondent to choose from. In any case, the principles underlying the use of the model as well as its power and importance should be evident.

PROBLEMS

The problems below illustrate several interesting applications of the Poisson distribution. It is worthwhile to note that the number *e* can be derived from the compound-interest problem; exploration along this line is an interesting exercise for the reader who wishes to understand more about the number *e*. The problems dealing with Poisson and χ^2 are examples of the use of the χ^2 test to determine that a certain distribution is reasonably close to a theoretical one. These Poisson-χ^2 problems are further exercises on the use of χ^2 and in this way do not differ from the applications of χ^2 discussed in the text.

1. **a.** A sociologist is studying a group of 100 people 60 years old. He knows the age-specific mortality rate for this group amounts to a probability of .05 dying within one year of the day the study starts. He is concerned with how many of these people will die while his study is continuing. Use the Poisson distribution to obtain the probabilities (1) that none of the people will die and (2) that one person will die. Continue calculating probabilities until the level is reached that enables the scientist to make a statement that he is 99 percent certain no more than x will die. What can he actually say about the effect of mortality on his group of 100, provided that the age-specific mortality rate is very accurate?

b. Discuss the problems involved in extending this study over a three- to five-year period. Can the same methods be used in dealing with the question of the number which might be expected to die? Remember that an age-specific mortality rate was used and also that certain assumptions must be met before a Poisson distribution is valid.

2. A group of grocery store managers from a given area met because they realized that mobility of persons in the city plays an important role in their business. They wished to investigate the hypothesis that some areas showed higher mobility rates than other areas. They selected 100 people in a valid statistical fashion and at the end of the year determined the people who were still living in the city. The following results were observed:

Number leaving	1	2	3	4	5	6	7
Number of stores	4	6	8	12	25	19	11

Number leaving	8	9	10	11	12	13 or more
Number of stores	8	3	2	1	1	5

These results may be treated in several ways. Use a Poisson model and determine whether it meets the Poisson assumption with $\bar{x}$ equal to the average rate of leaving for the city.

a. Use $(Pk) = \dfrac{\bar{x}e^{-\bar{x}}}{k!}$ and $\bar{x} \doteq 4$ leaving per year.

b. Calculate your own value of $\bar{x}$ and test it.

3. Analyze the following situation. It is believed that on the Canadian prairies towns more than 50 miles from one of the five major centers are established according to a chance pattern, as long as they lie in an area of sufficient moisture to allow agriculture to be the main pursuit. The following data were collected on the distribution of towns by dividing the nonarid areas into equal-sized areas, equal in terms of tillable acreage. The number of towns in these areas was determined. Formulate a Poisson model for the distribution of these towns in the areas, given 800 towns and 800 areas. Use the following results to test the hypothesis that trade centers are distributed randomly as long as they are not within a 50-mile radius of a major city.

Number of trade centers	0	1	2	3	4	5 or more
Number of areas having the given number of trade centers	320	300	100	50	10	20

4. In a project 100 tests at the 1 percent level are performed on independent samples. Knowing that the observations are completely random, use the Poisson and binomial distributions to fill in the following table:

PROBABILITY OF N ACCEPTANCES	NUMBER OF TIMES H_0 ACCEPTED					
	$N = 0$	$N = 1$	$N = 2$	$N = 3$	$N = 4$	$N = 5$ or more
Poisson						
Binomial						

5. What is meant when we say it is better to sample without replacement than with replacement? In this book, the question of one test or method being better than another has not really been discussed. This was first introduced as a meaningful question by R. A. Fisher.*

* See the Bibliography, R. A. Fisher, Article 2.757a and also 29.303a. (Fisher attacks Karl Pearson in the article "Method of Moments" and provides a good example of scientific conflict.)

CHAPTER 13

THE PROBABILITY OF THE UNION OF INTERSECTING EVENT SETS AND FURTHER APPLICATIONS OF THE POISSON DISTRIBUTION

IN A SENSE this chapter is an extension of the previous one; however, it requires the introduction of topics, important in their own right, such as the probability of the union of intersecting event sets and the probability of other special compound events. Some basic foundations are laid in the next two theorems.

13.1 COUNTING THE ELEMENTS IN INTERSECTING SETS

THEOREM 13.1.1. The grand total of the number of elements in sets that are at most singly intersecting is equal to the sum obtained by adding the sizes of the sets and subtracting the sizes of the intersections.

DEFINITION. Sets that are "at most singly intersecting" are sets containing no elements that belong to more than two of the sets. (See Figure 13.1.1.)

PROOF. The elements in the subsets constituting the intersections are counted twice in summing the sizes—once in each of the pairs of intersecting sets. Thus each element in an intersection is *over*-counted once. Subtracting the sum of the elements in the intersections eliminates the overcount, and the correct grand total remains. This completes the proof.

It will be convenient to call intersections of a pair of sets of the sort just considered *first-order intersections*. *Second*-order intersections are those subsets whose elements are simultaneously contained in three sets and, in general, $(r - 1)$st-order intersections are those whose elements are simultaneously contained in r sets.

Figure 13.1.1 / Venn Diagrams

Sets That Are at Most Singly Intersecting

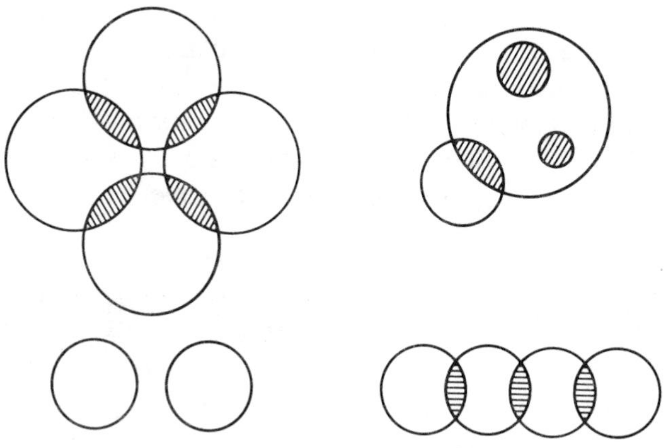

Examples of a Higher Order Intersection

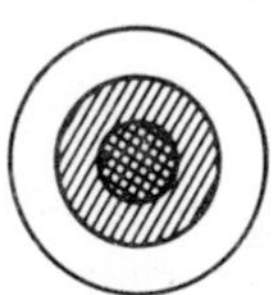

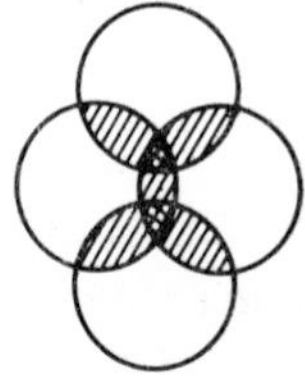

An element in any order of subset automatically belongs to subsets of all lower orders. For example:

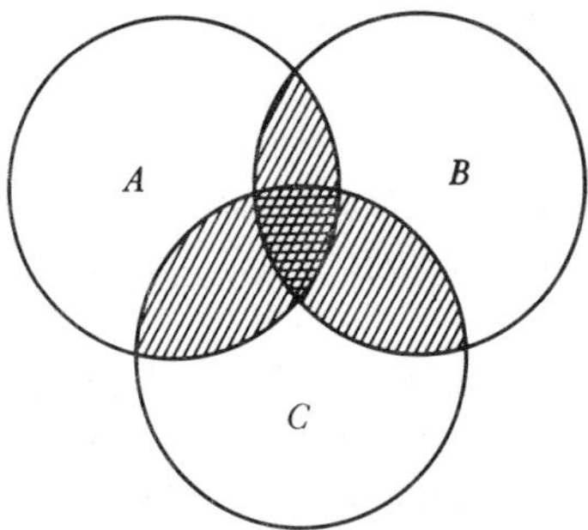

Note that the first-order intersection $A \cap B$ also contains $A \cap B \cap C$, as do $A \cap C$ and $B \cap C$.

We may now consider this theorem.

THEOREM 13.1.2. The grand total of elements in intersecting sets is equal to the sum obtained by adding their sizes minus the number of elements in their first-order intersections plus the number of elements in their second-order intersections $- \cdots \pm$ the number of elements in the subsets defined by the maximum order of intersections occurring.

PROOF. If the sizes of the sets are summed, the previous theorem suggests that the total should be adjusted by subtracting the number of elements in their first-order intersections. However, these first-order intersections are themselves sets for which the second-order intersections of the original sets are first-order intersections. Thus the subtraction removes a greater total of elements than is required and leaves a deficit in the total count that we may then attempt to restore by adding back the total of the number of elements in the second-order intersections. The same logic requires us alternately to add and subtract for each order of intersection the number of elements in the next higher order. The process is terminated when the size of the maximum order is added or subtracted, because it contains *no* intersections of a higher order than itself; hence adding or subtracting it involves no further overcount. This completes the proof.

To illustrate the theorem, the number of points in

$$E_1 \cup E_2 \cup E_3 = \mathscr{E}_1 + \mathscr{E}_2 + \mathscr{E}_3 - \mathscr{E}_{12} - \mathscr{E}_{13} - \mathscr{E}_{23} + \mathscr{E}_{123}$$
$$= \mathscr{E}_1 + \mathscr{E}_2 + \mathscr{E}_3 - [\mathscr{E}_{12} + \mathscr{E}_{13} + \mathscr{E}_{23}] + \mathscr{E}_{123}$$

where

$$\mathscr{E}_{ij} = \text{the number of points in } E_i \cap E_j$$
$$\mathscr{E}_{ijk} = \text{the number of points in } E_i \cap E_j \cap E_k$$

We may designate the sum of the sizes of the original sets as S_1, of the first-order intersections as S_2, and, in general, the sizes of the $(r-1)$st-order intersections as S_r. Then, if there are v sets of which the last is E_m,

$$S_1 = \sum_{i=1}^{v} \mathscr{E}_i$$

$$S_2 = \sum_{(i,j)=1}^{\binom{v}{2}} \mathscr{E}_{(ij)}$$

$$\vdots$$

$$S_v = \sum_{(i,j,k,\ldots,m)=1}^{\binom{v}{v}=1} \mathscr{E}_{(ijk,\ldots,m)}$$

where throughout $i < j < k < \ldots < m$ is a restriction needed to ensure that no intersection will be counted twice (recall that $E_i \cap E_j = E_j \cap E_i$).

The subscripts of the $\mathscr{E}$s are intended to indicate positions of intersections in their systematic ordering. For example, given the three sets E_1, E_2, E_3, a systematic ordering of the sizes of their first-order intersections could be $\mathscr{E}_{(12)=1}$, $\mathscr{E}_{(13)=2}$, $\mathscr{E}_{(23)=3}$. The possible number of such orders equals the number of ways in which subpopulations of size 2 may be selected from the elements 1, 2, 3, or $\binom{3}{2} = 3$. And, in general, the number of $\mathscr{E}_{(\ldots)}$ terms to be summed for any S_r, given v original sets, is $\binom{v}{r}$.

It is important to recognize that $\mathscr{E}_{(\ldots)} = 0$ is not excluded; that is, some sets and subsets might not have common intersections at all, so that the number of elements in their intersection equals 0.

This further implies that the number of original sets, ν, only limits —it does not determine—the magnitude of the highest order of intersections actually occurring. We only know a priori that $r_{\max} \leq \nu$.

13.2 THE PROBABILITY OF THE UNION OF EVENTS

We can now state the probability for the occurrence of at least one of a specified set of events without restriction to disjoint events. Our general definition of probability still applies—that is, the ratio of the number of elements in the primitive space qualifying as occurrences to the total number points in that space. Thus

$$P\left[\bigcup_{i=1}^{\nu} E_i\right] = \frac{S_1 - S_2 + S_3 - \cdots \pm S_\nu}{S}$$

$$= \frac{S_1}{S} - \frac{S_2}{S} + \frac{S_3}{S} - \cdots \pm \frac{S_\nu}{S}$$

For notational convenience, we may call these $p_i, p_{ij}, p_{ijk}, \ldots, p_{ijk\ldots m}$ respectively, so that

$$P\left[\bigcup_{i=1}^{\nu} E_i\right] = p_i - p_{ij} + p_{ijk} - \cdots \pm p_{ijk\ldots m}$$

We recall again that, in any specific case, the highest observed order intersections could range from 0 in the disjoint case to $\nu - 1$, where the simultaneous intersection of every set occurs. Hence the sequence of alternate *p*s may be truncated to conform to the highest order of observed intersections, and the remaining probabilities are understood to equal 0.

It will be even more convenient to identify the *p*s by bracketed subscripts indicating the number of intersecting sets. Thus $p_{(1)} = p_i$, $p_{(2)} = p_{ij}$, and, in general, $p_{(\mu)} = p_{ijk\ldots m}$.

Hence, Identity 13.2.1.

IDENTITY 13.2.1

$$P\left[\bigcup_{i=1}^{\nu} E_i\right] = \sum_{x=1}^{\mu} (-1)^{x+1} p_{(x)}$$

where μ = the maximum number of simultaneously intersecting sets.

Example

If four players take turns throwing a pair of dice, what is the probability, in one round of throws, that at least one of them will throw sum 3?

SOLUTION. The probability that the ith player will throw sum 3 is $\frac{2}{36}$ (that is, 2:1 or 1:2 out of 36 possibilities). The sum of the probabilities for all four of them is

$$p_{(1)} = 4\left(\frac{2}{36}\right) = \frac{8}{36}$$

The probability that any *specified* two of them will both throw sum 2 is

$$\frac{2}{36} \cdot \frac{2}{36} = \frac{4}{(36)^2}$$

and since there are $\binom{4}{2} = 6$ ways in which exactly two players can be chosen for sum 2,

$$p_{(2)} = 6 \cdot \frac{4}{(36)^2} = \frac{24}{(36)^2}$$

Similarly,

$$p_{(3)} = \binom{4}{3} \cdot \left(\frac{2}{36}\right)^3 = \frac{32}{(36)^3}$$

Finally,

$$p_{(4)} = \left(\frac{2}{36}\right)^4 = \frac{16}{(36)^4}$$

Hence the probability that at least one player will throw sum 3 is

$$P\left[\bigcup_{i=1}^{4} E_i\right] = \frac{8}{36} - \frac{24}{(36)^2} + \frac{32}{(36)^3} - \frac{16}{(36)^4}$$

$$= .22222222 - .0185185 + .00068587 - .00000952$$

$$= .20438$$

While the precision of the intermediate steps of the above computation may exceed practical necessity, it illustrates the theory.

13.3 MATCHES

If a sequence of 10 random selections is to be made from the integers 1 through 10 without replacement, what is the probability that the number 6 will be selected in the sixth trial?

Seven numbered balls are to be distributed randomly among seven cells without multiple occupancy. What is the probability that ball number three will occupy cell number three?

The events of interest in these examples are called matches. If we had two decks each of whose cards were numbered 1 to N, we might lay out one deck (called the target deck) and randomly assign one card from the other (the call deck) to each card from the first. Each case in which the cards had identical numbers would be called a match. Or, if one were asked to guess the values of each card drawn from such a deck, each correct guess would be a match. Statistical matching tests have interesting properties that are worth investigating.

We consider first a prototypical problem. If N balls are randomly distributed among N cells with the restriction of single occupancy, what is the probability that in the kth trial, cell number k will be occupied?

Solution. Notice that this is essentially a problem of arrangements. Our sample space $ consists of all possible arrangements of balls 1 through N among the N cells. Our event space E consists of all arrangements in which ball number k occupies cell number k. N elements can be arranged in $N!$ different ways; hence $S = N!$. Ball number k may occupy cell number k in only one way, but when that occurs the remaining $N - 1$ balls may be distributed among the remaining $N - 1$ cells in $(N - 1)!$ distinct ways. Hence

$$P[E] = \frac{(N-1)!}{N!} = \frac{1}{N}$$

Similarly, if we specified two cells, a and b, to be occupied by the trials corresponding to their own numbers,

$$P[\text{2 specified matches}] = \frac{(N-2)!}{N!} = \frac{1}{(N)_2}.$$

In general, for x specified matches, we would have Identity 13.3.1.

IDENTITY 13.3.1

$$P[x \text{ specified matches}] = \frac{(N-x)!}{N!} = \frac{1}{(N)_x}$$

Now let us consider the case in which only the *number* of matches rather than *which* matches is to be considered. Take the case of one match. We have already seen that

$$P[1 \text{ specified match}] = \frac{1}{N}$$

If we call the event in which a match occurs for the ith trial E_i, we might be tempted to reason

$$P\left[\bigcup_{i=1}^{N} E_i\right] = \sum_{i=1}^{N} P[E_i] = \sum_{i=1}^{N} \frac{1}{N} = \frac{N}{N} = 1$$

This would imply that the probability of at least one match is a certainty for any N—an assertion that our intuition rejects. The anomaly is caused by an overcount associated with the fact that the E_i are not exclusive sets and that intersections occur. The condition is met, for instance, if some single E_i occurs and also for any possible magnitude of the order of intersections. Thus if the fifth and seventh trials are both matches, then $E_5 \cap E_7$ occurs.

The sum of the probabilities of the intersections for any $(r-1)$st order of intersection consists in the present case of $\binom{N}{r}$ terms, each with a probability of $1/(N)_r$, so that Identity 13.3.2 is formed.

IDENTITY 13.3.2

$$p_{(r)} = \binom{N}{r} \cdot \frac{1}{(N)_r} = \frac{(N)_r}{r!} \cdot \frac{1}{(N)_r} = \frac{1}{r!}$$

Thus we observe the remarkable fact that $p_{(r)}$ is absolutely independent of N if $r \leq N$.

Applying Identity 13.2.1, then, we get to Identity 13.3.3.

IDENTITY 13.3.3

$$P\left[\bigcup_{i=1}^{N} E_i\right] = \sum_{x=1}^{N} (-1)^{x+1} p_{(x)} = \sum_{x=1}^{N} (-1)^{x+1} \frac{1}{x!}$$

This, then, is our formula for at least one match in N trials. Notice that, if we let N become large without limit,

$$1 - P\left[\bigcup_{i=1}^{N} E_i\right] = 1 - 1 + \frac{1}{2!} - \frac{1}{3!} + \cdots + \frac{(-1)^k}{k!} + \cdots = e^{-1}$$

by Identity 12.12 Corollary. Hence as $N \to \infty$

$$P\left[\bigcup_{i=1}^{N} E_i\right] = 1 - e^{-1}$$

It does not require a student of calculus to see that since $N!$ increases extremely rapidly with each increase in N, the terms soon add such negligible amounts that $1 - e^{-1}$ can be used as an extremely accurate estimate of the probability of at least one match, for even relatively small N. For $N = 8$, for instance, the term $1/N!$ changes the value of the probability by only .00002.

Since the probability of no occurrences is 1 minus the probability of at least one occurrence, then

$$P[0 \text{ matches}] = 1 - [1 - e^{-1}] = e^{-1}$$

For instance, in the random distribution of 10 balls among 10 cells, the probability that no trial would match the number of a cell is $e^{-1} = .36788$.

If a dozen married couples were randomly paired to be with members of the opposite sex at a dance, the probability that no one would be dancing with his own spouse is .36788. The probability that at least one married couple would be matched is $1 - .36788 = .63212$.

13.4 THE PROBABILITY OF EXACTLY *r* MATCHES

In this section we continue using one of the several meanings of E_i. Here E_i refers to a match of card i. The set defined by E_i is the set of all points such that there is a match of card i. The match of card i and the match of card j can then be indicated by $E_i \cap E_j$—that is, the set of all elements (points, events) where both matches occur.

We have seen by Identity 13.3.2 that the sum of the $\binom{N}{r}$ probabilities of the outcomes qualifying as r matches in N trials is

$$p_{(r)} = \frac{1}{r!}$$

regardless of the magnitude of N. The sum

$$\sum_{r<n} p_{(r)} = \sum_{r<n} \frac{1}{r!}$$

does not give us the probability of r matches in N trials because of overcounts caused by the intersections of the events. Our problem, then, becomes one of adjusting $p_{(r)}$ to eliminate the effects of overcounts.

Recalling that E_i is the event that a match occurs in the ith trial and that r matches require the intersection of r of these events, we may ignore all intersections of an order lower than $r - 1$, since these fail to qualify as r simultaneous occurrences and hence as r matches.

The condition that at least r matches have occurred is satisfied by the intersection of any r out of the N possible events. As we have seen, this can occur in any of $\binom{N}{r}$ different ways, each of which has the same probability $1/(N)_r$, so that the sum of the probabilities of those terms is

$$p_{(r)} = \binom{N}{r}\frac{1}{(N)_r} = \frac{1}{r!}$$

For instance, if we had decks of five cards each, a match of cards number i would be event E_i, so that a match of at least size 3 would occur with any combination of three simultaneous occurrences from among the five events E_1, E_2, E_3, E_4, and E_5. Typical sample points might be $E_1 \cap E_2 \cap E_3$ or $E_1 \cap E_4 \cap E_5$, and so forth, and there would be $\binom{5}{3} = 10$ such points. Thus $p_{(3)}$ incorporates the sum of the probabilities of 10 such points. These three-event intersections, however, may contain higher order intersections. For instance, the condition of at least three matches would be met not only by, say, $E_1 \cap E_2 \cap E_3$ but also by $E_1 \cap E_2 \cap E_3 \cap E_4$, or by $E_1 \cap E_2 \cap E_3 \cap E_5$, which are points in $p_{(r+1)} = p_{(4)}$. It could also be met by $E_1 \cap E_2 \cap E_3 \cap E_4 \cap E_5$, which is the maximum order intersection because it involves all of the events and has a probability of

$$p_{(r+2)} = p_{(r+N-r)} = p_{(2+5-2)} = p_{(5)}$$

Notice, then, that while $p_{(r+1)}$ contains only $\binom{N}{r+1}$ terms, each of these may be involved in more than one of the terms of $p_{(r)}$.

Thus $E_1 \cap E_2 \cap E_3 \cap E_4$, for example, a point in $p_{(4)}$, is involved in intersections with the following points in $p_{(3)}$:

$$E_1 \cap E_2 \cap E_3, \quad E_1 \cap E_2 \cap E_4, \quad E_1 \cap E_3 \cap E_4, \quad E_2 \cap E_3 \cap E_4$$

In other words, each point in $p_{(4)}$ is involved in $\binom{4}{3}$ of the intersections exemplifying occurrences of $p_{(3)}$. Thus in summing the points to obtain $p_{(3)}$ we have to be concerned not with one intersection of four events for each point in $p_{(3)}$ but with $\binom{4}{3} = 4$ of them.

More generally stated, each term in $p_{(r)}$ is involved in $\binom{r+1}{r}$ first-order intersections with points in $p_{(r+1)}$. And, even more generally stated, each term in $p_{(r)}$ is involved in $\binom{r+x}{r}(x-1)$st-order intersections with points in $p_{(r+x)}$.

The probability of exactly r matches, then, will be $p_{(r)}$ adjusted for all higher order intersections:

IDENTITY 13.4.1

$$P[r] = p_{(r)} - \binom{r+1}{r} p_{(r+1)} + \binom{r+2}{r} p_{(r+2)} - \cdots \pm \binom{N}{r} p_{(N)}$$

Of course, $p_{(N)}$ is the probability of a perfect matching of all N cards. Since there are $N - r$ terms after $p_{(r)}$, then the coefficient of $p_{(N)}$ is

$$\binom{r+N-r}{N-r} = \binom{N}{N-r} = \binom{N}{r}$$

Since

$$p_{(r)} = \frac{1}{r!} \quad \text{implies that} \quad p_{(r+x)} = \frac{1}{(r+x)!}, \quad \text{for any } r \leq N$$

we may obtain the probability for exactly r matches by the appropriate substitutions for the $p_{(r+x)}$ terms in Identity 13.4.1 as follows:

$$P[r] = \frac{1}{r!} - \binom{r+1}{r}\frac{1}{(r+1)!} + \binom{r+2}{r}\frac{1}{(r+2)!} - \cdots \pm \binom{N}{r}\frac{1}{N!}$$

$$= \sum_{x=0}^{N-r} \binom{r+x}{r}\frac{(-1)^x}{(r+x)!}$$

$$= \sum_{x=0}^{N-r} (-1)^x \frac{(r+x)_r}{r!}\cdot\frac{1}{(r+x)!}$$

$$= \frac{1}{r!}\sum_{x=0}^{N-r}\frac{(-1)^x}{x!}$$

However, if r remains finite and $N \to \infty$, then $N - r \to \infty$, and we obtain Identity 13.4.2.

IDENTITY 13.4.2

$$\frac{1}{r!}\sum_{x=0}^{\infty}\frac{(-1)^x}{x!} = \frac{1}{r!}\cdot e^{-1}$$

That is, we have our Poisson distribution in which $\lambda = 1$. Owing to the rapid convergence of the series, the approximation

$$P[r] \doteq \frac{e^{-1}}{r!} = p(r; \lambda = 1)$$

is excellent even for rather small N.* Since in statistical applications we are generally interested in cumulative probabilities at the tails of the distribution, we note

$$P[x|x \leq r] \doteq \sum_{x=0}^{r}\frac{e^{-1}}{x!} = e^{-1}\sum_{x=0}^{r}\frac{1}{x!}$$

$$= p[x \leq r; \lambda = 1] = C(x)$$

in the General Electric tables. And, of course,

$$P[r \leq x; \lambda = 1] = D(x)$$

* For a value as small as $N = 10$, the approximation is extremely accurate, and it might even suffice for an N as small as 6.

Example

A man who claimed that husbands and wives tend to "look alike" after they have been married for some time was asked to match the husbands and wives from 12 long-married couples. How many correct matches would he have to achieve for his claim to be credible at the .02 level?

Solution. We seek k such that $p(k \leq x; 1) = .02$. From the General Electric tables where $\lambda = 1$, $D(k) = .01899 < .02$, if $k = 4$. $D(3) = .08030 > .02$; hence $k = 3$ would not suffice. In other words, the claim would be quite credible if only four correct matches occurred.

What is to be noted is the decisiveness of results that are obtained with such a small N and small r. In short, this is a most powerful test, in the sense of yielding decisive results with amazingly small numbers of cases. Where cases are not easy to come by, an investigator might well consider the possibilities of this model. One potential area is in the assessment of sociometric relationships in small-group studies. For instance, after carefully determining the ranking of the group members for dominance ("pecking order"), the observer may wish to determine the social "reality perception" of individual members by having them assess the dominance ranks. Too few correct identifications would indicate poor reality perception.

In other areas it might be possible to use a matching model to determine whether a rank correlation exists where the conditions are not met for valid use of Spearman or Kendall correlation coefficients. The two variables could be ranked and a determination made as to whether the matches in rank exceeded the number that could be expected to occur by chance.

The versatility of matching tests is augmented by variations in matching models themselves. We shall not go into these variations here, but the reader should have little difficulty in understanding and applying those presented in Owen's *Handbook of Statistical Tables*, pp. 449–53. The essential feature of these is the opportunity to assess matches by membership in classes rather than depending upon unique identifiability of the elements to be matched. Thus in card matching one might be required to have a knowledge only of the suits rather than the unique value of each card such as "three of spades." It does not tax the imagination greatly to transfer these notions to such social categories as economic class or race.

13.5 THE PROBABILITY OF *m* EMPTY CELLS

In the matching models just considered, the implicit sample points are arrangements; this implies the restriction of single cell occupancy. One may investigate by very similar methods the probability of m empty cells given the random assignment of r balls among N cells without the restriction $r \leq N$. We shall assume that the reader now has sufficient confidence in the general methods to accept the end results, for the time being at least, without the proofs.*

By following Feller's method, the probability of finding exactly m cells empty in the random distribution of r balls in N cells is given by

$$p_m(r, N) = \binom{N}{m} \sum_{\nu=0}^{n-m} (-1)^\nu \binom{N-m}{\nu} \left(1 - \frac{m+\nu}{N}\right)^r$$

It is obvious that r/N is the average number of balls per cell. If r and N both become very large, but in such a way that r/N remains a value of moderate magnitude, then the following approximation formula is valid:

$$p_m(r, N) \doteq \frac{e^{-\lambda}\lambda^m}{m!}$$

where $\lambda = N\,e^{-r/N}$. Or

$$p_m(r, N) = p(m; \lambda = N\,e^{-r/N})$$

Hence

$$p_{m \leq x}(r, N) = D(m)$$

where $\lambda = N\,e^{-r/N}$, and

$$p_{x \leq m} = C(m)$$

* The skeptical reader is referred to Feller, *op. cit.*, pp. 91–95.

The following illustration should suggest other possibilities.

Example

A President of the United States disclaimed discriminating against any newsman in his press conference responses to questions. Out of a group of 147 newsmen in regular attendance during the first several years of his administration, 20 had never been recognized out of a total of 326 recognitions accorded to that group. Is there reason to suppose that the President was guilty of systematic avoidance? We will choose $\alpha = .05$.

*Solution.**

$$\frac{r}{N} = \frac{326}{147} \doteq 2.2177$$

$$\lambda = N\,e^{-2.2177} = 147(0.10886) \doteq 16$$

$$p_{20} = p(20 \leq x;\,16) = D(20) = .18775 > \alpha = .05$$

We are unable to reject H_0 that the President was impartial, since this many omissions could have occurred by chance 19 percent of the time.

If 24 newsmen had been ignored, then $D(24) = .037 < .05$, and there would be reason to suppose the President had shown favoritism or, more accurately, avoidance.

PROBLEMS

1. The children in a class choose a team of 10 of their class of 30 to represent them (see Chapter 5, Problem 2). Comparing the rank of class members and the order of choice of individuals gives a matching situation.

a. What is the probability of at least four matches?

b. What is the probability of no matches?

c. Formulate a test using matches and suggest how it might be interpreted.

* Values of e^x and e^{-x} may be obtained from tables, one of the most comprehensive and valuable of which is *Tables of the Exponential Function* e^x, N.B.S. Applied Mathematics Series 14, (Washington, D.C.: U.S. Government Printing Office, June 1951.)

2. Use the data given below, where two scales appear to calculate the probability of the observed or more than the observed number of matches.

RANKING ACCORDING TO	CLASS MEMBER											
	1	2	3	4	5	6	7	8	9	10	11	12
Scale 1	8	1	6	7	9	11	12	5	4	3	10	2
Scale 2	8	7	6	12	9	1	11	10	4	3	5	2

3. Refer to Chapter 12, Problem 3. Use the methods explained in Chapter 13 to determine the probable number of areas with no towns.

4. Given 500 categories and 500 people and assuming no a priori preference for categories, answer the following questions:

a. How many cells can be expected to be empty?

b. If a population is divided so that 20 percent of the population is in each of five age categories, 10 percent is in each of 10 occupational categories, 50 percent is in each of two sex categories, and 20 percent in each of five religion categories:

(1) Why are there 500 five-way categories? (Use the rules for product spaces.)

(2) If 300 of these cells are empty, what can be concluded?

5. With the primitive space containing the set $\{X|X$ is a digit 1 to $100\}$ as points, the probability of each point is .01. For each of the following events determine (1) the orders of intersection for the sets given; (2) the probability of the set (event given by direct counting and by the methods of Section 13.2 of the text). Use these sets:

$$X_1 = \{X|1 \leq X \leq 50\}$$

$$X_2 = \{X|1 \leq X \leq 40\}$$

$$X_3 = \{X|10 \leq X \leq 30\}$$

$$X_4 = \{X|1 \leq X \leq 10\}$$

$$X_5 = \{X|11 \le X \le 20\}$$
$$X_6 = \{X|21 \le X \le 30\}$$

Solve

a. $P[X_1 \cup X_2] =$
b. $P[X_1 \cup X_2 \cup X_3] =$
c. $P[X_4 \cup X_5 \cup X_6] =$
d. $P[X_3 \cup X_4 \cup X_5] =$
e. $P\left[\bigcup_{i=1}^{6} X_i\right] =$

CHAPTER 14

SOME TWO-SAMPLE TESTS

WE HAVE ALREADY considered a number of models in which the variables being tested may assume qualitative values. Now we consider models that require quantitative data but which nevertheless make such moderate assumptions about those data that they are regarded as nonparametric. To discuss these models we must draw on concepts from strong-assumption statistics—such as arithmetic mean and variance—but to develop these concepts meaningfully demands extensive discussion of topics that do not belong in this book. Since many readers will already have had at least an elementary exposure to strong-assumption statistics, we shall simply leave the special concepts undefined and proceed with our illustrative presentation of these "hybrid" models.

14.1 A RANDOMIZATION TEST FOR TWO INDEPENDENT SAMPLES

The randomization test for two independent samples that we are about to discuss is elegantly simple in its conception, requires no assumptions about normality or variance, as strong assumption statistics might; can be used even when the level of measurement is only ordinal; and makes use of all the information contained in the data. It can yield decisive results with amazingly small samples.

If the samples are small enough, computation is relatively simple. If they should be larger, it would be quite easy to write a computer program to do the job, or, as a second choice, use an approximation method.*

The model is best developed by a concrete example. The respondents from two groups—one group judged to be leader types and the other a randomly formed control group—were individually and independently exposed to an identical social situation requiring a decision. A concealed observer recorded the decision times as follows:

DECISION TIME IN SECONDS

Leaders	0.7	1.0	1.3	1.5	—
Control group	1.2	1.4	1.8	2.0	2.3

The substantive issue to be resolved is whether leaders make decisions more quickly than the members of a general population undifferentiated as to leaders and nonleaders. In other words, do leaders, on the average, tend to be differentially more rapid decision-makers?

Statistically, we might ask, "If four leaders had been randomly assigned without multiple occupancy to the set of nine scores achieved, is a set with as low an average score as that actually observed for the leaders a rare event?" The four leaders could have been assigned to the nine scores in as many ways as four indistinguishable balls may be assigned to nine cells without multiple occupancy—that is, in $\binom{9}{4}$ ways.

This, then, represents the number of points in a uniform space of samples of size $r = 4$, drawn without replacement and without regard to order from a population of $n = 9$ elements.

If we set $\alpha = .05$, then the number of points in the region of rejection, however it may be defined, is

$$\alpha\binom{n}{r} = .05\binom{9}{4} = .05(126) \doteq 6$$

* For an approximation formula, see Siegel, *op. cit.*, p. 155.

The region of rejection may now be defined as the six points in the sample space with the six lowest arithmetic means. Since the same number of scores are in each point, we do not need to calculate the mean. The sums of the scores in each point will yield exactly the same information.

Starting with the four lowest scores, their sums may be tabulated in order of magnitude as follows:

$$.07 + 1.0 + 1.2 + 1.3 = 4.2$$
$$.07 + 1.0 + 1.2 + 1.4 = 4.3$$
$$.07 + 1.0 + 1.3 + 1.4 = 4.4$$
$$.07 + 1.0 + 1.2 + 1.5 = 4.4$$
$$.07 + 1.0 + 1.3 + 1.5 = 4.5^*$$
$$.07 + 1.0 + 1.4 + 1.5 = 4.6$$

The sum with the asterisk is the sum of the scores actually observed for the "leaders." Since it falls in the region of rejection, we reject H_0 that there is no difference between the leaders and the control group, and conclude that leaders tend to make decisions more quickly.

Tie scores need not create any special problems. A distinction is implicitly made between tie scores, because each recurrence of that score is handled as a unique element in computing the sums for the sample space. Too many tie scores could create the problem of getting sufficient discrimination in the sums to set the region of rejection precisely where one wants it, but this would be an indirect effect.

If the data are only ordinal (that is, ranked) then those ranks can be used as though they were real-number scores. The procedures are identical except that the sums are obtained from the ranks rather than the scores themselves. Since the ranks are all integers, the arithmetic is simpler. Redoing this problem with ranks is suggested as an exercise for the reader. A good example may be found in Hodges and Lehman.* In ranked form, this is called the *Wilcoxon two-sample test.* If one uses ranks when real-number scores are available, information may be lost, although if extreme scores overly weight the mean of the scores, ranking might even rectify a misleading result. Careful considerations would be necessary to make this determination.

* J. L. Hodges, Jr., and E. L. Lehman, *Basic Concepts of Probability and Statistics* (San Francisco: Holden-Day, Inc., 1964), pp. 303–06.

14.2 RUNS

In linear arrangements of objects that are distinguishable between classes but not within classes (for example, blue books and red books), a continuous sequence of indistinguishable objects is called a *run*. Various patterns of runs have associated probabilities, under the null hypothesis that the objects were randomly arranged, and this fact provides the conceptual basis for the statistical models known as runs tests.

One application of runs analysis is the *Wald-Wolfowitz runs test*, which, like the randomization test, is used to decide whether two samples of quantitative data may be regarded as randomly drawn from a common population. In some cases, this test will not be as sensitive to specific items as parametric tests, but it compensates for this by not requiring assumptions that might not be true. For example, two samples with the same mean might be quite different in the distribution of the observations about the mean. A test that shows the means to be the same might require the *assumption* that the distributions are the same for each sample.

It is necessary for the data to be on at least an ordinal scale of measurement. Consider two samples that are combined to form a single collection of variates which are then arranged into a single, ranked arrangement but with each variate identified as to the sample from which it came. Thus two samples, A and B, might have contained scores as follows:

Sample A: 1, 2, 11, 12, 13, 14, 15
Sample B: 3, 4, 5, 7, 9, 10

A combined ranking which would identify the samples could be:

1	2	3	4	5	7	9	10	11	12	13	14	15
A	A	B	B	B	B	B	B	A	A	A	A	A

This reveals a total of three runs, an A run of size 2, a B run of size 6, and an A run of size 5. The stochastic problem becomes one of determining the probability that a random arrangement of seven As and six Bs would yield as few or fewer than three runs.

Consider for the moment the two extreme possibilities. The minimum number of runs would be two, and these could occur in two different ways. All of the As could precede all of the Bs, or all of the Bs could precede all of the As. We intuitively and correctly suppose that this would occur by chance only rarely under the null hypothesis and that it would suggest that the two samples had indeed been drawn from different populations.

At the other extreme, the maximum number of runs would occur if none of the elements in the smaller sized sample were adjacent to each other. For example, if one had an equal number of *A*s and *B*s, then the maximum number of runs would be achieved if they alternated *ABABAB*.... Such an orderly sequence would indicate intentional rather than random mixing, particularly where an actual arrangement is an observed one (for instance, a seating arrangement of men and women) rather than being a set of variates drawn for two mixed samples. Thus a very systematic alternation would lead to a maximum number of runs, which, like a very small number, would be an unlikely event if it were caused by random factors. Between the maximum and the minimum number of runs are various numbers of runs of varying magnitudes of probability. The stochastic foundations of runs tests require the determination of the probabilities associated with various numbers of runs.

14.3 NUMBER OF RUNS

First consider the numbers of runs. If there is an even number of runs, it must start with one type of element and end with the other. Conversely, if the arrangement starts with a run of one of the elements and ends with a run of the other, it must be characterized by an even number of runs. If we represent the total number of runs by k and the runs of the two elements by n_1 and n_2, respectively, then if there is an even number of runs, $n_1 = n_2$ and $n_1 + n_2 = k = 2n_1$. Moreover, two such sets of runs of size k may occur—one starting with one element and the other starting with the other element.

If there is an odd number of runs, then the arrangement must start and end with the elements involved in the greater number of runs. Conversely, if the arrangement starts and ends with the same elements, it contains an odd number of runs. If n_1 refers to the smaller run element, then $n_2 = n_1 + 1$. If n_1 refers to the larger run element, then $n_1 = n_2 + 1$.

If we let v represent the number of runs of the element with the minimum number, then $k = 2v$ for an even number of runs and $k = 2v + 1$ for an odd number of runs.

14.4 LEMMA FOR THE ANALYSIS OF RUNS

THEOREM 14.4.1. Given r indistinguishable balls and n distinguishable cells, so that $n < r$, the number of distinguishable distributions in which no cell remains empty is $\binom{r-1}{n-1}$. Translated into sample space meaning, this gives us the number of unordered samples of size r that contain every element at least once, if sampling occurs with replacement. It also represents the total number of sets of occupancy numbers that can occur if every cell has an occupancy number of at least one.

PROOF. In this case, we may regard the two end cell walls fixed and two end balls fixed adjacent to them. The remaining $n - 1$ indistinguishable cell walls must then be distributed among the $r - 1$ spaces between the r balls in such a manner that no two walls may occupy the same space.* Asking the number of ways in which $n - 1$ indistinguishable objects may be distributed without multiple occupancy among $r - 1$ cells is the same as asking how many distinguishable samples of size $n - 1$ can be drawn without replacement and without regard to order, from a population of $r - 1$ different elements. This is, of course, $\binom{r-1}{n-1}$. No cells are empty, because every cell wall is separated by at least one ball.

14.5 THE PROBABILITY OF n RUNS

We will consider the problem in terms of runs of αs and βs. Saying that there are n_1 alpha runs is the same as saying that there are n_1 cells among which r_1 alphas may be distributed under the condition that there shall be at least one alpha in every cell. In other words, we are asking in how many distinguishable ways r_1 indistinguishable alphas may be distributed among n_1 distinguishable cells, if no cell is to remain empty. We have seen from Theorem 14.4.1 that the number of distinguishable ways in which r_1 indistinguishable objects may be distributed among n distinguishable cells, under the condition that no cell shall remain empty, is $\binom{r-1}{n-1}$. Hence our alphas may be distributed in $\binom{r_1-1}{n_1-1}$ distinguishable ways.

* In effect, we are temporarily regarding the balls as cell walls and the cell walls as indistinguishable balls to be distributed in the cells formed by the balls.

For each of these there are by analogous consideration $\binom{r_2-1}{n_2-1}$ distinguishable arrangements of the betas. Thus for a given sequence of alpha and beta runs that is fixed with respect to the positions* (but not the sizes) of the runs, there are $\binom{r_1-1}{n_1-1}\binom{r_2-1}{n_2-1}$ distinguishable arrangements conforming to the stipulation n_1 alpha runs and n_2 beta runs.

Now if there is an even number of runs, the sequence may start with alphas and end with betas or start with betas and end with alphas in which case there are twice as many arrangements as for a fixed sequence.

Recalling by Theorem 6.3.1 that the number of distinguishable ways in which a objects of one sort and b of another may be arranged is given by

$$\binom{a+b}{a} = \binom{a+b}{b}$$

it is evident that the total number of distinguishable arrangements of r_1 alphas and r_2 betas is obtained from

$$\binom{r_1+r_2}{r_1} = \binom{r_1+r_2}{r_2}$$

if neither numbers nor lengths of runs are specified. Hence when there is an even number, ($k = 2\nu$), of runs, the probability of occurrence of exactly that number is given by

$$P_{2\nu} = \frac{2\binom{r_1-1}{\nu-1}\binom{r_2-1}{\nu-1}}{\binom{r_1+r_2}{r_1}}$$

If $k = 2\nu + 1$—that is, if the number of runs is odd—then the number of arrangements conforming to the stipulation exactly k runs is

$$\binom{r_1-1}{\nu-1}\binom{r_2-1}{\nu+1-1} + \binom{r_1-1}{\nu+1-1}\binom{r_2-1}{\nu-1}$$

where the left-hand terms yield the number of arrangements if there are ν alpha runs and $\nu + 1$ beta runs, and the right-hand terms yield the number of arrangements if there are $\nu + 1$ alpha

* For example, a sequence in which it is specified that the first run must be an α run, the second a β run, and so forth.

runs and v beta runs. Thus the probability of exactly k runs, where $k = 2v + 1$, is given by

$$P_{2v+1} = \frac{\binom{r_1-1}{v-1}\binom{r_2-1}{v} + \binom{r_1-1}{v}\binom{r_2-1}{v-1}}{\binom{r_1+r_2}{r_1}}$$

The probability of k or fewer runs is

$$P[x \leq k] = P[k] + P[k-1] + P[k-2] + \cdots + P[2]$$

Stated differently, the probability of k or fewer *even* runs may be expressed as

$$P[2x \leq k] = \frac{2}{\binom{r_1+r_2}{r_1}} \sum_{x=1}^{v} \binom{r_1-1}{x-1}\binom{r_2-1}{x}$$

The probability of k or fewer *odd* run terms may be expressed as

$$P[2x+1 \leq k] = \binom{r_1+r_2}{r_1}^{-1} \sum_{x=1}^{v} \left[\binom{r_1-1}{x-1}\binom{r_2-1}{x} + \binom{r_1-1}{x}\binom{r_2-1}{x-1}\right]$$

In Table F of Siegel,* critical values of k (labeled r therein) are given for the .05 significance level for numbers of elements $r_1 = 2$ to $r_1 = 20$ alphas and $r_2 = 2$ to $r_2 = 20$ betas (labeled therein n_1 and n_2).

Example

The director of a series of regular sessions of socio-drama wished to test the hypothesis that those who participate in the dramas tend to become more outgoing than those who attend merely as spectators. Out of some 30 persons enrolled for the sessions he randomly chose seven to be frequent participants in the dramas and six to be limited to the role of spectator during the experimental period. All 30 enrollees of the session were provided with ample informal opportunity and encouragement to get to know one another when the dramas were not being conducted. Initial and terminal tests were given in which each individual in

* Siegel, *op. cit.*, pp. 252–253.

the experimental and control groups was asked to list all the enrollees in the session whom he felt he trusted and regarded as friends. We shall suppose that the first test showed no significant difference between the experimental and control groups and that the numbers selected by the respondents in the second test are those indicated in sample A (experimental) and sample B (control) in Section 14.2.

We set $\alpha = .01$ and we have

H_0: Groups A and B do not differ with respect to "outgoingness"

H_1: One group is more outgoing than the other

The total number of runs observed was $k = 3$. Since $k = 2v + 1$ for the odd runs in the series,

$$v = \frac{k-1}{2} = \frac{3-1}{2} = 1$$

$$r_1 = 7 \text{ elements (scores)}$$

$$r_2 = 6 \text{ elements}$$

$$\binom{r_1 + r_2}{r_1} = \binom{7+6}{7} = \binom{13}{6} = 1716$$

$$P[2x + 1 \leq 3] = \frac{1}{1716} \sum_{x=1}^{1} \binom{7-1}{x-1}\binom{6-1}{x} + \binom{7-1}{x}\binom{6-1}{x-1}$$

$$= \frac{\binom{6}{0}\binom{5}{1} + \binom{6}{1}\binom{5}{0}}{1716} = \frac{(1 \cdot 5) + (6 \cdot 1)}{1716} = \frac{11}{1716}$$

For the even-run segment of the series, $k = 2v$ and

$$v = \frac{k}{2} = \frac{2}{2} = 1$$

and

$$P[2x \leq 2] = \frac{2}{1716} \sum_{x=1}^{1} \binom{7-1}{x-1}\binom{6-1}{x}$$

$$= \frac{2}{1716}\binom{6}{0}\binom{5}{1} = \frac{2 \cdot 1 \cdot 5}{1716} = \frac{10}{1716}$$

Combining the odd and even segments gives

$$P[x \leq k] = \frac{11 + 10}{1716} = \frac{21}{1716} = .01224 \doteq .01 \leq .01 = \alpha$$

We therefore reject H_0 and accept H_1 that one group is more outgoing, presumably the experimental one.

Ordinarily one would use a table rather than actually calculate the cumulative probabilities.* Tables published for use with runs characteristically list the critical numbers of runs associated with selected confidence levels rather than the probabilities associated with specified numbers of runs, because the marginal tabs are used to identify the sizes of the samples involved (n_1 and n_2 correspond to r_1 and r_2 of our notation).

Runs tests can be used obviously with a low level of measurement such as ordinal and hence with arrangements. In practice, this means arrangements of elements of two sorts, but there is no barrier in principle to a larger number of categories. Arrangement applications could be illustrated by runs of the sexes in a theater line or races at a lunch counter.

Another possible application is the detection of autocorrelated error terms in the analysis of time series. Too few runs in the time sequence of values falling both above and below the regression function would lead one to conclude that the null hypothesis of autocorrelated error runs could not be rejected, thereby casting doubt on the validity of the regression coefficients and the coefficient of correlation.

As in the case of many of the other statistical models, the application potential of the runs test is largely determined by the creative imagination of the investigator.

PROBLEMS

1. The following data were observed on a reaction-speed test:

Leader	.7	1.0	1.3	1.5	—
Control group	1.2	1.4	1.8	2.0	2.3

* Such tables are to be found in Appendix of Siegel, *op. cit.*, and in Lieberman and Owen, *op. cit.*, pp. 373–82.

a. Use the runs test to make a statistical test of these data. Why do the results of the runs test differ from the results obtained in the first part of the chapter?

b. Rank the individuals. Use the ranks to get means and establish a statistical distribution. Compare this test with the two tests mentioned in part a.

c. With a sample of size 9, there will be four fastest reaction speeds. A table like the following can be formed:

	Leader	Control	Total
Fastest			4
Slower			5
Total	4	5	9

Use the χ^2 and Fisher exact tests to formulate conclusions about the data given for this problem.

d. Construct a table comparing all five tests and clarifying any differences in the generality of the H_0 tested. (*Note:* The two tests using means are more specific in what they test than are the other three tests.)

2. Persons are often fooled into thinking there is something sacred about "measured" values as opposed to rank or run information. The following data are an example of a use where this is not true.* These data are scores on an endurance test.

College athletes	.70	.6	.55	.45	.45	.3
Construction workers	.54	.50	.48	.46	.53	—

a. Do all parts of Problem 1.

b. Draw substantive conclusions based on the runs test.

* See Scheffe and Seigel on randomization and see Hammersley and Handscomb on the Monte Carlo Method.

BIBLIOGRAPHY

PART ONE

The references below are those that will help the reader gain a second perspective on points that are difficult to understand; they may also serve as sources for extra problems. The chapter on probability in Smith and Dice's *Modern College Mathematics* may prove particularly valuable for supplementary work for those who have difficulty with set concepts and probability. The book by Feller, *An Introduction to Probability Theory and Its Applications*, is the advanced work most directly related to the present book. Cramér's *Mathematical Methods of Statistics* is a good advanced reference on statistics. *Monte Carlo Methods*, by Hammersley and Handscomb, tells what to do if a probability problem is too complicated to solve analytically.

Allendoerfer, Carl B., and C. O. Oakley, *Fundamentals of Freshman Mathematics.* New York: McGraw-Hill, 1965.

Cramér, H., *Mathematical Methods of Statistics.* Princeton, N.J.: Princeton University Press, 1961.

Feller, William, *An Introduction to Probability Theory and Its Applications* (2nd ed.), Vol. I. New York: Wiley, 1959.

Fisher, Ronald A., *Statistical Methods for Research Workers.* New York: Hafner, 1958.

Fisz, Marek, *Probability Theory and Mathematical Statistics.* New York: Wiley, 1963.

Hammersley, J. M., and D. C. Handscomb, *Monte Carlo Methods.* New York: Barnes & Noble, 1965.

Hodges, J. L., and E. L. Lehman, *Basic Concepts of Probability and Statistics.* San Francisco: Holden-Day, 1964.

Hoel, Paul G., *Introduction to Mathematical Statistics.* New York: Wiley, 1954.

Hogg, Robert U., and Allen T. Craig, *Introduction to Mathematical Statistics.* New York: Macmillan, 1962.

Kattsoff, Louis O., and Albert J. Simone, *Finite Mathematics.* New York: McGraw-Hill, 1965.

Kemeny, John G., J. Laurie Snell, and G. L. Thompson, *Introduction to Finite Mathematics.* Englewood Cliffs, N. J.: Prentice-Hall, 1957.

Lipschutz, Seymour, *Probability.* New York: McGraw-Hill (Schaum's series), 1968.

McGinnis, Robert, *Mathematical Foundations for Social Analysis.* Indianapolis, Ind.: Bobbs-Merrill, 1966.

Richardson, C. H., *An Introduction to Statistical Analysis.* New York: Harcourt, Brace, 1944.

Siegel, Sidney, *Nonparametric Statistics for the Behavioral Sciences.* New York: McGraw-Hill, 1956.

Shanahan, Patrick, *Introductory College Mathematics.* Englewood Cliffs, N.J.: Prentice-Hall, 1963.

Smith, William K., and Stanley F. Dice, *Modern College Mathematics.* Boston: Allyn and Bacon, 1963.

Spiegel, Murray R., *Theory and Problems of Statistics.* New York: Schaum, 1961.

Thorp, Edward O., *Elementary Probability.* New York: Wiley, 1966.

PART TWO

The books below are recommended for broadening one's understanding of mathematical concepts as used in the social and behavioral sciences. Kamke's *Theory of Sets* is a good though quite advanced treatment of the theory of counting with transfinite numbers; it is an excellent example of how a difficult topic can be developed clearly and logically. *Contributions to Mathematical*

Statistics, prepared in the memory of R. A. Fisher—probably the first applied statistician to develop a solid theoretical approach to the question of why one statistical procedure is better than another—presents articles which show a real conflict over which statistical way is better.

Ayres, Frank, *Theory and Problems of Modern Algebra*. New York: Schaum, 1965.

Coleman, James S., *Introduction to Mathematical Sociology*. New York: Free Press, 1964.

Fisher, R. A., *Contributions to Mathematical Statistics*. New York: Wiley, 1950.

Gordon, Charles K., *Introduction to Mathematical Structures*. Belmont, Calif.: Dickenson, 1967.

Kamke, E., *Theory of Sets*, trans. Frederick Bagemial. New York: Dover, 1950.

Kemeny, John G., H. Mirkil, J. L. Snell, and G. L. Thompson, *Finite Mathematical Structures*. Englewood Cliffs, N.J.: Prentice-Hall, 1963.

———, A. Schleifer, ———, ———, *Finite Mathematics with Business Applications*. Englewood Cliffs, N.J.: Prentice-Hall, 1962.

———, and J. Laurie Snell, *Mathematical Models in the Social Sciences*. Boston: Ginn, 1962.

Lazarsfeld, Paul F., and N. W. Henry, *Readings in Mathematical Social Science*. Chicago: Science Research Associates, 1966.

Lipschutz, Seymour, *Theory and Problems of Finite Mathematics*. New York: Schaum, 1966.

———, *Theory and Problems of General Topology*. New York: Schaum, 1965.

———, *Theory and Problems of Set Theory and Related Topics*. New York: Schaum, 1964.

Luchins, Abraham S., and Edith H. Luchins, *Logical Foundations of Mathematics for Behavioral Scientists*. New York: Holt, 1965.

Massarik, Fred, and Philburn Ratoosh, eds., *Mathematical Explorations in Behavioral Science*. Homewood, Ill.: Irwin and Dorsey Press, 1965.

Polya, G., *Induction and Analogy in Mathematics*, Vol. I. Princeton, N.J.: Princeton University Press, 1954.

Polya, G., *Patterns of Plausible Inference*, Vol. II. Princeton, N.J.: Princeton University Press, 1954.

Springer, Clifford H., Robert E. Herlihy, Robert T. Mall, and Robert I. Beggs, *Probabilistic Models*, Vol. IV. Homewood, Ill.: Irwin, 1968.

Whitworth, William Allen, *Choice and Chance with One Thousand Exercises*. New York: Hafner, 1959.

PART THREE

The works below list tables of statistical and mathematical values.

Computation Laboratory Staff, *Tables of the Cumulative Binomial Probability Distribution.* Cambridge, Mass.: Harvard University Press, 1955.*

Fisher, Ronald A., and Frank Yates, *Statistical Tables for Biological, Agricultural and Medical Research.* New York: Hafner, 1957.

General Electric Company, Defense Systems Department, *Tables of the Individual and Cumulative Terms of Poisson Distribution.* Princeton, N.J.: Van Nostrand, 1962.

Lieberman, Gerald J., and Donald B. Owen, *Tables of the Hypergeometric Probability Distribution.* Stanford, Calif.: Stanford University Press, 1961.

N.B.S. Applied Mathematics Series No. 31, *Table of Natural Logarithms for Arguments Between Zero and Five to Sixteen Decimal Places.* Washington, D.C.: U.S. Government Printing Office, 1953.

N.B.S. Applied Mathematics Series No. 53, *Table of Natural Logarithms for Arguments Between Five and Ten to Sixteen Decimal Places.* Washington, D.C.: U.S. Government Printing Office, 1958.

N.B.S. Applied Mathematics Series No. 14, *Table of the Exponential Function* e^x. Washington, D.C.: U.S. Government Printing Office, 1961.

Owen, D. B., *Handbook of Statistical Tables.* Reading, Mass.: Addison-Wesley, 1962.

U.S. Department of Commerce, *Handbook of Mathematical Functions with Formulas, Graphs, and Mathematical Tables.* Washington, D.C.: U.S. Government Printing Office, 1964.

* Additional tables of binomial probability values are listed in Chapter 9, Section 9.4.

APPENDIX A: DISTRIBUTION OF χ^2 PROBABILITY*

n	·99	·98	·95	·90	·80	·70	·50	·30	·20	·10	·05	·02	·01	·001
1	$\cdot 0^{3}157$	$\cdot 0^{3}628$	·00393	·0158	·0642	·148	·455	1·074	1·642	2·706	3·841	5·412	6·635	10·827
2	·0201	·0404	·103	·211	·446	·713	1·386	2·408	3·219	4·605	5·991	7·824	9·210	13·815
3	·115	·185	·352	·584	1·005	1·424	2·366	3·665	4·642	6·251	7·815	9·837	11·345	16·266
4	·297	·429	·711	1·064	1·649	2·195	3·357	4·878	5·989	7·779	9·488	11·668	13·277	18·467
5	·554	·752	1·145	1·610	2·343	3·000	4·351	6·064	7·289	9·236	11·070	13·388	15·086	20·515
6	·872	1·134	1·635	2·204	3·070	3·828	5·348	7·231	8·558	10·645	12·592	15·033	16·812	22·457
7	1·239	1·564	2·167	2·833	3·822	4·671	6·346	8·383	9·803	12·017	14·067	16·622	18·475	24·322
8	1·646	2·032	2·733	3·490	4·594	5·527	7·344	9·524	11·030	13·362	15·507	18·168	20·090	26·125
9	2·088	2·532	3·325	4·168	5·380	6·393	8·343	10·656	12·242	14·684	16·919	19·679	21·666	27·877
10	2·558	3·059	3·940	4·865	6·179	7·267	9·342	11·781	13·442	15·987	18·307	21·161	23·209	29·588
11	3·053	3·609	4·575	5·578	6·989	8·148	10·341	12·899	14·631	17·275	19·675	22·618	24·725	31·264
12	3·571	4·178	5·226	6·304	7·807	9·034	11·340	14·011	15·812	18·549	21·026	24·054	26·217	32·909
13	4·107	4·765	5·892	7·042	8·634	9·926	12·340	15·119	16·985	19·812	22·362	25·472	27·688	34·528
14	4·660	5·368	6·571	7·790	9·467	10·821	13·339	16·222	18·151	21·064	23·685	26·873	29·141	36·123
15	5·229	5·985	7·261	8·547	10·307	11·721	14·339	17·322	19·311	22·307	24·996	28·259	30·578	37·697
16	5·812	6·614	7·962	9·312	11·152	12·624	15·338	18·418	20·465	23·542	26·296	29·633	32·000	39·252
17	6·408	7·255	8·672	10·085	12·002	13·531	16·338	19·511	21·615	24·769	27·587	30·995	33·409	40·790
18	7·015	7·906	9·390	10·865	12·857	14·440	17·338	20·601	22·760	25·989	28·869	32·346	34·805	42·312
19	7·633	8·567	10·117	11·651	13·716	15·352	18·338	21·689	23·900	27·204	30·144	33·687	36·191	43·820
20	8·260	9·237	10·851	12·443	14·578	16·266	19·337	22·775	25·038	28·412	31·410	35·020	37·566	45·315
21	8·897	9·915	11·591	13·240	15·445	17·182	20·337	23·858	26·171	29·615	32·671	35·343	38·932	46·797
22	9·542	10·600	12·338	14·041	16·314	18·101	21·337	24·939	27·301	30·813	33·924	37·659	40·289	48·268
23	10·196	11·293	13·091	14·848	17·187	19·021	22·337	26·018	28·429	32·007	35·172	38·968	41·638	49·728
24	10·856	11·992	13·848	15·659	18·062	19·943	23·337	27·096	29·553	33·196	36·415	40·270	42·980	51·179
25	11·524	12·697	14·611	16·473	18·940	20·867	24·337	28·172	30·675	34·382	37·652	41·566	44·314	52·620
26	12·198	13·409	15·379	17·292	19·820	21·792	25·336	29·246	31·795	35·563	38·885	42·856	45·642	54·052
27	12·879	14·125	16·151	18·114	20·703	22·719	26·336	30·319	32·912	36·741	40·113	44·140	46·963	55·476
28	13·565	14·847	16·928	18·939	21·588	23·647	27·336	31·391	34·027	37·916	41·337	45·419	48·278	56·893
29	14·256	15·574	17·708	19·768	22·475	24·577	28·336	32·461	35·139	39·087	42·557	46·693	49·588	58·302
30	14·953	16·306	18·493	20·599	23·364	25·508	29·336	33·530	36·250	40·256	43·773	47·962	50·892	59·703
32	16·362	17·783	20·072	22·271	25·148	27·373	31·336	35·665	38·466	42·585	46·194	50·487	53·486	62·487
34	17·789	19·275	21·664	23·952	26·938	29·242	33·336	37·795	40·676	44·903	48·602	52·995	56·061	65·247
36	19·233	20·783	23·269	25·643	28·735	31·115	35·336	39·922	42·879	47·212	50·999	55·489	58·619	67·985
38	20·691	22·304	24·884	27·343	30·537	32·992	37·335	42·045	45·076	49·513	53·384	57·969	61·162	70·703
40	22·164	23·838	26·509	29·051	32·345	34·872	39·335	44·165	47·269	51·805	55·759	60·436	63·691	73·402
42	23·650	25·383	28·144	30·765	34·157	36·755	41·335	46·282	49·456	54·090	58·124	62·892	65·205	76·084
44	25·148	26·939	29·787	32·487	35·974	38·641	43·335	48·396	51·639	56·369	60·481	65·337	68·710	78·750
46	26·657	28·504	31·439	34·215	37·795	40·529	45·335	50·507	53·818	58·641	62·830	67·771	71·201	81·400
48	28·177	30·080	33·098	35·949	39·621	42·420	47·335	52·616	55·993	60·907	65·171	70·197	73·683	84·037
50	29·707	31·664	34·764	37·689	41·449	44·313	49·335	54·723	58·164	63·167	67·505	72·613	76·154	86·661
52	31·246	33·256	36·437	39·433	43·281	46·209	51·335	56·827	60·332	65·422	69·832	75·021	78·616	89·272
54	32·793	34·856	38·116	41·183	45·117	48·106	53·335	58·930	62·496	67·673	72·153	77·422	81·069	91·872
56	34·350	36·464	39·801	42·937	46·955	50·005	55·335	61·031	64·658	69·919	74·468	79·815	83·513	94·461
58	35·913	38·078	41·492	44·696	48·797	51·906	57·335	63·129	66·816	72·160	76·778	82·201	85·950	97·039
60	37·485	39·699	43·188	46·459	50·641	53·809	59·335	65·227	68·972	74·397	79·082	84·580	88·379	99·607
62	39·063	41·327	44·889	48·226	52·487	55·714	61·335	67·322	71·125	76·630	81·381	86·953	90·802	102·166
64	40·649	42·960	46·595	49·996	54·336	57·620	63·335	69·416	73·276	78·860	83·675	89·320	93·217	104·716
66	42·240	44·599	48·305	51·770	56·188	59·527	65·335	71·508	75·424	81·085	85·965	91·681	95·626	107·258
68	43·838	46·244	50·020	53·548	58·042	61·436	67·335	73·600	77·571	83·308	88·250	94·037	98·028	109·791
70	45·442	47·893	51·739	55·329	59·898	63·346	69·334	75·689	79·715	85·527	90·531	96·388	100·425	112·317

For odd values of n between 30 and 70 the mean of the tabular values for $n-1$ and $n+1$ may be taken. For larger values of n, the expression $\sqrt{2\chi^2}-\sqrt{2n-1}$ may be used as a normal deviate with unit variance, remembering that the probability for χ^2 corresponds with that of a single tail of the normal curve. (For fuller formulæ see Introduction.)

APPENDIX B: ALGOL COMPUTER PROGRAM FOR A 2 × 3 CELL FISHER EXACT TEST

WE PRESENT here a working program for a 2 × 3 cell Fisher exact test as discussed in Section 8.8. Input/output instructions vary greatly with local computer installations and are not part of the ALGOL language. They have nevertheless been retained to show where input/output instructions are required. The format instructions have been left in for their instructive value. The program was originally written to be run with the B. C. ALGOL 60 compiler prepared at the University of California at Berkeley. The program was run-tested and reflects exigencies of compiler limitations. Its primary value here is for the algorithm it contains, since computer installations that support ALGOL are not too common in the United States. The very close similarity of PL/I to ALGOL should make the translation fairly simple.

```
BEGIN

COMMENT

    THIS PROGRAM FINDS THE EXACT AND THE CUMULA-
TIVE UP AND DOWN PROBABILITIES FOR THE HYPER-
GEOMETRIC MODEL OF A SAMPLE DRAWN WITHOUT
REPLACEMENT FROM A POPULATION CONTAINING 3 DIS-
TINCT TYPES OF ELEMENTS, I.E. A SAMPLE OF SIZE EN
DRAWN FROM A POPULATION OF SIZE N CONTAINING KWUN
ELEMENTS OF ONE SORT, KTU ELEMENTS OF ANOTHER
SORT, AND N-KWUN -KTU RESIDUAL ELEMENTS. THIS PRO-
GRAM FINDS THE PROBABILITY THAT SUCH A SAMPLE WILL
CONTAIN RWUN ELEMENTS OF THE FIRST SORT AND RTU
ELEMENTS OF THE SECOND SORT.
    IF THIS PROGRAM IS USED FOR A 2 BY 3 CONTINGENCY
TABLE, N = THE TOTAL NUMBER OF CASES, EN = A MAR-
GINAL TOTAL IN THE SHORT DIMENSION, KWUN AND KTU
ARE MARGINAL TOTALS IN THE LONG DIMENSION AND
RWUN AND RTU ARE CELL VALUES IN THE SAME COLUMN
AS EN AND THE SAME ROWS RESPECTIVELY AS KWUN AND
KTU. CHOOSE SMALLEST VALUES FOR KWUN AND KTU TO
SAVE MACHINE TIME.
    ORDER OF INPUTS IS N, EN, KWUN, KTU, RWUN, RTU,
AND ONE SET (=2) TITLE CARDS;

REAL PROCEDURE BICOF (N,R);

    VALUE N,R;

    INTEGER N,R;

BEGIN

    REAL INT;

    INT:= 1;

IF R=O THEN GO TO OUT;
```

```
    IF R >N-R THEN R=N-R;

    N:=N+1;

    R:=R+1;

CORKSCREW:

    N:=N-1;

    R:=R-1;

    INT  := (INT/R) X N;

    IF R > 1 THEN GO TO CORKSCREW;

OUT:

    BICOF  := INT;

END;

    PROCEDURE TEXT (S); STRING S; CODE;

    INTEGER N, EN, KWUN, KTU, RWUN, RTU, I, KPROD,
    UPDIF, LODIF, XWUN, XTU, CONST, UPWUN, AUGCONST,
    LOCONST;

    REAL DENOM, RAY, EXPROB, CUMPROB, CUMDOWN;

    REAL FORMAT (TRUE, 20, 7);

    INPUT ( N );

    INPUT (EN);

    INPUT (KWUN);

    INPUT (KTU);
```

```
    INPUT (RWUN);

    INPUT (RTU);

    KPROD := (KWUN + 1) X (KTU + 1);

    I := 0;

    DENOM := BICOF (N, EN);

    UPDIF := N - KWUN - KTU;

    XWUN := -1;

    CONST := UPDIF - EN;

    UPWUN := KTU + 1;

BEGIN

    ARRAY PROB [1:KPROD] ;

ESCALATOR:

    XWUN := XWUN + 1;

    IF XWUN > KWUN THEN GO TO FINALE;

    AUGCONST := CONST + XWUN;

    LOCONST := EN-XWUN+1;

    RAY := BICOF (KWUN, XWUN) / DENOM;

    LODIF := EN-XWUN;

    XTU := -1;

INCYC:

    XTU := XTU + 1;
```

```
    IF XTU > KTU THEN GO TO ESCALATOR;

    I:= I + 1;

    PROB [I]:= IF XTU = 0 THEN RAY X BICOF (UPDIF, LODIF)
    ELSE (PROB [ I-1 ] X (UPWUN - XTU) X (LOCONST - XTU))
    / (XTU X (AUGCONST + XTU));

IF XWUN = RWUN AND XTU = RTU THEN EXPROB :=
    PROB [ I ];

    GO TO INCYC;

FINALE:

    CUMPROB := 0;

    FOR I:= 1 STEP 1 UNTIL KPROD DO

BEGIN

    IF PROB [ I ] ≤ EXPROB THEN CUMPROB := CUMPROB +
    PROB [ I ];

END;

    CUMDOWN := 1-CUMPROB + EXPROB;

    NLCR; NLCR; NLCR;

    REAL FORMAT (TRUE, 10, 7);

    TITLE;

    NLCR; NLCR;

    SPACES (20);

TEXT (THE POINT PROBABILITY=);

    OUTPUT (EXPROB);

    SPACES (5);
```

```
TEXT (CROSSCHECK OF POINT PROBABILITY = );

    OUTPUT (BICOF(KWUN, RWUN) X BICOF(KTU, RTU) X
    BICOF(UPDIF, (EN-RWUN-RTU))/DENOM);

    NLCR; NLCR;

    SPACES (20);

TEXT (THE PROBABILITY THAT A DISTRIBUTION WOULD BE
    AS PROBABL  );

TEXT (E OR LESS PROBABLE THAN THIS =);

    OUTPUT (CUMPROB);

    NLCR; NLCR;

    SPACES (20);

TEXT (THE PROBABILITY THAT A DISTRIBUTION WOULD BE
    AS PROBABL  );

TEXT (E OR MORE PROBABLE THAN THIS =);

    OUTPUT (CUMDOWN);

    NLCR; NLCR; NLCR;

    INTEGER FORMAT (3);

TEXT (THE PARAMETERS OF THE DISTRIBUTION TESTED
    WERE:);

    NLCR; NLCR;

    SPACES (20);

TEXT (N=);

    OUTPUT (N);
```

```
    NLCR; NLCR;
    SPACES (20);
TEXT (EN =);
    OUTPUT (EN);
    NLCR; NLCR;
    SPACES (20);
TEXT (KWUN =);
    OUTPUT (KWUN);
    NLCR; NLCR;
    SPACES (20);
TEXT (KTU =);
    OUTPUT (KTU);
    NLCR; NLCR;
    SPACES (20);
TEXT (RWUN=);
    OUTPUT (RWUN);
    NLCR; NLCR;
    SPACES (20);
TEXT (RTU=);
    OUTPUT (RTU);
END;
END;
```

APPENDIX C: BASIC LANGUAGE PROGRAM FOR THE 3-DIMENSIONAL χ^2 CONTINGENCY TABLE

```
READY
LIST


CHI3       12:24  W.REG.  05/05/69  MON

100 PRINT
110 PRINT
120 PRINT "THREE DIMENSIONAL CHI-SQUARE TABLE OF DECLARED SIZE"
130 PRINT "E X F X G -- MAXIMUM = 10 X 10 X 10. VARIABLES ARE"
140 PRINT "I, J, AND K. I = 1 TO E; J = 1 TO F; K = 1 TO G."
150 PRINT "MODEL IS FROM FUNDAMENTALS OF NONPARAMETRIC STATISTICS"
160 PRINT "BY ALBERT PIERCE.  PROGRAM WRITTEN BY AUTHOR."
170 PRINT
180 PRINT
190 PRINT "          E FOR YOUR TABLE IS";
200 INPUT E
210 PRINT "          F FOR YOUR TABLE IS";
220 INPUT F
230 PRINT "          G FOR YOUR TABLE IS";
240 INPUT G
250 PRINT
260 PRINT "DATA FOR THIS PROGRAM MUST BE STORED IN FILE TRY."
270 PRINT
280 PRINT "       IS YOUR DATA STORED IN FILE TRY (TYPE YES OR NO)";
290 INPUT Q$
300 IF Q$="YES" THEN 350
310 PRINT
320 PRINT
330 PRINT "PROGRAM RUN TERMINATED FOR LACK OF DATA"
340 STOP
350 REM DATA IS IN FILE
360  PRINT
370  PRINT
380 PRINT "      NUMBER OF CASES TO BE PROCESSED IS";
390 INPUT N
400  PRINT
410  PRINT
420  FOR I=1 TO E
430  FOR J=1 TO F
440  FOR K=1 TO G
450  LET R(I,J,K)=0
460  NEXT K
470  NEXT J
480  NEXT I
490 DEF FNP(X)=(((X-R(I,J,K))↑2)/X)
500  FOR Z=1 TO N
510 INPUT:TRY:I,J,K
520  LET R(I,J,K)=R(I,J,K)+1
530  NEXT Z
540 PRINT
550  FOR I=1 TO E
560  LET T(I)=0
570  NEXT I
580  FOR J=1 TO F
590  LET U(J)=0
600  NEXT J
610  FOR K=1 TO G
620  LET V(K)=0
630  NEXT K
640 GOSUB 1670
650  FOR I=1 TO E
660  FOR J=1 TO F
670  FOR K=1 TO G
680  LET T(I)=T(I)+R(I,J,K)
690  LET U(J)=U(J)+R(I,J,K)
700  LET V(K)=V(K)+R(I,J,K)
710 LET A(I,J)=A(I,J)+R(I,J,K)
720 LET B(I,K)=B(I,K)+R(I,J,K)
```

```
730 LET C(J,K)=C(J,K)+R(I,J,K)
740  NEXT K
750  NEXT J
760  NEXT I
770 PRINT "COLUMN TOTALS"
780 PRINT
790 FOR I=1 TO E
800 PRINT "       TAU( I =";I;") =";T(I)
810  NEXT I
820  PRINT
830  FOR J=1 TO F
840 PRINT "       TAU( J =";J;") =";U(J)
850  NEXT J
860 PRINT
870  FOR K=1 TO G
880 PRINT "       TAU( K =";K;") =";V(K)
890 NEXT K
900  PRINT
910  PRINT
920 PRINT "     OBSERVED AND EXPECTED CELL VALUES"
930 PRINT
940 PRINT
950 PRINT " I";"  J";"  K";"  R","E(I,J,K)","E(IJ:K)","E(IK:J)",
960 PRINT "E(JK:I)"
970 PRINT
980 LET N2=N↑2
990  LET C2=Ø
1ØØØ LET P1=Ø
1Ø1Ø LET P2=Ø
1Ø2Ø LET P3=Ø
1Ø3Ø  FOR I=1 TO E
1Ø4Ø  FOR J=1 TO F
1Ø5Ø  FOR K=1 TO G
1Ø6Ø LET WØ=(T(I)*U(J)*V(K))/N2
1Ø7Ø GOSUB 123Ø
1Ø8Ø PRINT I;J;K;R(I,J,K),WØ,W1,W2,W3
1Ø9Ø LET C2=C2+FNP(WØ)
11ØØ  NEXT K
111Ø  NEXT J
112Ø  NEXT I
113Ø  PRINT
114Ø  PRINT
115Ø PRINT "CHI-SQUARE =";C2;"WITH";(E-1)*(F-1)*(G-1);
116Ø PRINT "DEGREES OF FREEDOM"
117Ø PRINT
118Ø PRINT
119Ø PRINT "N =";N
12ØØ PRINT
121Ø PRINT
122Ø GO TO 131Ø
123Ø REM SUBROUTINE TO COMPUTE PARTIALS
124Ø LET W1=(A(I,J)*V(K))/N
125Ø LET W2=(B(I,K)*U(J))/N
126Ø LET W3=(C(J,K)*T(I))/N
127Ø LET P1=P1+FNP(W1)
128Ø LET P2=P2+FNP(W2)
129Ø LET P3=P3+FNP(W3)
13ØØ RETURN
131Ø REM END PARTIAL SUBROUTINE
132Ø PRINT "COLUMN TOTALS FOR PARTIALS"
133Ø PRINT
134Ø FOR I=1 TO E
135Ø FOR J=1 TO F
136Ø PRINT "       TAU(I =";I;",J =";J;") =";A(I,J)
137Ø NEXT J
138Ø NEXT I
139Ø PRINT
14ØØ FOR I=1 TO E
141Ø FOR K=1 TO G
```

```
1420 PRINT "       TAU(I =";I;",K =";K;") =";B(I,K)
1430 NEXT K
1440 NEXT I
1450 PRINT
1460 FOR J=1 TO F
1470 FOR K=1 TO G
1480 PRINT "       TAU(J =";J;",K =";K;") =";C(J,K)
1490 NEXT K
1500 NEXT J
1510 PRINT
1520 PRINT
1530 PRINT "CHI-SQUARES FOR PARTIALS WITH TWO VARIABLES CONSTANT"
1540 PRINT
1550 PRINT
1560 PRINT "CHI-SQUARE(IJ:K) =";P1;"WITH";(E+F-1)*(G-1);
1570 PRINT "DEGREES OF FREEDOM"
1580 PRINT
1590 PRINT "CHI-SQUARE(IK:J) =";P2;"WITH";(E+G-1)*(F-1);
1600 PRINT "DEGREES OF FREEDOM"
1610 PRINT
1620 PRINT "CHI-SQUARE(JK:I) =";P3;"WITH";(F+G-1)*(E-1);
1630 PRINT "DEGREES OF FREEDOM"
1640 PRINT
1650 PRINT
1660 STOP
1670 REM SUBROUTINE TO ZERO PARTIALS
1680 FOR I=1 TO E
1690 FOR J=1 TO F
1700 LET A(I,J)=0
1710 NEXT J
1720 NEXT I
1730 FOR I=1 TO E
1740 FOR K=1 TO G
1750 LET B(I,K)=0
1760 NEXT K
1770 NEXT I
1780 FOR J=1 TO F
1790 FOR K=1 TO G
1800 LET C(J,K)=0
1810 NEXT K
1820 NEXT J
1830 RETURN
1840 END

READY
RUNBIG


CHI3      12:31  W.REG.  05/05/69  MON


THREE DIMENSIONAL CHI-SQUARE TABLE OF DECLARED SIZE
E X F X G -- MAXIMUM = 10 X 10 X 10. VARIABLES ARE
I, J, AND K. I = 1 TO E; J = 1 TO F; K = 1 TO G.
MODEL IS FROM FUNDAMENTALS OF NONPARAMETRIC STATISTICS
BY ALBERT PIERCE.  PROGRAM WRITTEN BY AUTHOR.


          E FOR YOUR TABLE IS ? 2
          F FOR YOUR TABLE IS ? 2
          G FOR YOUR TABLE IS ? 3

DATA FOR THIS PROGRAM MUST BE STORED IN FILE TRY.

        IS YOUR DATA STORED IN FILE TRY (TYPE YES OR NO) ? YES


        NUMBER OF CASES TO BE PROCESSED IS ? 177
```

COLUMN TOTALS

```
TAU( I = 1 ) = 47
TAU( I = 2 ) = 130

TAU( J = 1 ) = 152
TAU( J = 2 ) = 25

TAU( K = 1 ) = 70
TAU( K = 2 ) = 52
TAU( K = 3 ) = 55
```

OBSERVED AND EXPECTED CELL VALUES

I	J	K	R	E(I,J,K)	E(IJ:K)	E(IK:J)	E(JK:I)
1	1	1	1	15.9622	13.0508	2.57627	16.9944
1	1	2	11	11.8576	9.69492	12.8814	11.6836
1	1	3	21	12.5417	10.2542	24.904	11.6836
1	2	1	2	2.62536	5.53672	.423729	1.59322
1	2	2	4	1.95027	4.11299	2.11864	2.12429
1	2	3	8	2.06279	4.35028	4.09605	2.9209
2	1	1	63	44.1508	47.0621	57.5367	47.0056
2	1	2	33	32.7977	34.9605	31.774	32.3164
2	1	3	23	34.6899	36.9774	22.3277	32.3164
2	2	1	4	7.26164	4.35028	9.46328	4.40678
2	2	2	4	5.39436	3.23164	5.22599	5.87571
2	2	3	3	5.70558	3.41808	3.67232	8.0791

CHI-SQUARE = 54.2795 WITH 2 DEGREES OF FREEDOM

N = 177

COLUMN TOTALS FOR PARTIALS

```
TAU(I = 1 ,J = 1 ) = 33
TAU(I = 1 ,J = 2 ) = 14
TAU(I = 2 ,J = 1 ) = 119
TAU(I = 2 ,J = 2 ) = 11

TAU(I = 1 ,K = 1 ) = 3
TAU(I = 1 ,K = 2 ) = 15
TAU(I = 1 ,K = 3 ) = 29
TAU(I = 2 ,K = 1 ) = 67
TAU(I = 2 ,K = 2 ) = 37
TAU(I = 2 ,K = 3 ) = 26

TAU(J = 1 ,K = 1 ) = 64
TAU(J = 1 ,K = 2 ) = 44
TAU(J = 1 ,K = 3 ) = 44
TAU(J = 2 ,K = 1 ) = 6
TAU(J = 2 ,K = 2 ) = 8
TAU(J = 2 ,K = 3 ) = 11
```

CHI-SQUARES FOR PARTIALS WITH TWO VARIABLES CONSTANT

.

CHI-SQUARE(IJ:K) = 38.9411 WITH 6 DEGREES OF FREEDOM

CHI-SQUARE(IK:J) = 17.2575 WITH 4 DEGREES OF FREEDOM

CHI-SQUARE(JK:I) = 45.0859 WITH 4 DEGREES OF FREEDOM

```
RUNNING TIME:    Ø4.5 SECS  I/O TIME :    32.1 SECS

READY
OLD

PROBLEM NAME: TRY

READY
LIST


TRY          12:37  W.REG.  Ø5/Ø5/69  MON

1ØØ 1,1,3, 1,1,2, 1,1,3, 1,1,2, 1,1,3, 1,1,3, 1,2,2
1Ø1 1,2,1, 1,1,2, 1,1,2, 1,1,3, 1,2,3, 1,2,3, 1,1,3
1Ø2 1,1,3, 1,2,3, 1,1,3, 1,1,2, 1,1,3, 1,2,3, 1,1,2
1Ø3 1,2,3, 1,1,3, 1,2,3, 1,2,2, 1,1,2, 1,1,3, 1,1,3,
1Ø4 1,1,3, 1,1,2, 1,1,2, 1,1,3, 1,1,3, 1,2,2, 1,1,3
1Ø5 1,1,3, 1,1,1, 1,1,3, 1,1,3, 1,1,2, 1,1,3, 1,2,3
1Ø6 1,1,3, 1,2,1, 1,1,2, 1,2,2, 1,2,3, 2,1,1, 2,1,3
1Ø7 2,2,2, 2,1,1, 2,1,3, 2,1,1, 2,1,1, 2,1,2, 2,1,1
1Ø8 2,1,1, 2,1,1, 2,1,1, 2,1,1, 2,1,2, 2,1,3, 2,1,2
1Ø9 2,2,2, 2,1,2, 2,1,1, 2,1,3, 2,2,1, 2,1,1, 2,1,3
11Ø 2,1,1, 2,1,2, 2,1,1, 2,1,1, 2,1,1, 2,1,1, 2,1,2
111 2,1,2, 2,1,2, 2,1,1, 2,1,2, 2,1,1, 2,1,1, 2,1,1
112 2,1,2, 2,1,3, 2,1,3, 2,1,1, 2,2,1, 2,1,2, 2,1,1
113 2,1,1, 2,1,1, 2,1,1, 2,1,1, 2,1,1, 2,1,1, 2,1,1
114 2,1,2, 2,1,2, 2,1,1, 2,1,3, 2,1,1, 2,1,1, 2,1,1
115 2,1,2, 2,1,1, 2,1,1, 2,1,2, 2,2,2, 2,1,2, 2,1,1
116 2,1,3, 2,1,1, 2,1,1, 2,1,2, 2,2,1, 2,1,1, 2,1,3
117 2,1,1, 2,1,3, 2,1,1, 2,1,1, 2,1,1, 2,1,2, 2,1,1,
118 2,2,1, 2,1,2, 2,1,2, 2,1,1, 2,1,1, 2,1,1, 2,1,1
119 2,1,2, 2,1,3, 2,1,2, 2,2,3, 2,1,3, 2,1,2, 2,2,2
12Ø 2,1,1, 2,1,1, 2,1,1, 2,1,3, 2,1,2, 2,1,3, 2,1,1
121 2,1,3, 2,2,3, 2,1,2, 2,1,1, 2,1,1, 2,1,3, 2,1,3
122 2,1,1, 2,1,1, 2,1,2, 2,2,3, 2,1,2, 2,1,2, 2,1,1
123 2,1,3, 2,1,2, 2,1,2, 2,1,2, 2,1,1, 2,1,3, 2,1,2
124 2,1,3, 2,1,1, 2,1,1, 2,1,2, 2,1,1, 2,1,1, 2,1,3
125 2,1,1, 2,1,3,
9999 END

READY
BYE
OFF AT 12:39
```

APPENDIX D: BASIC LANGUAGE PROGRAM FOR THE 2 × 3 CELL FISHER EXACT PROBABILITY MODEL*

* This program was written too late to be mentioned in the text. The model is developed on pp. 127–130.

```
GENERAL ELECTRIC 400 TIME SHARING


ON AT -- 12:34   TTY:17


TIME SHARING WILL GO DOWN AT 1300 HRS


USER.NUMBER -- V720

TYPE OLD OR NEW:OLD:HYP3

READY
RUN


HYP3      12:35  W.REG. JULY 14, 69 MON

DO YOU WANT THE EXPLANATORY PARAGRAPHS OMITTED (TYPE YES OR NO)? NO


THIS PROGRAM FINDS THE EXACT AND CUMULATIVE UP AND DOWN PROB-
ABILITIES FOR THE FISHER EXACT TEST OF 2 X 3 CELLS. THE INPUTS
REQUIRED ARE: N= THE TOTAL NUMBER OF CASES, N1=THE SAMPLE
SIZE IN THE SHORT DIMENSION, K1 AND K2 ARE ROW TOTALS IN THE LONG
DIMENSION, AND R1 AND R2 ARE CELL VALUES AT THE INTERSECTION OF N1
AND K1 AND N1 AND K2. ASSIGN K1 AND K2 TO SMALLEST VALUES TO SAVE
MACHINE TIME.

STATISTICAL MODEL IS FROM FUNDAMENTALS OF NONPARAMETRIC STAT-
ISTICS BY ALBERT PIERCE. PROGRAM WRITTEN BY AUTHOR.

CHOOSE TABLE VALUES SO THAT N1=<N-N1.

THE RESPECTIVE VALUES OF N,N1,K1,K2,R1,R2 ARE? 72,36,12,24,3,9


      THE POINT PROBABILITY = 8.13641E-4


THE PROBABILITY OF A DISTRIBUTION AS PROBABLE OR LESS PROBABLE
THAN THAT OBSERVED = 2.00602E-3


THE PROBABILITY OF A DISTRIBUTION AS PROBABLE OR MORE PROBABLE
THAN THAT OBSERVED = .998808



RUNNING TIME:   02.1 SECS  I/O TIME :   08.4 SECS

READY
RUNNH
DO YOU WANT THE EXPLANATORY PARAGRAPHS OMITTED (TYPE YES OR NO)? YES

STATISTICAL MODEL IS FROM FUNDAMENTALS OF NONPARAMETRIC STAT-
ISTICS BY ALBERT PIERCE. PROGRAM WRITTEN BY AUTHOR.

CHOOSE TABLE VALUES SO THAT N1=<N-N1.

THE RESPECTIVE VALUES OF N,N1,K1,K2,R1,R2 ARE? 72,36,12,24,6,12


      THE POINT PROBABILITY = 5.12426E-2


THE PROBABILITY OF A DISTRIBUTION AS PROBABLE OR LESS PROBABLE
THAN THAT OBSERVED = 1.
```

```
THE PROBABILITY OF A DISTRIBUTION AS PROBABLE OR MORE PROBABLE
THAN THAT OBSERVED = 5.12426E-2



RUNNING TIME:   01.7 SECS  I/O TIME :   08.7 SECS

READY
LISTNH
100   PRINT "DO YOU WANT THE EXPLANATORY PARAGRAPHS OMITTED (TYPE ";
110   PRINT "YES OR NO)";
120   INPUT Z$
130   IF Z$="YES" THEN 290
140   PRINT
150   PRINT
160  PRINT "THIS PROGRAM FINDS THE EXACT AND CUMULATIVE UP AND ";
170  PRINT "DOWN PROB-"
180 PRINT  "ABILITIES FOR THE FISHER EXACT TEST OF 2 X 3 CELLS.";
190  PRINT " THE INPUTS"
200 PRINT "REQUIRED ARE: N= THE TOTAL NUMBER OF CASES, N1=THE";
210  PRINT " SAMPLE"
220 PRINT "SIZE IN THE SHORT DIMENSION, K1 AND K2 ARE ROW TOTALS IN";
230 PRINT " THE LONG"
240 PRINT "DIMENSION, AND R1 AND R2 ARE CELL VALUES AT THE INTER";
250 PRINT "SECTION OF N1 "
260 PRINT "AND K1 AND N1 AND K2. ASSIGN K1 AND K2 TO SMALLEST VALUES ";
270 PRINT "TO SAVE"
280 PRINT "MACHINE TIME."
290 PRINT
300 PRINT "STATISTICAL MODEL IS FROM FUNDAMENTALS OF NONPARAMET";
310 PRINT "RIC STAT-"
320 PRINT "ISTICS BY ALBERT PIERCE. PROGRAM WRITTEN BY AUTHOR."
330 PRINT
332 PRINT "CHOOSE TABLE VALUES SO THAT N1=<N-N1."
340 PRINT
350 PRINT "THE RESPECTIVE VALUES OF N,N1,K1,K2,R1,R2 ARE";
360 INPUT N,N1,K1,K2,R1,R2
370 DIM P(1000)
380 LET P1=(K1+1)*(K2+2)
390 LET I=0
400 LET N0=N
410 LET R0=N1
420 GOSUB 980
430 LET D0=Q
440 LET U=N-K1-K2
450 LET X1=(-1)
460 LET C=U-N1
470 LET U1=K2+1
480 REM ESCALATOR
490 LET X1=X1+1
500 IF X1>K1 THEN 740
510 LET A=C+X1
512 IF A=>0 THEN 520
514 PRINT "YOUR DATA VALUES ARE INVALID. PROGRAM RUN TERMINATED."
516 STOP
520 LET L=N1-X1+1
530 LET N0=K1
540 LET R0=X1
550 GOSUB 980
560 LET Y=Q/D0
570 LET L0=N1-X1
580 LET X2=(-1)
590 REM INCYC
600 LET X2=X2+1
610 IF X2>K2 THEN 480
620 LET I=I+1
630 IF X2=0 THEN 660
640 LET P(I)=(P(I-1)*(U1-X2)*(L-X2))/(X2*(A+X2))
```

```
650 GO TO 700
660 LET N0=U
670 LET R0=L0
680 GOSUB 980
690 LET P(I)=Y*Q
700 IF X1<>R1 THEN 730
710 IF X2<>R2 THEN 730
720 LET E0=P(I)
730 GO TO 590
740 REM FINALE
750 LET C0=0
760 FOR I=1 TO P1
770 IF P(I)=<E0 THEN 790
780 GO TO 810
790 LET C0=C0+P(I)
800 NEXT I
810 LET C1=1-C0+E0
820 PRINT
830 PRINT
840 PRINT "       THE POINT PROBABILITY =";E0
850 PRINT
860 PRINT
870 PRINT "THE PROBABILITY OF A DISTRIBUTION AS PROBABLE OR LESS";
880 PRINT " PROBABLE"
890 PRINT "THAN THAT OBSERVED =";C0
900 PRINT
910 PRINT
920 PRINT "THE PROBABILITY OF A DISTRIBUTION AS PROBABLE OR MORE ";
930 PRINT "PROBABLE"
940 PRINT "THAN THAT OBSERVED =";C1
950 PRINT
960 PRINT
970 STOP
980 REM BINOMIAL COEFFICIENT SUBROUTINE
990 IF R0>N0-R0 THEN 1010
1000 GO TO 1020
1010 LET R0=N0-R0
1020 LET Q=1
1030 IF R0=0 THEN 1090
1040 LET N0=N0+1
1050 FOR R=R0 TO 1 STEP -1
1060 LET N0=N0-1
1070 LET Q=(Q/R)*N0
1080 NEXT R
1090 RETURN
1100 END

READY
RUNNH
DO YOU WANT THE EXPLANATORY PARAGRAPHS OMITTED (TYPE YES OR NO)? YES

STATISTICAL MODEL IS FROM FUNDAMENTALS OF NONPARAMETRIC STAT-
ISTICS BY ALBERT PIERCE. PROGRAM WRITTEN BY AUTHOR.

CHOOSE TABLE VALUES SO THAT N1=<N-N1.

THE RESPECTIVE VALUES OF N,N1,K1,K2,R1,R2 ARE? 110,58,19,38,10,21
YOUR DATA VALUES ARE INVALID. PROGRAM RUN TERMINATED.


RUNNING TIME:    01.0 SECS   I/O TIME :    07.8 SECS

READY
```

INDEX